# A CAPITALIST'S
# LAMENT

# A CAPITALIST'S
# LAMENT

## How Wall Street Is Fleecing You
## and Ruining America

# LELAND FAUST

Skyhorse Publishing

Skyhorse Publishing books may be purchased in bulk at special discounts for sales promotion, corporate gifts, fund-raising, or educational purposes. Special editions can also be created to specifications. For details, contact the Special Sales Department, Skyhorse Publishing, 307 West 36th Street, 11th Floor, New York, NY 10018 or info@ skyhorsepublishing.com.

Skyhorse® and Skyhorse Publishing® are registered trademarks of Skyhorse Publishing, Inc.®, a Delaware corporation.

Visit our website at www.skyhorsepublishing.com.

10 9 8 7 6 5 4 3 2 1

Library of Congress Cataloging-in-Publication Data is available on file.

Cover design by Rain Saukas

Print ISBN: 978–1–5107–1362–8
Ebook ISBN: 978–1–5107–1363–5

Printed in the United States of America

To Don Hill for being a marvelous mentor, perfect partner, and fabulous friend and for having the great strength of character to allow me to take credit for so much of what we did together.

To Susan for listening to "Econ 101" at the dinner table for all these years and helping me refine, organize, and coherently express my ideas. More importantly, for steadfastly standing by my side as a pillar of support and love for just shy of fifty years.

# Table of Contents

# SECTION I

# The Lay of the Street

ONE

# America: We Have a Problem

Wall Street is fleecing you and ruining America. You may think Wall Street's perpetual activity and financial innovations help the free-enterprise system, but in fact they cause irreparable harm to the country. This story of how Wall Street completely fools you as it skillfully makes a killing for itself, turning your money into theirs, is too vastly important to ignore. We will all continue to be at great risk and suffer if we do not force changes to this toxic system.

Investors, big and small, are continually being fleeced and have very few people on their side. Whether you have nothing to invest and are interested only in good public policy and consumer protection, or you have a nest egg of $10,000 or $10,000,000,000 (yes, many of the most wealthy are taken in, too), you need to know how the Wall Street system really works, how the benefits are distributed, how much risk is routinely taken, how Wall Street uses the media to promote its charade, and how it shamelessly misleads investors and the public.

If after reading this book you think the title is hyperbole, then I have failed in my mission. Wall Street has ingeniously convinced a large segment of the public that to oppose Wall Street is to be against the great American free enterprise system. Not so! I am a hard-core capitalist, but I am not an apologist for Wall Street's horrendous behavior. I am not a populist trying to change our core beliefs. As an

3

independent investment advisor, I've been both a West Coast outsider and a clear-eyed insider in the financial world. Unlike Ralph Nader and Michael Moore, who berate the system itself, I'm outraged precisely because I support our regulated but essentially free market economy. I'm not someone who failed and then rails. I've worked very successfully in the industry and observed it over my entire professional career. I know it inside and out. I have represented real people with their real money and financial lives on the line. I have had to make the tough decisions on the spot. I am not a journalist or an academic looking at events or the system with the luxury of hindsight.

This book is not about bashing the American economic system; it is about bashing business as usual on Wall Street. Too many people think that free enterprise, or capitalism, has failed. I completely disagree. The free enterprise system has produced the greatest amount of economic prosperity for the greatest number of people in history. If you don't support free enterprise, please turn in your iPad and your smartphone, stop watching cable television, and never go to Google. Self-interest serves us all well. But selfish interest—taking advantage of the system by illegal or immoral actions—harms us all.

I am outraged that Wall Street constantly puts its own interests ahead of those of its customers and society. Smooth-talking yet well-credentialed hucksters selling the false promise of easy gains have hijacked our system in order to earn higher fees for themselves. Wall Street continually makes outrageous predictions designed to impress you and entice you to buy. But it is mostly a giant casino where games of chance masquerade as investments. This culture of gambling exposes us all to risks that no one should take.

Let's be clear. We are not talking about boiler-room operations and swampland shysters. We are talking about the largest, most prominent and renowned Wall Street players: brokerage firms, financial advisors, mutual fund complexes, financial center banks, insurance companies, analysts, consultants, rating agencies, government agencies, government-sponsored enterprises, the financial press and broadcast media, and many financial economists. When Wall Street firms and their employees forget whose interest they are supposed to protect and instead act only in their own selfish interest, the problem is not just unscrupulous or unethical behavior but the criminal practices that go with it.

Today Wall Street does not create wealth; it takes it from others. Wall Street's unsavory tactics assume many guises—alluring come-ons, airbrushed risks, high stakes gambling, distortions, half-truths, false promises, misleading statements, falsified research, outlandish predictions, white lies, bold lies, tricks to overcharge customers, bad deals, and outright fraud. The financial-services industry seduces Main Street investors—and surprisingly even the big players, including major corporations and other institutional investors— getting them to take chances that no one should ever consider.

- Wall Street takes advantage of uninformed customers by charging hidden fees and markups on their products. It tells clients they are paying less when in fact they are paying more. Financial prospectuses feature a picture of a grandfather and his granddaughter, implying he is investing for her security—when in fact the fund advertised is chock-full of risky investments.
- Wall Street celebrities, worshipped by the media, use their status to hype forecasts that mislead the investing public. They consistently get the big things wrong, yet no one in the financial press seems to know or care or hold anybody accountable. Most Wall Street experts confidently predicted that the stock market would increase in 2008; instead we saw the worst decline in seventy years. A Nobel Prize winner predicted that the S&P 500 Index would fall to 400 from 1000, only to see a rise to almost 2100 by the date he specified.
- Wall Street is a world where the largest firm in the industry can recommend to its customers stocks that its own internal memoranda refer to as "dogs." It's a world where hedge fund operators make hundreds of millions of dollars managing funds in which their investors lose billions. It's where the most popular television personality can give his advice on the one single best stock

to own, only to see it decline by 50 percent over the next year and by 95 percent over the next two years. It's where employees of the major firms do not even try to protect their clients and customers; they go out of their way to harm them in order to help either a few favored clients or themselves. It's where too many people have disdain for their very own clients and customers, display arrogance without limit, and have a sense of entitlement that never ends.

- Wall Street sells risky products to nonprofit organizations. When university endowments or charitable foundations suffer needless losses, services are diminished. Pension plans depend upon their investments to provide retirement benefits. They are in jeopardy because Wall Street sold unsophisticated representatives of state and local governments risky products, incurring higher fees and losses. Now pensioners or taxpayers are on the hook for the losses.

- Wall Street siphons money from the productive segments of society, misallocates government resources, and is destroying America's social fabric. Wall Street's ability to extract money from the economic system is really like toll taking, exacting tribute for the use of their services. This makes America less productive and less competitive.

- Wall Street's compensation practices have caused a huge brain drain. Too many of the "best and brightest" pursue careers in finance rather than in productive careers in engineering, chemistry, manufacturing, or education. Unlike the wealth earned by Bill Gates (Microsoft), Sam Walton (Walmart), Steven Jobs (Apple), or Mark Zuckerberg (Facebook), who all created new companies and products and services, the fortunes amassed by hedge fund operators represent very little contribution to the economy. And Wall Streeters then have the audacity to complain about the possibility of being forced to pay the same tax rate as other wealthy people.

- Wall Street created the Internet (or dot-com) bubble and then the severe downturn in 2000–2002. Wall Street followed that with the subprime mortgage bust. That in turn caused the market crash in 2008, which led to the Great Recession.

The Great Recession did not arise from weaknesses in the underlying economy. It was produced by the actions of Wall Street firms. Wall Street's culture of debt has been totally out of control and has put us all at greater risk. It has recklessly borrowed money on its own while encouraging its customers to borrow even more. This has destabilized the economy as downturns in markets lead to greater losses that in turn increase the risk of insolvency or bankruptcy. Without excessive debt used by both Wall Street and its customers, the Great Recession of 2008 would have been far less severe or might not have happened at all.

The potential for insolvency, a severe decline in lending activity, substantial losses by the major banks, and the mere possibility that the banking system could collapse in 2008 led to massive government guarantees and bailouts. These bailouts in turn diverted government money from what I hope we all think are better uses—better educational programs, more research into renewable energy, improvements to our infrastructure, lower taxes, and decreased government deficits.

Meanwhile, daily scandals continue to rock the financial world: high-profile bankruptcies, mismanaged pension funds, sky-high compensation, old-boy favoritism, insider trading, stock-option giveaways, and massive bailouts. Lapses in accountability are the rule. Wall Street passes off poor analysis as fact and undue risk as opportunity. Making foolish or outlandish or just plain wrong predictions is of no consequence. Wall Street luminaries with poor track records still garner celebrity status.

Wall Street's ever-increasing emphasis on short-term performance and get-rich-quick schemes increases everyone's risk, destroys morale, and lessens the incentive for long-term investments, which can lead to lower productivity. Individuals and the society are economically more secure and more productive if we take a long-term approach to investing. We should want to reward hard work rather than speculation.

Has Wall Street learned anything from the Great Recession or from the continuing scandals? Sadly, not much. There has been the *appearance* of renewed scrutiny of banks, brokerage houses, investment advisors, funds, and customer lending. But appearances do not add up to fundamental change. In fact, manipulation lives on, adapting itself to evolving conditions.

Fundamental overhaul of the system is needed to rebuild the great financial engine that once powered prosperity. But pundits, politicians, and regulators suggest only meager reforms that do nothing to eliminate the systemic rot that is leading us to financial disaster yet again. Wall Street's actions have a profound impact on all segments of our society, and when they threaten the banking system in the United States, the repercussions are felt around the world. Who was served when Iceland's government pension plans lost billions investing in subprime mortgages, or when Goldman Sachs helped Greece hide its true government deficit while earning a fee of $300 million?

These misdeeds have led to the public's growing lack of trust in the free enterprise system. Wall Street's sense of entitlement, its ceaseless pursuit of selfish interest, and its relentless extracting of huge sums from the economy are leading to class warfare as I have never seen before. The Occupy Wall Street movement rightfully voiced its discontent with "the system." But many or even most of the protestors had no clear understanding of the problems, which would be difficult enough to solve if we were united and much harder if we are at each other's throats.

Wall Street as it now behaves does not merit our support. But we do need a well-functioning financial system to raise capital to help companies grow, to place debt instruments, and to make liquid markets for investors. "Shut it down" is no answer; it's not as if we can eliminate Wall Street and all will be fine. We need it to function differently. Government needs to be part of the solution, but instead it is just as guilty as, and perhaps even guiltier than, Wall Street. More regulation and socialism waste time and money and reduce productivity. They simply provide more work for bureaucrats who merely check boxes on forms.

I have seen a lot more red tape since the Great Recession, but I haven't seen a lot of meaningful reform. Part of the problem is that Wall Street's bad behavior did not start with the market crash leading to the Great Recession in 2008, nor with the dot-com bust in 2000, but much earlier.

I've been a firsthand observer of Wall Street misbehavior for over forty years. I started my firm in 1978 with nothing and grew it until I managed about $2 billion. Along the way we succeeded in many ways. First and most important, we helped our clients' assets grow and protected them against the substantial and unexpected market crashes. For the only four years I was eligible, I was named by *Barron's* to its annual list of the Top 100 Independent Investment Advisors in the country. For its entire life, from 1997 through 2010, I managed the CSI Equity Fund, which consistently out-performed most other mutual funds in its class. For much of its life, our fund received a five-star rating from Morningstar, and for many years we had better performance than Warren Buffett's famed Berkshire Hathaway.

When I started my company, I had the old-fashioned idea that the good guys win—that those who gave sound advice through careful research, reasoned analysis, and rational planning would prevail. But since then I have grown increasingly disillusioned, even outraged, by the ugly truth: Wall Street couldn't care less about its investors.

True reform is possible only when the problems are recognized for what they really are. Capitalism and free markets are not at fault—business as usual on Wall Street is what's wrong. The only way for investors to protect themselves is to understand what they're actually getting into—among many other things, to learn how much is being charged in fees, to see through the hype and worthless forecasts and predictions, to resist the dangerous allure of derivatives and hedge funds, to understand the role of the too-compliant financial media, to spot brokers' and money managers' conflicts of interest, and to avoid short selling, leverage, and IPOS.

That's my mission in this book: to promote reform and to help you get ahead instead of getting taken for a ride.

# SECTION II

# The Triumph of Selfish Interest

# TWO

# Big Is Not Beautiful

In 2011, MF Global, a highly reputable commodities futures brokerage, filed for the eighth-largest bankruptcy in US history. The *San Francisco Chronicle* published my thoughts at the time, which were the germ of the ideas developed in this book. Here is the article that ran in the newspaper:

"The stunning reality is that five years into the financial meltdown, it's business as usual on Wall Street—outlandish rewards for insiders with downside for almost everyone else. Occupy Wall Street protesters are right—something is wrong—but they're not sure what. Here's what I say: A rigged game affects not just the 99 percent, but everyone, and with global repercussions.

"I recently had a chance to explain these problems on 'Street Soldiers,' a radio program devoted to keeping inner-city residents 'alive and free.' It's not the usual forum for an independent investment adviser who has managed more than $1.5 billion in assets for clients from the 1 percent. The radio show host wanted his listeners to hear from a Wall Street 'soldier' who had broken ranks to publicly challenge his industry's out-of-control practices. Maybe I could explain what is wrong on Wall Street and why CEOs get eight-figure bonuses while hardworking Americans lose their homes and jobs.

"Make no mistake—as I told the listeners—I'm a hard-core capitalist. But capitalism has been hijacked, and I'm infuriated. For capitalism to work, people who assume risk should reap the rewards of success, but they also must suffer when losses occur.

"If you're unconvinced, let's revisit the latest debacle—the implosion of yet another Wall Street darling, MF Global. The fallout of its bad bets on European bonds is hitting home hard, even in rural America, where many of its agricultural customers work. As the eighth-largest bankruptcy filing in U.S. history, MF Global represents just about everything that is wrong on Wall Street.

1.  *The cult of a Wall Street superstar:* In 2010, Jon Corzine, the former chairman of Goldman Sachs and former governor of New Jersey, became CEO of MF Global. His goal was to transform the little-known futures broker into a powerhouse investment bank. It took him only 19 months to blow up an institution that dates back to 1793.
2.  *Gambling disguised as investing:* Speculation ruled once Corzine got going. MF was not after long-term returns but an immediate killing. In the midst of the euro crisis, it made an astonishing $6.3 billion bet on European bonds. But the bonds declined, putting the company's very existence on the line and taking down its customers too.
3.  *The bail-me-out syndrome:* MF's management must have thought there was no way it could lose because surely the Europeans would bail out the weaker countries so they wouldn't default on the bonds. Imagine MF's shock when the huge bailouts didn't materialize.
4.  *Enormous conflicts of interest:* The Commodity Futures Trading Commission, chaired by a former Corzine colleague at Goldman Sachs, was supposed to ensure that MF kept customer funds segregated from the firm's own investments. But apparently the commission didn't act when signs of trouble first appeared or start enforcing restrictions until $1.2 billion had vanished from customer accounts.
5.  *Leverage on a grand scale:* Some investment banks scaled back their borrowing after the financial meltdown, but not MF Global.

It continued leveraged investments at pre-2008 levels— reportedly at a rate of 40 to 1. Excessive borrowing allowed management to go for the big score, but proved fatal when the markets moved against MF's bets, requiring more collateral.

6. *Failure of regulators and the reform law:* Where was the oversight by the Securities and Exchange Commission, the CFTC and FINRA, the largest independent regulator of security firms? Reforms such as the Sarbanes-Oxley and Dodd-Frank protection laws had no effect.

7. *Misappropriation of client funds:* Investigators want to know how MF tapped clients' segregated accounts for $1.2 billion to cover its financial losses. After it declared bankruptcy, 33,000 clients found their accounts frozen. How would you like that in today's volatile markets? Shouldn't someone do jail time instead of getting a slap-on-the-wrist fine?

8. *Worthless rating agencies:* Post-meltdown, it's the same old game—investment firms hire rating agencies to rate their own debt. In August, MF was rated a good investment. Within 60 days, the firm declared bankruptcy.

9. *Golden parachutes soaring high:* Corzine didn't risk much of his money on MF stock, but he received lots of stock options. Later, after taking home compensation of $14.25 million in 2010, he voluntarily declined his $12 million golden parachute. Why is he entitled to anything extra for leadership that resulted directly in bankruptcy?

10. *Breakdown of morality:* Even if something is legal, that doesn't mean it is right. MF's management crossed the line for their own potential gain—putting personal interest ahead of protecting shareholders and customers.

"Wall Street will keep sucking huge sums out of our economy and putting 100 percent of us at risk unless the rules change. Stiff jail time if you cheat or steal. Whopping personal fines paid by wrongdoers, not their corporations. Fireproof walls that protect customers from a firm's risky bets. Most important, we must stop gambling and start investing again to build valuable companies. Unless we take back Wall Street and restore true capitalism, we're living with a time bomb. The next crisis will make 2008 look like a warm-up.

"Imagine how big the Occupy camps will be if that happens."

In the four years since I wrote those words, there have been two interesting developments. First, MF Global's customers were able to recover much of their stolen funds as result of litigation against banks and accounting firms. Second, in April 2015 reports circulated that Jon Corzine had plans to start his own hedge fund. In the great Wall Street tradition, massive failure and even wrongdoing don't hinder a Wall Street luminary from reinventing himself over and over.

In this respect, Wall Street is quite different from other industries. A problem with one drug firm does not imply that all drug firms act badly. Similarly, a breach of ethics or poor practices at one law firm does not implicate all law firms. Even in the extremely competitive world of college football recruiting, one coach breaking the rules doesn't suggest that everyone is cutting corners.

But on Wall Street, bad behavior is not an aberration—it's endemic. Almost all the major firms are continually engaged in questionable if not illegal practices. In July 2012, the *Wall Street Journal* reported that criminal investigators were looking into charges that at least nine major financial institutions (including Citigroup, UBS, Deutsche Bank, HSBC, JPMorgan Chase, and the Royal Bank of Scotland) were working together to rig global interest rates. In 2015, Citigroup, JPMorganChase, Barclays, and the Royal Bank of Scotland, among others, agreed to plead guilty to price fixing on foreign exchange markets. And for many years the Internal Revenue Service has pursued tax evasion by thousands of US citizens maintaining off-shore accounts with Credit Suisse and UBS.

We also know that a significant number of the major financial institutions in the United States, and many abroad, orchestrated the events that led to the market crash in 2008 and the Great Recession. Through December 2015, the major global banks had paid fines or settlements of about $300 billion for their actions.

1. Bank of America paid a $17 billion fine for its role in selling mortgage securities and paid $11.8 billion to settle claims arising from foreclosure violations.
2. HSBC paid a $2 billion fine for money laundering that assisted a Mexican drug cartel and admitted to the Swiss authorities that it held accounts that aided tax dodgers.
3. Merrill Lynch paid a $100 million fine for issuing public statements on seven companies expressing positive views while it privately expressed negative views on all of them. It placed a "buy" rating on a stock when its private analysis referred to the company as "such a piece of crap."
4. For over a decade, Morgan Stanley paid one of its funds' advisors for work never performed. It paid a $604 million verdict for fraud in advising a renowned Wall Street investor.
5. UBS rigged foreign-exchange rates and acted unlawfully in precious metal trades. It also paid a $780 million fine to the Department of Justice for aiding tax evasion.
6. Citigroup lost $50 billion in 2007–2008 gambling on collateralized debt obligations, leading to a massive government bailout and a reduction (through 2015) of 87 percent of the value of its stock. It also paid over $4.5 billion to settle claims of investors in Enron and WorldCom.
7. JPMorgan Chase paid $2.6 billion to settle claims for its failure to properly supervise the activities of Bernard Madoff's Ponzi scheme. It also paid a fine of $13 billion to the Department of Justice for its role in selling toxic mortgage securities.
8. Wells Fargo Bank set aside $2 billion to settle government allegations that it had wrongfully foreclosed on mortgages. It was also sued by the US Attorney for fraudulently certifying loans for more than ten years.

These penalties might appear large, but they are relatively insignificant, just a normal cost of doing business. If one of these banks pays a $100 million fine, it's the equivalent to someone making $100,000 per year paying about $120. How bad would you feel if you could avoid criminal and civil liability for such a trivial payment? What if your uncle (in the financial world, the banks' shareholders) paid it for you?

In 2014 the four largest financial firms in the United States—Citigroup, Bank of America, Wells Fargo Bank, and JPMorgan Chase—had average revenues of approximately $85 billion, with average profits of about $14 billion. Many of those very same banks received massive government bailouts following their despicable deeds. The government loans and guarantees were made under the pretext that the entire economic system would crash all around us without government intervention. All of the major banks took money under the Troubled Asset Relief Program (TARP), but those amounts were small when compared to the secret loans these large banks received from the Federal Reserve Bank. Only later audits of the Federal Reserve revealed the true extent of the bailout. The CEOs of the major financial institutions seemed to know they could rely on crony capitalism.

Does size matter when it comes to honesty? Let's see what the leaders of the largest financial institutions had to say. It sure looked like they felt free to issue to the public bogus statements as to their firms' financial health. My thanks to *Bloomberg Markets* of January 2012 for compiling the following quotes and statistics:

1. *September 21, 2008.* John Mack, Morgan Stanley CEO, said, "Morgan Stanley is in the strongest possible position."—TARP funding: $10 billion; highest borrowing from the Fed: $107 billion (eight days later).
2. *December 31, 2008.* Lloyd Blankfein, Goldman Sachs CEO, indicated, "Our deep and global client franchise, experienced and talented people and strong balance sheet position our firm well."—TARP funding: $10 billion; highest borrowing from the Fed: $69 billion (fifteen days later).
3. *January 16, 2009.* Vikram Pandit, Citigroup CEO, observed, "We have an irreplaceable franchise." —TARP funding: $45 billion; highest borrowing from the Fed: $99.5 billion (four days later).

4. *January 22, 2009*. Kenneth Lewis, Bank of America CEO, told us, "The diversity and strength of our company is allowing us to continue to invest in our businesses to drive future profit growth."—TARP funding: $45 billion; highest borrowings from the Fed: $91.4 billion (thirty-five days later).
5. *February 23, 2009*. Jamie Dimon, JPMorgan Chase CEO, stated, "We believe we have a fortress balance sheet."—TARP funding: $25 billion; highest borrowings from the Fed: $48 billion (three days later).
6. *March 6, 2009*. John Stumpf, Wells Fargo CEO, remarked, "We couldn't feel better about the future."—TARP funding: $25 billion; highest borrowings from the Fed: $45 billion (eight days earlier).

These are the same executives who constantly complain about government regulation and interference. Furthermore, working for a huge institution does not mean you know what is really happening. In April 2013, *Fortune* ran an article entitled "The Running of the Bull—Speaking fluent gibberish is an essential business tool. Especially if you're a banker." JPMorgan Chase had incurred a $6 billion loss in derivatives trades. The trader, who had to get approval for his plan before executing it, made a presentation to the bank's senior management. According to a report issued by a US Senate subcommittee, the trader's presentation included the following:

"Sell the forward spread and buy protection on the tightening move."

"Use indices and add to existing position."

"Go long risk on some belly tranches, especially where defaults may realize."

"Buy protection on HY and Xover in rallies and turn the position over to monetize volatility."

Since I am not an expert in derivatives and options, this makes no sense to me. Apparently I am not alone. The Senate report indicated that not a single person who was interviewed understood the meaning either. Didn't matter—the plan was approved. Everyone at JPMorgan was happy until the $6 billion evaporated.

If we just pay attention and look at what is all around us every day, we can certainly see that big is not beautiful. And my personal experiences show how some of the large Wall Street firms really work.

The big firms incur a lot of expenses to impress their customers with their claimed special expertise. A number of years ago one of my law clients served as a co-trustee of a large family trust. The trustees, despite my disapproval, chose one of the major brokerage firms to advise them on their investments and their investment managers, as well as to execute trades. Once a year the firm flew the trustees and their attorneys from California to New York for some daytime meetings and evening entertainment. We were often introduced to the heads of various departments, given presentations and written materials, and invited to bring up our questions and comments.

One year we were given a private luncheon with the firm's chief economist in the firm's private dining room on one of the upper floors of the World Trade Center, with sweeping views of the Hudson River and New Jersey. The economist gave us his predictions for the year ahead and shared other insights. I returned home and picked up the *Wall Street Journal* on Monday to learn that the chief economist had been fired on Friday, the day after our meeting.

This firm's research department analyzed investment advisors and recommended the ones with the best performance records over the prior few years. When the chosen advisors performed well, the brokerage firm would take full credit for recommending them. When the chosen advisors performed poorly, the brokerage firm would replace them with new advisors. Somehow, no matter how poorly the chosen advisors performed, the brokerage firm was able to get its customers to forget who made the bad recommendations in the first place. One of the chosen advisors had been in the top 1 percent in his category in the three years prior to the client retaining his services. Over the next three years he fell to the bottom 1 percent, but with no repercussions to the brokerage firm that had recommended him.

Each year the head of the brokerage firm's department that picked the advisors made a presentation to us. She included so-called "scatter graphs" that showed the performance of a universe of managers in comparison to the risk they were taking. A typical chart would look like this:

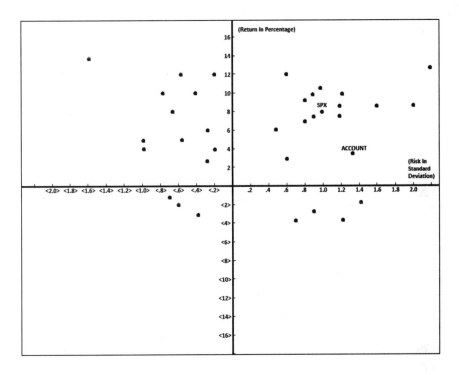

A manager whose performance is represented on a scatter graph like this one wants his dot to be as high on the chart as possible and as far to the left, representing higher returns with lower risk. In the words of the trade, you want to be in the "northwest quadrant." In making her presentation, she showed us where my client's advisors were located. None of them were in the northwest quadrant for the period during which they managed my client's assets. The lawyer for one of the other trustees innocently asked for the names of the firms in the northwest quadrant and asked why they had not been suggested to us. The department head said she didn't know, would look into it, and would get back to us. We never found out, but fortunately we didn't need to. Once we got home to California the other lawyer said he was stunned by her lack of knowledge. He then joined me in recommending terminating the client's entire relationship with the brokerage firm.

The client hired new consultants who provided much better service and advice than did the old brokerage firm, but it came at a price to the trustees and their attorneys. No more junkets to New York with the best tickets to the hottest Broadway shows. I still remember the noise and the smoke from our seats close to the stage for *Miss Saigon*. Since then I've had to pay for my own theater tickets in New York.

Too many of us believe our money is safe when entrusted to large insurance companies that have been in business for many years. We feel comfortable with names we know and the delusion that they employ smart, experienced professionals who act in their customers' interest. But my personal experience with the investment departments of some major life insurance companies leaves me wondering what some of these life insurance companies really have to offer.

In 1997 my firm started a mutual fund investing in stocks of companies throughout the world. The fund performed very well in both the good years and the leaner years that followed. After five years the two most highly respected mutual fund rating companies gave our fund top ratings. Lipper rated our fund in the top 1 percent of its class, and Morningstar awarded us its highest rating: five stars. Because of this strong performance, an insurance agent suggested to John Hancock Life Insurance that our fund be included as an investment option in the variable life insurance policies that Hancock (and so many other life insurance companies) had started to offer. Obviously, we were delighted at the prospect of national exposure and an opportunity to manage significantly more assets.

Before we could be included, we had to complete Hancock's standard RFP (request for proposal), consisting of about 40 pages of detailed questions concerning our qualifications, experience, method of investing, past performance, and prior regulatory problems (if any). After our RFP had been reviewed by the Hancock home office, we had to meet with a team of their executives so we could answer even more questions and provide even more detail about the operation of our fund.

Hancock sent about eight people from their headquarters in Boston to our office in San Francisco to meet with my partner and me. During the interview, one of Hancock's representatives expressed concern over the proportion of our fund invested in consumer companies because we had a higher percentage invested in consumer companies than did the S&P 500 Index. We indicated our goal was good returns and protection of our investors' money. We did not see our role as just mimicking the S&P 500 Index. If that was our goal, we should just go out of business and have our clients buy index funds. Hancock's representative made it clear that she was very upset with our approach, despite the fact that we had done so well.

At the time of our meeting, John Hancock managed a large cap growth fund that over the prior ten years had underperformed the S&P 500 Index by a staggering 9 percent per year, ranking it in the lowest 4 percent of all equity funds. It returned an average of 3.6 percent per year during one of the best decades in American history, while the S&P 500 returned approximately 12.7 percent per year. $10,000 invested for 10 years with this Hancock fund increased to about $14,000, while $10,000 invested in the S&P 500 increased to about $33,000. Ouch! Apparently Hancock's fund managers thought they could take advantage of short-term swings in stock prices. Between 1997 and 2000 their fund ranked in the bottom 25 percent in three of those four years, and their average annual portfolio turnover was 135 percent. That's a lot of short-term trading, and it resulted in terrible performance. After awarding the Hancock Large Cap Growth Fund its lowest rating, Morningstar observed, "There's no reason to buy or keep this fund."

Shortly after our meeting, a major investment industry journal published its rankings of mutual fund performance over the past five years. As luck would have it, Hancock operated a fund in the same category as ours. The good news—ours was the second-best performer (of about 100 funds) in the category. Hancock's fund was in the lowest 2 percent, and its return to investors trailed ours by an average of 9 percent per year for each of the five years. That's a huge difference. Over the five-year period, every investor in our fund was about 54 percent ahead of investors in their fund. For every $15,400 our clients had, theirs had about $10,000. I would be the first to acknowledge that top performance requires some luck as well as good analysis, but horrible performance is just bad work.

We had a similarly instructive, yet disappointing, experience with Penn Mutual Life Insurance. Someone suggested to the executives of Penn Mutual that our fund be added to the platform Penn Mutual administered for owners of its variable life insurance policies. What could be better than having a major life insurance company with thousands of agents recommending your product?

I flew to the headquarters of Penn Mutual and met with a number of the top executives in their variable life insurance division. The meeting went very well—the technical discussions went smoothly, and we seemed to have good personal rapport. The Penn Mutual executives were satisfied with how we managed our fund and volunteered that our fund would provide them with a competitive advantage. Their agents could differentiate themselves from their competitors by offering their customers a successful product not available elsewhere. Based on what they had seen in writing and in our discussions, the Penn Mutual executives said they were ready to go.

Then came the unexpected glitch. I guess I was naive, for I was totally unprepared for their request. In order for our fund to be included on their platform, we had to agree to sponsor a portion of their next company meeting with their insurance agents. The initial cost was $50,000. I respectfully declined their offer to "pay to play," and we have had no communications since.

Unfortunately, I now know that pay to play is all too common. I certainly was not the only firm asked to contribute to the cost of a firm's meetings. How many decisions are major financial institutions making based on extracting $50,000 from their investment partners to help defray the costs of their overhead? What happened to fiduciary duty?

Lots of investors believe they will prosper by investing with the large mutual fund complexes. Perhaps they should reconsider. The August 24, 1998, issue of *Forbes* contained this article: "The fund industry's dirty secret: Big is not beautiful." The author examined the forty-five largest stock mutual funds starting in 1993 and tracked their performance over the next five years. His conclusion: only one of those forty-five funds had beaten the S&P 500 Index over the five years, and that one only by two thirds of 1 percent per year. Taken together, the forty-five giant funds represented mediocrity at best. Interestingly enough, the one fund that had previously beaten the S&P 500 Index by two thirds of 1 percent per year underperformed by approximately 5 percent per year for the next five years.

The experience of those forty-five large funds about twenty years ago was not an aberration but part of a continuing pattern. In September 2014, *Time* magazine published statistics compiled by the S&P Dow Jones Indices showing the performance of actively managed large cap mutual funds for the seven years ending in June 30, 2014. During those recent seven years, the S&P 500 Index beat on average 62 percent of the actively managed funds each year. In one year the Index outperformed 85 percent of the active managers.

Longer-term results show the same thing. In March 2011 *Scientific American* reported that a study in the *Journal of Economics and Portfolio Strategy* tracked 452 actively managed mutual funds for twenty years from 1990 to 2009 and found that only thirteen of them beat the market average. In November 2010 S&P Indices published results of its study for the five years ending September 30, 2010. It reported that only 4.1 percent of large cap funds maintained a top-half ranking over five consecutive twelve-month periods. By random chance, 6.25 percent should have achieved that. The same study found that 14.2 percent of large-cap funds with a top-quartile ranking over the five years ending in September 2005 maintained a top quartile ranking over the next five years. Random results would have produced 25 percent.

Purchasing a hot mutual fund has often been a losing venture for investors as a whole even if the fund's long-term record outpaces the index. How can that be? This occurs when a fund builds its reputation by producing great results when it is a relatively small fund, attracts a lot of new investors, and then has poor performance when it is much larger fund. The following numerical example will illustrate.

### Changes in Stock Index

|  | Index—Start of Year | Index Return | Index—End of Year |
|---|---|---|---|
| Year 1 | 100 | 10% | 110 |
| Year 2 | 110 | 5% | 115.50 |
| Year 3 | 115.50 | 2% | 117.80 |

### Changes in Value of Fund

|  | Fund—Start of Year | Fund Return | Fund—End of Year |
|---|---|---|---|
| Year 1 | 100 | 20% | 120 |
| Year 2 | 120 | 15% | 138 |
| Year 3 | 138 | <8%> | 126.92 |

### Investments of Fund

| Year | Amount Invested | Start of Year Price Per Share | Start of Year Total Value of Fund | Annual Return | End of Year Price Per Share | End of Year Value of Fund |
|---|---|---|---|---|---|---|
| Year 1 | 100,000 | 100 | 100,000 | 20% | 120 | 120,000 |
| Year 2 | 500,000 | 120 | 620,000 | 15% | 138 | 713,000 |
| Year 3 | 2,000,000 | 138 | 2,713,000 | <8%> | 126.96 | 2,495,960 |

| Total Invested | 2,600,000 |
|---|---|
| Total Ending Value | 2,495,960 |
| Net Loss to Investors | 104,040 |

As we can see from the tables, over its three-year life, the fund's shares have increased from $100 per share to $127 per share, for total return to the original investors of 27 percent. The index, however, has returned only 17.8 percent. The original investors are ahead both in absolute and relative terms. But they are the only ones, and their aggregate investments are much smaller than those who came later after the fund had done well. Because the fund had hot performance during the first two years, much more money came in at the start of year three. Those who paid $120 per share at the start of the second year have seen their investment increase to $127. But had they held the index, those last two years their value would have increased to $128.50 per share. Obviously those who invested at the start of the third year have lost in both an absolute sense (8 percent) and in a relative sense (10 percent). The table shows the total invested in the fund over the three years was $2,600,000, while the ending value was $2,495,960. The investors as a whole lost money even though the fund has beaten the index. Hot funds often end up costing investors this way.

Goldman Sachs (Goldman), founded in 1869, has for many years been viewed as the gold standard (pun intended) of Wall Street firms. Its reputation and reach extend throughout the world. *Fortune* ran a cover story in February 2014 entitled "Why Everyone Still Wants to Work at Goldman Sachs." The article describes Goldman as "the ultimate career destination." It's really easy to understand why: it comes with enormous prestige and huge compensation.

But perhaps Goldman truly represents what's so wrong with Wall Street today. It embodies conflicts of interest and its customers be damned (what I call "selfish interest"), gambling masquerading as investing (what I call "the ultimate con job"), and shameless hucksterism (what I call "Wall Street pornography"). Unfortunately for Goldman's customers, none of this is new. There is a long record of Goldman engaging in activities that are unlawful, unethical, or harmful to its customers. As I spend more and more time in the financial services industry, I repeatedly see Goldman's great influence. But unfortunately I see mostly Goldman behaving badly.

As we see a pattern in Goldman's actions, keep asking yourself the same question that I ask myself. What would have happened if my small firm engaged in any one of these practices? Could it even have survived, let alone continued, as the most admired member of the community?

In the late 1990s, an accounting firm occasionally referred some of its clients to us. One of that firm's clients had previously retained a small investment advisory firm to manage her assets. The relationship between the client and the investment advisor turned sour when she discovered the advisor had stolen from some of his other clients. The client now had to choose a new investment advisor, and the accountant recommended our firm. The initial meetings with this prospective client went very well. She was, quite reasonably, very hesitant to hire another small independent firm because of what had just occurred. She indicated she would feel safer with a large and established firm, even though she trusted the accountant and knew we had a good working relationship. The client had liked our presentation and approach to investing, but she decided to play it safe and trust all of her money to Goldman's management. Fortunately for my firm, before the client transferred all her funds to Goldman, the accountant was able to persuade her to give 90 percent to Goldman and 10 percent to our firm.

This was a large account even for Goldman. According to its monthly reports to the client, it assigned about ten professionals to the relationship. Both Goldman and my firm were instructed to manage the account as if it represented all of the client's assets and to maintain both equities and fixed income in whatever percentages we deemed the best. These relationships started early in 2000, just before the dot-com bubble was about to burst. Over the next three years the S&P 500 Index declined about 37 percent as part of the worst stock market slump in twenty-eight years.

The client then decided to review the performance of her accounts with Goldman and with our firm. Fortunately for our clients, we had allocated their accounts conservatively, had chosen individual equities that lost much less than average, and had maintained a diversified portfolio of high quality investments. Over the three years, the client's account with us was just slightly up (about 4.5 percent). Given the environment, that performance was strong. How did Goldman do? It had, as instructed, maintained a balance of equity and fixed income investments. However, Goldman loaded most of the equity investments into technology and healthcare companies, two sectors that suffered significantly. Over the three years the client lost about 37 percent of her account value at Goldman even though a significant portion was in fixed income. The equity portion of the Goldman portfolio incurred losses well in excess of the 37 percent decline in the overall stock market.

No matter how large Goldman was, no matter how much its executives earned, no matter how much PR it churned out, no matter how many executives it assigned to its clients' accounts, no matter how large its clients were, and no matter how envied and admired the firm was by the Wall Street community, this client lost big time. Based on this performance, she concluded that she wasn't so safe with Goldman after all and happily for us decided to place her entire account under our management.

We can also learn about Goldman from an employee's perspective. A friend of mine had worked a number of years in the financial services industry both as an analyst and a client account manager. He was happy in his job when he was approached by Goldman with an offer to play a significant role in one of its branch offices. Even though I was not a big fan of Goldman, I thought he had no option but to accept the offer. He probably would have continued to be happy and successful where he was employed, but that did not really matter. If he didn't accept the offer from Goldman, he would always be haunted by the thought that he turned down the golden ring. After considering all his options, he accepted the offer.

We kept in touch as his career with Goldman moved ahead. After he had been there for a while we talked about his experiences. Knowing full well what I thought of Goldman, he told me that I was wrong in my appraisal. He said it was even worse than I had imagined! Goldman was constantly pushing products on customers and selling more complicated instruments when simpler ones would have served the clients' needs and lowered their costs. Generally, Goldman took steps to increase its revenues at the expense of its customers. He also said he saw a lot of people at the top making lots of money but unwilling to share even relatively small amounts with those in the middle or at the bottom.

In the spirit of full disclosure, I must describe part of my personal experience in selling my own investment management firm a few years ago. Fortunately, because of the amount of money we managed, our strong performance history, our roster of numerous sports stars and other celebrities, and our own success, some larger firms expressed interest in acquiring our business. Despite the fact that my investment bankers knew my views of Goldman, they wanted to see what its interest might be. Although I thought it was excruciatingly unlikely that we could ever be happy to cut a deal with Goldman, I agreed to explore the opportunity. We had some discussions, correspondence, and meetings after which Goldman made us an offer. It was literally about one-half of what we had been offered by others. Obviously, that's all they thought it was worth. In evaluating the offer my partners and I thought that Goldman believed we should be happy with their offer for the privilege of being able to join their organization. It's said that every man has his price. Fortunately, I was not put to the test here.

Let's turn to some of Goldman's actions reported in the press over the last twenty years. What follows represents just a small sample from my files.

*May 1996.* Goldman commences coverage of Sun Microsystems with a buy recommendation. It maintains that recommendation when the stock reaches $60 per share. Only in May 2002, when Sun is trading at $7 per share, does it lower the buy rating.

*May 2000.* Goldman analysts divide thirty-two Internet commerce companies into three groups based on their likelihood of survival. All but one of the eight highest-ranked companies are Goldman investment banking clients. None of the fifteen rated least likely to survive is represented by Goldman. (Perhaps Goldman could argue that it underwrote the best companies and therefore its analysts' rankings are unbiased.) From the time of the grouping in May 2000 through

December of that year, the eight companies Goldman favored lose on average 73 percent of their market value, and the fifteen least favored suffer an average loss of 72 percent.

*July 2004.* Goldman pays a $2 million fine to settle Securities and Exchange Commission (SEC) charges of improperly trying to promote initial public stock offerings before receiving required regulatory approvals.

*July 2004.* Goldman pays a $5 million fine to the National Association of Securities Dealers (NASD) for overcharging investors when buying corporate bonds and paying them too little when selling bonds. These transactions with big institutional customers feature prices that exceeded regulatory guidelines.

*April 2006.* The cover story of *Barron's* refers to Goldman as a "Tower of Power" that is "very good at making lots of money." In a preview of coming attractions (we had to wait about two years until the financial world, Goldman included, started to unravel) *Barron's* reported, "Sure, Goldman's trading risks have risen—and management has promised they will continue to rise. But that's only because Goldman has figured out where the world of high finance is going, and is heading there faster than the competition." I can only conclude that whatever they figured didn't quite work out. Without later government bailouts, no more Goldman. This cover story pointed out the real reason why Goldman was such a wonderful employer. In the first quarter of 2006 Goldman reports that average compensation was more than $800,000 for all of its 23,000 employees. We also know that the average pay for about 400 managing partners was over $5 million then.

*August 2007.* Goldman pays $2 billion to bail out its own Global Equities Opportunities hedge fund, acknowledging that this computer-generated fund malfunctioned. The $3.6 billion fund loses about $1.5 billion when its computer models fail to predict market turbulence. Three Goldman funds fall by as much as 30 percent in just two weeks. By way of comparison, the S&P 500 Index for 2007 through mid-August is down about 1 percent.

*November 2007.* Goldman begins marketing efforts to raise $6 billion for a new hedge fund. Why would it want to go through administrative red tape and expense to raise a new hedge fund rather than just continue with existing funds? Two significant reasons. It does not wish investors to be constantly reminded of the losses they have incurred. A new fund starts with a clean slate. Also, Goldman cannot earn its 20 percent of the fund's profits when huge losses remain on the books. Starting a new fund resets gains and losses to zero, and 20 percent of each dollar of new profit can then be paid to Goldman.

*January 2008.* Goldman enters into a $1.3 billion option trade for Libya's sovereign wealth fund controlled by Muammar Gaddafi. Apparently no standard contracts are used. By June 2008 the options are worth approximately $25 million, for a loss of about 98 percent in six months. If Goldman performs this well advising a notorious world leader with major amounts at stake, I can only wonder what it would do for you or me. Later came revelations that Goldman gave a paid internship to a top Libyan official's relative while it was carrying out this losing trade on behalf of the Libyan government's fund. Goldman says that the internship had nothing to do with its relationship with the Libyan investment authority.

*May 2008.* Goldman analysts predict that oil could hit $200 a barrel within six months. In October 2008, as oil prices continue to decline, Goldman revises its prediction to $50 per barrel. It falls to about $40 per barrel by the end of the year.

*August 2008.* Goldman pays a $22.5 million fine to settle with New York State over its role in selling auction-rate securities. Goldman also agrees to buy back $1.5 billion of those securities.

*December 2008.* Crony capitalism works well for Goldman (and other huge firms) as the financial crisis reaches its worst point. The November 2009 issue of *Vanity Fair* runs an article detailing the government bailout of Wall Street. "Morgan Stanley's Nides [Tom Nides, chief administrative officer] had a cynical view: Paulson will keep us alive because if he doesn't, then Goldman will go." The Paulson to which he was referring was Henry Paulson, then Secretary of the Treasury and former head of Goldman.

*April 2009.* Goldman pays part of a $586 million settlement for market manipulation claims arising from IPOs during the technology bubble in the late 1990s and 2000.

*May 2009.* Goldman agrees to pay a $60 million settlement for claims by Massachusetts regulators that it participated in unfair and deceptive lending practices involving subprime mortgages.

*December 2009.* Goldman reports that Whitehall Street International, its international real-estate investment fund, lost 98 percent of its $1.8 billion value.

*January 2010.* A Goldman executive admits that the firm violated well-established laws and regulations by trading ahead of, and even against, its own clients.

*January 2010.* Goldman reports record profits of approximately $13.3 billion for its fiscal year ending in 2009. In fall 2008 the Federal Reserve Bank of New York agrees that American International Group (AIG) could pay Goldman 100 percent for its trading positions. Without this agreement, Goldman's positions with AIG are essentially worthless. Goldman receives approximately $13 billion, the largest single payment to creditors of AIG. In essence, taxpayers enable Goldman to earn a record amount. Goldman then pays bonuses of about $13 billion.

*February 2010.* The Federal Reserve begins investigating Goldman's structuring of currency swaps for Greece. Goldman is criticized by European regulators for structuring transactions so that Greece could hide some of its budget deficit and not be in violation of the European Union Treaty. Goldman arranges for a $6 billion cross-currency swap and is paid a $300 million fee.

*April 2010.* Lloyd Blankfein, Goldman's CEO, testifies before the US Senate about the firm's selling securities to clients while at the same time betting against them. Sen. Carl Levin stated, "You shouldn't be selling junk. You shouldn't be selling crap. You shouldn't be betting against your own customers at the same time you're selling to them."

*April 2010.* In testimony before the United States Senate, the head of Goldman's structured products group trading testifies, "We did not cause the financial crisis. . . . I do not think that we did anything wrong." (This reminds me of the testimony the CEOs of the major tobacco companies gave to the US Congress. Each and every one of them denied, under oath, that cigarettes were addicting.) During that same hearing, Sen. Carl Levin asks the former head of Goldman's mortgage department about an internal email referencing a product that Goldman had sold to investors while betting against it. That email had described the product as "one shitty deal."

*May 2010.* Goldman is censured by the SEC for more than 400 violations connected with clients' trades on short sales and is fined $450,000. (Doesn't that seem like a trivial amount to Goldman, which had annual revenue of $32.9 billion and net earnings of $8.4 billion in 2010?)

*June 2010.* The SEC inquires into another Goldman mortgage-backed securities deal. In one internal email an employee said that one potential investor was "too smart to buy this kind of junk." Goldman sells this product to other investors while going short itself. Less than eighteen months later the issuer's credit rating plunges, resulting in losses for the investors and gains for Goldman.

*July 2010.* Goldman pays a $550 million fine to settle claims of the SEC over its handling of the mortgage-linked product known as Abacus. As part of that settlement, Goldman is forced to admit that it made a "mistake" in the marketing of that security. That "mistake" was selling to one group of customers an investment pool that had been specifically designed to fail in order to help other clients.

*September 2010.* Goldman pays a fine of about $31 million to United Kingdom regulators for misleading investors and costing them as much as $1 billion.

*December 2010.* The US Senate investigates Goldman's trading activity in 2007 in the credit insurance market. The Senate subcommittees investigation shows internal Goldman documents encouraging a "short squeeze strategy" to drive down prices of certain credit default swaps. This would enable Goldman to purchase them at artificially low prices. *Financial Times* reports that a Goldman executive wrote "start killing the … shorts in the street," indicating that "this will have people totally demoralized." The executive went on to say that this strategy would "cause maximum pain" on the existing holders of certain credit insurance. In a dog-eat-dog commercial world, should it be okay to "kill," "demoralize," and "cause maximum pain?"

*March 2011.* The cover of *Bloomberg Markets* includes this statement: "Goldman Sachs is an also-ran when it comes to managing other people's money." Bloomberg reports that 74 percent of Goldman's separate accounts trail their peers.

*October 2011.* Goldman receives a $20 million fee for advising El Paso on its $21 billion sale to Kinder Morgan. This would appear to be part of Goldman's normal business. The only trouble is—Goldman also owns a $4 billion stake in Kinder Morgan. A slight change in the terms of the merger would be worth a lot more to Goldman than its $20 million fee.

*March 2012.* A twelve-year veteran of Goldman quits and writes an article in the *Wall Street Journal* titled, "Why I Am Leaving Goldman Sachs." He says the integrity problem was just too big to ignore, and he identifies two ways to become a leader at Goldman. One is to persuade your clients to invest in stocks or other products that Goldman is trying to get rid of. The second is to get clients to trade whatever will bring the biggest profit to Goldman. He wrote that at sales meetings no time was spent discussing how to help customers. Rather, all discussions focused on how Goldman could make the most money. The ex-Goldman employee is called disingenuous by many Wall Street insiders for having spent twelve years at the firm and only then complaining that nothing had changed. He isn't attacked on the substance, but only on why it took him so long to speak out.

*April 2012.* Goldman agrees to pay $22 million to settle regulatory charges that one of its analysts shared confidential information with a favored client.

*April 2013.* A Goldman trader pleads guilty to wire fraud for hiding $8.3 billion of unauthorized trades, on which Goldman lost $118 million. Even in a firm as massive as Goldman, how is it possible to hide trades of $8.3 billion? Yes, the trader entered fabricated trades into the system to offset the real trades, but wouldn't any trades so large raise eyebrows? The Commodities Futures Trading Commission (CFTC) cites Goldman for failing to inform them until after the CFTC opened its investigation that the employee had attempted to conceal the positions.

*August 2013.* The CFTC, the Justice Department, and a US Senate panel investigate allegations that Goldman engages in abusive practices in aluminum warehouses. Industrial users such as Coca-Cola complain that the warehouses had artificially slowed the release of aluminum to limit supply and drive up prices. Multiple lawsuits follow.

*August 2013.* In a civil case, a former Goldman trader is found liable for defrauding European banks in 2007 in connection with their investments in mortgage-backed securities. This is nothing but symbolic as the trader himself has virtually no money to pay the judgment. One former SEC litigator says that after this judgment "they are laughing in the executive suites of Wall Street." And why not? No top executives are sued, and Goldman pays $550 million of its shareholders' money to avoid further liability and to avoid all criminal prosecutions both for the company and its executives.

*August 2013.* Goldman places numerous erroneous orders in the stock options market. Some estimate that Goldman incurs hundreds of millions of dollars of losses. Somehow, miraculously, about a day later the New York Stock Exchange cancels most of the trades retroactively. I guess because Goldman is big, powerful, important, revered, and influential, it is able to get the trades reversed. In 2012 Knight Capital loses huge amounts because of a coding error, and that firm is effectively put out of business. In the famous "flash crash" of 2010, trades are not canceled when innocent investors are significantly harmed.

*January 2014.* Goldman pays about $3.4 billion in penalties to the US government for its role in the residential mortgage securities debacle. From 2005 to 2008 Goldman issued approximately $121 billion of those securities.

*March 2014.* The SEC investigates Goldman for unlawfully dividing new bond issues among its investors. The demand for high-quality corporate bonds made them a valued asset, and the SEC alleged that Goldman favored some large asset-management firms at the expense of smaller bond investors.

*August 2014.* Goldman settles for about $1.2 billion a lawsuit with the Federal Housing Financing Agency for failing to disclose the risk of mortgage bonds that it sold before the financial crisis of 2008.

*October 2014.* The Federal Reserve Bank of New York fires an employee for being too hard in her investigation of Goldman's practices. The Fed had concluded that the deal under examination was "legal, but shady." The deal was this: Banco Santander, a huge Spanish bank, wanted its financial statements to look better. It paid Goldman $40 million to temporarily hold shares of a Brazilian subsidiary to enable it to meet European bank regulators' rules.

*November 2014. Financial Times* reports that a US Senate report blasted Goldman and others for its practices with commodities, exposing "themselves to catastrophic financial risks, environmental disasters and potential market manipulation by investing in oil, metals, and power plant businesses."

Can we learn something from these incidents? Maybe we can't rely on the large Wall Street firms for much other than attempting to maximize their own profits. The culture does not promote serving the customers' best interests and being paid a reasonable fee. Rather, the culture is one of the client, the customer, the public, and even the shareholders be damned. Wall Street's culture encourages deceit and profiteering. Conflicts of interest, overcharging, market manipulation, misleading or fraudulent statements, outright lies, unethical behavior, and criminal behavior are all too common. With explicit or implicit government guarantees, Wall Street can run amok and rest content that it gets to keep all its profits while the public will absorb any significant losses.

Far too often on Wall Street it's ethics be damned. In December 2013 *The Economist* reported the results of a survey finding that more than half of the international financial services executives they polled said that behaving ethically would harm their chances of promotion and their companies' performance.

So many major Wall Street firms, no matter how much wrong-doing they engage in, are so well described by Will Rogers when he observed, "If you can build a business up big enough, it's respectable."

In the February 11, 2013, edition of the *New Republic,* Michael Lewis summarized the financial markets crash of 2008 and subsequent Wall Street and government actions. Specifically referring to Goldman, he observed:

"Stop and think once more about what has just happened on Wall Street: its most admired firm conspired to flood the financial system with worthless securities, then set itself up to profit from betting against those very same securities, and in the bargain helped to precipitate a world historic financial crisis that cost millions of people their jobs and convulsed our political system. In other places, or at other times, the firm would be put out of business, and its leaders shamed and jailed and strung from lampposts. (I am not advocating the latter.) Instead Goldman Sachs, like the other too-big-to-fail firms, has been handed tens of billions in government subsidies, on the theory that we cannot live without them. They were then permitted to pay politicians to prevent laws being passed to change their business, and bribe public officials (with the implicit promise of future employment) to neuter the laws that were passed—so that they might continue to behave in more or less the same way that brought ruin on us all."

What could I possibly add?

# THREE

# Nonstop Conflicts of Interest

Today we are witnessing the never-ending triumph of selfish interest on Wall Street. A significant portion of its employees are committed almost exclusively to enriching themselves and have no interest in protecting their customers, clients, and shareholders. The long-term health of their industry or the society at large is of no concern. The question is "How much can I grab now?" There's been a breakdown of morality—people may (or may not) be doing what is legal, but certainly what they are doing is wrong. We need to change what is legal, too.

Far too many people on Wall Street are failing to exercise their fiduciary duty. Fiduciary duty is a legal term describing your obligation to act in someone else's best interest, not your own. As a fiduciary you are charged with prudently managing other people's assets with the same care as you would manage your own. Client first, no excuses. We should think of fiduciary duty as the golden rule of Wall Street. Unfortunately, today it is fools' gold.

Wall Street's apologists argue that not all financial firms have a legal fiduciary duty to their customers and clients. In many cases that is technically correct, but that doesn't make it right. Wall Street pretends to have its customers' interests at heart, and then it pays huge sums to lobbyists to defeat congressional attempts to pass laws making fiduciary duty universal on Wall Street. If financial firms were already acting in their customers' and clients' best interest, why would they fight attempts to help weed out the players who are not?

Here are just a few everyday practices in which Wall Street places its own interests ahead of its customers and clients or puts one group of customers' interests ahead of those of others.

1. Selling mutual funds with the highest commissions.
2. Encouraging speculation with borrowed money.
3. Encouraging short-term trading.
4. Selling multiple products when fewer would do just as well.
5. Selling products, including hedge funds, with much higher fees.
6. Creating complex products with higher fees when simpler products would do the same job at lower cost.
7. Allocating shares of oversubscribed IPOs to favored customers.
8. Trading on inside information.
9. Front running clients. That is, buying or selling before your clients do. This allows you to get better prices for your own transactions and benefit from their actions.
10. Unloading investments a firm no longer wishes to own while advising clients to buy the same positions, or buying while advising clients to sell.
11. Advising one group of customers to pursue one course of action while advising another group to do just the opposite.
12. Using terms like "insurance" to sell risky products that really have nothing to do with insurance.
13. Choosing which advisor or which product to recommend based on the fees or commissions received.
14. Making extremely risky bets with other people's money in order to increase the chances of higher compensation.
15. Rigging benchmarks like the LIBOR (London Interbank Offered Rate), on which so many others interest rates depend.
16. Calling risky investments "safe."
17. Selling bonds from their own inventory instead of buying them on the market.

18. Selling shares of companies they are underwriting, on which they receive higher commissions.

Wall Street looks out for itself, not its customers. In 2009 a reporter for a major financial publication asked me how my clients had reacted to the stock market crash of 2008 and whether I had shifted priorities because of that crash and the recession that followed. Some of our clients had lost faith in the stock markets and required adjustments to their portfolios. But I was happy to report that our firm has lost very few, if any, clients as a result of the crash. We had clearly protected our clients' money much better than most of our competition had. I told the reporter that our clients' loyalty was in large part attributable to their appreciation of an important part of our firm's culture—that if we took care of our clients, they would take care of us. Although I told the reporter I knew that sounded both self-serving and trite, she said my attitude was an interesting contrast to that of a high-ranking executive of a major brokerage she had recently interviewed. He told her that the great stock market decline compelled his firm to increase its efforts to protect two important constituencies: the shareholders and the employees. No mention was made of the customers; clearly their well-being was not even worth considering.

In a true free enterprise system, the owners of capital know that they are rewarded for success and penalized for failure. If the owners themselves are not making the decisions, then their chosen representatives are supposed to act on their behalf in a fiduciary capacity. But too many actors on Wall Street and in the corporate boardrooms and executive suites have abandoned this fiduciary duty. They have maneuvered themselves into positions where they take enormous risks with other people's money, are rewarded if they succeed, and incur no financial consequences if they fail. The losses are passed along to the firms' shareholders. In extreme cases the liabilities are passed along to the government, as we saw with the massive Wall Street bailouts in 2008 and 2009.

Sometimes this perversion of the free enterprise system is called "crony capitalism," a system with a close relationship between business and government. If only this were limited to Wall Street, we might be able to fix it. Unfortunately, it's essentially everywhere today. Subsidies exist for oil companies, but also for solar power companies. On Wall Street this relationship just seems to be more extreme.

"Moral hazard" is another appropriate term to use when analyzing Wall Street's behavior. This describes the situation where there is no price to be paid for bad behavior or bad results. The person entering into a transaction knows that he will be protected against risk—that some other party will pay the cost. This has also been referred to as "private gains and socialized losses" or "heads I win, tails you lose." Clearly someone protected from loss behaves differently than someone exposed to personal liability, so I guarantee the results will be skewed. Wouldn't you make large high-risk bets with someone else's money? If you win you get massive compensation. And if you lose your employer gets stuck with a big bill, and you just move across the street to another firm and start again.

Timothy Geithner, Secretary of the Treasury from 2009 to 2013, was president of the Federal Reserve Bank of New York during 2008, when the federal bailouts of the Wall Street firms began. In an opinion piece he wrote for the *Wall Street Journal* in May 2014, he explained his support for the bailouts: "We put out the financial fire, not because we wanted to protect the bankers, but because we wanted to prevent mass unemployment." Obviously, no one knows whether that's true or not, but any restrictions on bonuses were temporary or nonexistent. Why did we reward those who caused the problem with multimillion-dollar bonuses at taxpayer expense?

Alan Greenspan, former chairman of the Federal Reserve, in testifying before Congress on what he thought caused the financial meltdown in 2008–2009, said he found a "flaw in the model that I perceived is the critical functioning structure that defines how the world works." He thought that the executives of the Wall Street firms would do what they were supposed to: protect the interest of their firms and refrain from things that would jeopardize their businesses. But he was wrong.

Why? Because all the incentives for Wall Street executives were working the wrong way—the pay packages and stock ownership plans for Wall Street executives were in conflict with the best interest of companies that employed them. In October 2008 Greenspan expressed "shocked disbelief" that lending institutions failed to protect their shareholders' equity. Later *Fortune* observed that "this bubble was catastrophic because self-interest failed." Really? I think self-interest worked all too well.

*Fortune* then observed that "the *firm's* interest in its own profits should have stopped the housing bubble insanity." But who is the "firm"? As our economic system evolved, the firm was an entity controlled by its owners and operated for their benefit. Now major public companies are owned by a diffuse group of shareholders, none of whom individually (and as a practical matter, even collectively) can control management and its policies. Today the firm is controlled by management, not owners. That changes everything. Management all too often runs the firm in its own self-interest, not for the owners (the shareholders) whose interests often are not aligned with that of the management. Management cares most about its salaries, stock options, bonuses, perks, and tenure. Management wants to solidify its power and the financial rewards that come with that power.

Today, most management could not care less about the shareholders' long-term success. The captains of Wall Street find themselves in a position where the divorce of management from ownership allows them to pursue their personal self-interest at the cost of the shareholders' interest and to make huge personal gains with essentially no personal risk. They are able to pass the risk to others—namely the shareholders of the enterprises whose interests they are supposed to advance. Greenspan and *Fortune* were wrong, again. Self-interest did not fail. Management acting in its self-interest contributed greatly to the financial collapse.

When investors risk their own capital, gains in one year are reduced by losses suffered in subsequent years. This has not been the case for Wall Street's employees, who enjoy amazingly huge compensation even in years with poor performance or substantial losses. If losses ever become too large so that bonuses are curtailed, employees simply move to other firms and start again with continued high compensation.

The result of "heads I win, tails you lose" is not a failure of unregulated capitalism. It is a failure of the shareholders' representatives to exercise their fiduciary duty. No one with his or her own money at stake would have taken "bet the company" risks that Wall Street continues to take. Who would risk their own money by (a) leveraging their investments twenty-five to one (or in Bear Sterns' case, thirty-six to one), so that a 4 percent decline in asset value would result in bankruptcy; (b) paying an outside manager $50,000,000 for gambling with their money; (c) awarding large bonuses in a year in which there were large losses; (d) rewarding those who put short-term profits ahead of long-term viability of their firms?

Similarly, would any sane person have issued a sub-prime mortgage with his own money? Who would make a loan to someone who (a) clearly had no ability to repay the principal; (b) could not even pay the interest under the loan once the initial ("teaser") rates were adjusted (and maybe could not even pay at the teaser rate); (c) had no equity in the property, so that even if the property actually maintained its value, the lender would lose about 10 percent of his investment in the event of foreclosure; or (d) had either no credit history or horrible credit history? Who would loan his own capital and assume that prices could *never* fall? Strange, but true: at least one of the highly regarded rating agencies had its computer model programmed so that it would not accept even the slightest decrease in housing prices. Who would believe that a pool of unsafe mortgages becomes safe only because there are a lot of them in the pool? (Later the default rate on subprime mortgages was over 43 percent.)

The investment rating agencies are supposed to make unbiased evaluations of securities offerings, but they get paid by the very companies they rate—a seemingly unresolvable conflict of interest. In September 2011, the Securities and Exchange Commission threatened legal action against Standard & Poor's, alleging violations of federal securities law regarding the rating of collateralized debt obligations like the ones at the center of the subprime crisis. S&P gave its highest rating, AAA, to $1.6 billion of CDOs (Collateralized Debt Obligations). Those instruments didn't really deserve that high rating, but that wasn't the entire problem here. Just nine days before issuing this high rating, Standard & Poor's had placed $7.4 billion of similar securities on a credit watch. Within a few months Standard & Poor's downgraded this very issue. In 2015 Standard & Poor's agreed to a penalty of $1.5 billion for these violations.

We also see bias in the recommendations made by the major brokerage firms. As one example, in late 2000 and early 2001 Morgan Stanley Dean Witter led the pack with absolutely no sell ratings and 670 buy ratings on individual stocks. Let's think about that. In a deteriorating market the firm's many analysts could not find one single company whose stock they thought was overpriced and merited being sold.

How about today? Wall Street firms continue to encourage buy ratings in order to help their underwriting departments get and maintain business. In December 2014, Citigroup, Goldman Sachs, and eight other firms were fined a total of $43.5 million for offering favorable stock research in the hopes of winning the underwriting business for an IPO of Toys "R" Us. *Fortune,* in its February 5, 2001, issue, explained the matter very simply. "'You're making seven figures,' confesses one analyst. 'So why would you ever take the risk of pissing someone off?'" Negative ratings on a corporate client of a securities firm, or general concern about the economy or the stock market, can be a sure path to unemployment. A former colleague of mine who had previously worked as the chief economist for an independent investment advisor was told he would be fired if he continued to issue reports with a message of caution.

Much of the problem with excessive risk taking on Wall Street came about when the Wall Street firms changed their ownership structures. When these firms were founded, and for many years afterward, they were partnerships. The executives running the firms had their own assets on the line. They would bear the losses for any deals gone sour. That all changed when the Wall Street firms became public corporations. Now the risk of any loss was transferred to the shareholders. No firm owned by its own executives would ever leverage itself thirty-five or even forty to one and then gamble in ways that could destroy the firm. Who with his own money would buy an asset for $100 and face bankruptcy if its value fell to $97? In November 2008, Michael Lewis said he doubted that "any partnership would have sought to game the ratings agencies or leap into bed with loan sharks or even allow mezzanine C.D.O.'s to be sold to its customers."

The current Wall Street generation can justify what it does as simply part of the culture. An article in *Business Week* way back on October 5, 1998, entitled "Wall Street's Spin Game—Stock analysts often have a hidden agenda" began with the story of how Donaldson Lufkin & Jenrette, then a prestigious Wall Street firm, fired a top-ranked analyst because he criticized some bank mergers. The analyst was asked, "What happens when there's a conflict between objective analyses and the demands of investment bankers?" The analyst responded, "There's no conflict. That's been settled. The investment bankers won." That analyst said Donaldson Lufkin & Jenrette offered him $450,000 (in 1998) for a five-year agreement not to talk about the firm. He turned it down. What did Donaldson Lufkin & Jenrette fear if a former employee disclosed non-confidential information? The *Business Week* article concluded that "analysts who try to provide an honest and unconflicted opinion are becoming scarcer and scarcer on Wall Street."

Even further back, the *Los Angeles Times* ran a story about stockbrokers in July 1992. It reached this conclusion: "But the main reason dishonest brokers are allowed to stay with big firms, industry insiders say, is that many are top money-makers from their employers. Critics say there is little financial incentive to weed out 'big producers' who resort to unethical salesmanship."

Another conflict of interest arises when consulting firms advise their clients on the selection of investment advisors and proceed to recommend affiliates. A Securities and Exchange Commission study in May 2005 showed undisclosed financial ties between consultants for pension funds and the money management firms they recommended—firms that agreed to direct stock trades through the consulting firms' brokerage arms. The SEC also found disguised kickbacks when money managers sponsored conferences for consultants. Nothing changed after the market crash and recession. In January 2012 *Financial Times* ran an article entitled "A Bank Run for the Benefit of its Owners? Dream On." Consultants for many pension funds continued to receive what amounted to undisclosed kickbacks for recommending money managers.

A consultant might replace one fund manager or investment advisor with another because of direct conflicts of interest or because the consultant prefers his own friends. An institutional client of my firm brought in a new consultant after suffering poor investment results. One manager in particular, who had the largest share of the client's assets, had performed very poorly. So the consultant completely cleaned house and terminated all of the advisors, including our firm. The consultant made no effort to meet with us despite the fact that the account we managed outperformed those of all of the other managers and was well ahead of the benchmark used in evaluating our performance. Terminations for no good reason happen every day, and investment managers live in constant fear of their clients' consultants.

Occasionally the opposite happens and investment managers selected by a consultant will be retained regardless of their poor performance. Sometimes the consultant does not wish to lose his share of "pay to play." Other times the consultant does not wish to acknowledge his mistake in selecting a poorly performing manager. Maintaining the status quo draws less attention to the problem. What's in the clients' best interest is an afterthought.

Sometimes a consultant's recommended managers fail to perform well, so the consultant advises replacing those managers with new and better ones. But when the replacements fail, the consultant acts like he had nothing to do with the selection, even though he personally chose them. Somehow the clients don't get the joke.

Wall Street would be a better deal for not only its customers and clients but for society at large if a fiduciary standard applied to all advice. You don't need to exploit conflicts of interest to survive. You can be a fiduciary and thrive. When the captains of Wall Street act like true owners and when fiduciary duty rules, we can worry much less about a repeat performance of the crash of 2008. Until then, continue to be concerned—very concerned.

# FOUR

# So Much for So Little

Wall Street firms continually breach their fiduciary duty by deceiving their customers and clients about the cost of their services and products. Customers are almost universally clueless and overcharged every day on a massive scale.

Occasionally an accomplished Wall Street actor has pangs of guilt and changes his ways. One successful broker abandoned his sales job and became an even more successful investment manager. In an interview years later he reflected on his experiences as a stockbroker for major firms. He had been concerned about the poor performance of his customers' accounts and went to his boss to discuss his uneasiness. His boss told him, "You're confused about your job." He should not fret over customers' performance. Rather, his job was to bring in money to the firm. The concerned broker said another broker told him, "Your job is to turn your clients' money into your own." That, I'm afraid, remains the dominant ethic on Wall Street today.

I know of no better place to start discussing deceptive fee practices than with the class C shares of many mutual funds sold by retail brokers. Obviously, mutual fund managers and their sales forces must be paid. Sales commissions can be paid to the brokers at the time of sale (the "load"). Fees can also be paid to the brokers on a trailing basis through annual marketing fees. And the fund managers are paid annual management fees for operating the fund.

When the mutual fund industry started, almost all funds charged sales commissions. For many years the sales commissions were at least 5 percent (and as much as 8.5 percent) of the amount invested. The remainder of the investors' money went into the fund. Gradually, with deregulation of the securities industry in the 1970s, new competition entered in the form of mutual funds offered by discount brokers (such as Schwab and Fidelity), and new marketing practices evolved (such as automated telephone purchases and redemptions and eventually Internet access) that did not employ salesmen or brokers. The new funds did not charge any commissions and came to be known as "no-load" because 100 percent of the investors' money went to work for them.

Numerous academic and professional studies have evaluated the performance of load versus no-load funds. The results have been crystal clear for a long time: the managers of the no-load funds are just as proficient as those of the load funds, but the average no-load funds have better returns than the average load funds. The difference in performance is attributable to the load.

These negative findings posed a direct threat to a significant source of traditional brokers' income. So the marketing departments of the load funds developed a brilliant strategy to deal with the threat. They created class C shares for their mutual funds. How do class C shares differ from class A shares (for which the load is paid on purchase) and B shares (for which the load is paid on redemption)? Class A shares continued to bear a sales commission (still about 5 percent), but under certain circumstances about to be discussed, the commission is reduced or waived. Here's how the sales pitch goes:

For many years our firm's mutual funds have been sold with a commission. But now we understand that those commissions can adversely affect the returns to our investors. We want to fix that, and we have devised a way that will provide you with a commission-free (no-load) product, provided you are a long-term investor. And, of course, you should be a long-term investor when you buy mutual funds. You don't want to be trading in and out of the funds all the time and incurring all the expense that entails. Besides, long-term investing should produce better results and is more tax-efficient. So we have created a new class of shares for our mutual funds. The original A and B shares will continue to be sold with a commission. The new class C shares will have no-load as long as you maintain your investment for at least five years. But you must stay in for five years or you will have to pay an exit penalty. It's 5 percent of your cost in the first year, 4 percent in the second year, etc., until you are free to leave without any penalty after five years.

Based on that pitch, sales of the class C shares soared and those of the class A shares cratered. Why would the brokers prefer to sell shares with no commission over those with a commission? They clearly were not looking to drastically reduce their incomes. The answer lies in a small detail buried in the official documents for these funds, but which the brokers neglect to tell their customers during the sales presentation. The class C shares come with an extra annual management fee of 0.75 percent. Let's analyze this. If an investor redeems class C shares toward the end of his first year, he would pay the 5 percent redemption penalty plus the extra 0.75 percent management fee. If he redeems the class C shares toward the end of the second year, he incurs a 4 percent redemption penalty, plus an additional 1.5 percent management fee during the two years. If the customer stays in for ten years, he pays no commissions and no exit penalty. But by then he has paid extra management fees totaling 7.5 percent, more than the 5 percent commission he avoided. In other words, no matter when investors redeem their shares, they'll still wind up paying more, sometimes a lot more, than they would for a true no-load fund.

If you purchased class C shares in a mutual fund and did not understand the fees you were paying, you're certainly not alone. Over the years I have explained the economics of the class C shares to well over 100 friends, clients, and prospective clients. Before I explained the cost breakdown, only one of those people understood the true cost of the class C shares. I have also spoken extensively on this issue in public, and very few members of my audiences knew the real economics of the class C shares. It's a dirty little secret of the financial industry today, and it sure could be costing you.

Another trick that some of the mutual fund sponsors use is called incubation. Although it is legal, it clearly misleads investors. Mutual-fund sponsors provide seed money to a number of their managers who operate private investment pools that are technically mutual funds. The sponsors then wait and see which of these private investment pools establish good track records and which do not. They then kill the poor performers and go public and promote the good ones. With good track records and the name of a well-known sponsor behind them, these funds have a much easier time attracting investors. After going public, most of the incubator funds don't maintain exceptional performance, but rather become just average funds. But by building assets before they revert to the average, they are often able to sustain themselves profitably for a very long time even if the investors don't prosper.

Many customers think the Wall Street firms make lots of money selling stocks, options, derivatives, and other exotic products but make very little selling bonds. That is simply wrong. Part of this confusion arises from the difference in the way bonds and stocks are purchased for the brokerage firms' customers. When stocks are purchased, the brokerage firm typically goes into the market, purchases the shares, and adds a commission that is separately stated on the customers' confirmation statements. The customers see the details of the transactions.

A bond purchase uses a different mechanism. Sometimes the brokerage will sell bonds to its customers out of its own inventory, and its profit on the transaction will be the difference between what it paid to acquire the bonds and what it charges the customer. Alternatively, the brokerage firm will go into the market, purchase the bonds, mark them up internally, and then transfer them to the customers. In neither case do the customers see on a confirmation statement how much the brokerage firm made. By law the brokerage firm must disclose the charge if requested, but retail customers rarely ask. While a retail customer might pay a $10 commission to purchase $100,000 of common stock, he may pay $500 or more to purchase $100,000 of bonds. At the extreme, as we shall see, markups can be as high as 5 percent.

Years ago I was introduced to a business manager for some high-profile entertainers. He told me he had worked for years with a brokerage firm that could get favorable prices for bond offerings not generally available to other firms' customers. I told him I had my doubts and suggested he give me a call the next time he was presented with a special offering at a great price. A few weeks later he told me his client could acquire a zero-coupon bond maturing at $1,000 for about $550. I checked with my bond trader at Charles Schwab and Company. He could get me the bond for about $525. So much for being special or favorably priced. I relayed this information to the business manager, who was completely dumbfounded.

Most customers would not know the bond was available at $525. Even if they learned that, they might not stop to think that $25 on this transaction is 5 percent and would represent about $5,000 on a bond purchase of $100,000. On a twelve year zero-coupon bond, this difference of $25 translates into earning about 5.1 percent per year instead of 5.5 percent per year. How do the brokers get away with this? The customers don't know the market and trust their brokers to be fair. No one wants to believe that his broker would take advantage of him. The prevailing attitude is: Sure, there are brokers who manipulate the system for their own good, but not mine.

Seemingly insignificant differences in fees and other costs of maintaining investments can make a huge difference over time. In May 2015 *Financial Times* reported that in 2014 the asset-weighted average expense ratio of all Vanguard funds was .14 percent, whereas for Franklin Templeton it was .87 percent. At first glance you might think that this difference of .73 percent per year would make little difference. But let's look at some numbers. If you invested $3000 per year for 30 years and earned a gross return of 7 percent per year, then your average Vanguard account would earn a net of 6.86 percent per year and have an ending balance of approximately $295,000. With an average Franklin Templeton account, you would earn a net of 6.13 percent per year and have an ending balance of about $258,000. And that's with a difference of just .73 percent per year. And please don't tell me that Franklin Templeton makes up that difference by better performance.

As I write this, Morningstar covers thirty-eight Franklin Templeton equity funds (after combining funds with multiple classes of shares) with an average rating of 2.9 stars. It rates forty-four Vanguard equity funds with an average of 3.6 stars. Where would you rather put your money?

Another technique brokers use to generate extra fees is called crossing trades or just crossing. This is selling a security (usually a bond) from one customer's account to another. There certainly are instances when this could be appropriate or even helpful. If one customer desires to sell a bond, and if another customer needs to purchase a similar bond, then a transaction within the "family" could actually be better by avoiding the cost and bother going into the open market. Unfortunately, those are not the circumstances when most crossing is done.

More often the broker decides he can make more money by convincing a customer to sell a bond for no good reason and to replace it with another. With crossing, the bond is transferred from the account of one customer to another. The brokerage firm pays the selling customer less than it charges the purchasing customer and pockets the difference. The brokerage firm then goes out into the open market to buy a replacement bond for the selling customer and earns a spread on that transaction too.

The temptation for brokers to cross trades is so great because the rewards can be so high. I was introduced to a highly successful broker who marketed himself as a bond specialist with a who's who list of celebrity clients. When I met him, he showed me actual portfolios he had put together so I could understand his investment philosophy and process. Apparently he thought it would help his business development to share with a stranger the portfolios of some of his superstar customers with *their actual names on the accounts.* Since I had always been very careful to maintain client confidentiality, you can imagine how unimpressed I was by this display. Needless to say, we did no business together. A few years later numerous lawsuits were filed against this broker for crossing trades and violations of the securities law.

Multiple layers of fees are another problem for Wall Street's customers. Fees upon fees upon fees can be charged for an underlying investment. Retail customers pay brokers or institutional customers pay consultants to choose their investments. These salesmen or advisors sometimes place their customers' or clients' money in funds of funds, which in turn invest in the actual operating funds. For example, a consultant to a pension plan (charging a fee of 1/4 percent of assets under management) recommends an investment advisor (charging a fee of 1/2 percent of assets under management). The investment advisor in turn recommends a fund of funds consisting of private equity partnerships or hedge funds (charging a fee of 1 percent of the assets invested plus 10 percent of the profits). The private equity partnerships or hedge funds (charging a fee of 2 percent of assets plus 20 percent of the profits) make the final investments. The total cost to the client of these four fees is 3 3/4 percent annually, plus 30 percent of profits.

Annuities are investments (mostly issued by insurance companies) that provide a stream of payments to the holder at specific intervals, usually annually, quarterly, or monthly. But annuities come with serious disadvantages, so I would only recommend them for two kinds of investors: spendthrifts and people who want the security of knowing they will not outlive their money. For spendthrifts, contributions to an annuity are in essence locked away and out of the investors' control (out of sight, out of mind), to be returned to them later. For those wanting lifetime security, an annuity provides a steady income stream.

Illiquidity is a major disadvantage with annuities. Once an investor purchases an annuity, his investment becomes illiquid for a long time unless he is willing to incur significant penalties. In order to withdraw his own funds during the first seven to ten years (sometimes longer) after the investment is made, an investor typically has to pay a surrender charge, which can be as high as 10 percent. The surrender charges often decline over time, but they remain substantial. A typical surrender charge schedule might look something like this: 10 percent in the first year, 8 percent in the second year, and then declining percentages over the next eight years.

Annuities also have tax disadvantages. To the extent personal investments generate dividends or long-term capital gains, these are taxed at favorable rates. But all distributions from an annuity in excess of the cost are taxed as ordinary income and thus are more costly to the holder.

Why do Wall Street brokers and insurance salesmen push annuities on customers who don't need them? It is quite clear—the commissions (typically in the range of 7 percent to 10 percent) are very high compared with those on other products. The surrender charges for annuities are imposed so that the issuing financial institutions have the investors' money long enough to earn enough to pay the commissions. There is a common saying in the financial world that "annuities are not bought, they are sold." In most of the cases I have personally seen, annuities were pushed on unsuspecting customers who liked the sound of guaranteed lifetime income without understanding the substantial costs involved.

It only gets worse when brokers convince their customers to invest in annuities with funds held in IRA or other retirement accounts. The owners of annuities pay no income taxes on the buildup of the annuities' value until funds are withdrawn. But with IRA accounts there are already no taxes on the buildup of the accounts' value until withdrawal. By selling an annuity inside an IRA, the broker is putting a tax-deferred vehicle inside another tax-deferred vehicle. Why would a broker do this? Because he finds clients who have money in IRA accounts but no substantial investable funds elsewhere. The broker is taking advantage of his clients' lack of financial sophistication in order to earn high fees. One broker I confronted about this practice indignantly advised me that it was legal and done by his firm all the time. Unfortunately, that's true, but that doesn't make it right. It's about time we change the law too.

Wall Street has its own selfish reasons for creating new and more complicated investment vehicles to sell. The customers do not understand them and must rely on their brokers to evaluate them. This

makes the brokers look smarter and more important to the investment process and enables them to charge more through embedded
fees the customers almost never see.

One popular Wall Street invention is the structured note. This is
a debt obligation of the issuing institution, but it also has characteristics of an equity investment. The amount paid at maturity is
typically linked to the performance of an equity index. For example,
a structured note might provide for a payment at maturity of the
principal amount plus twice the percentage increase in the S&P 500
Index, capped at a maximum of 16 percent, but with the principal
amount reduced on a one-to-one basis by any percentage decline in
the index. This provides the investor with leverage on the upside but
more limited exposure on the downside. For example, if the S&P 500
Index increased 7 percent between the time of purchase and maturity of the structured note, the holder would receive $1,140 on each
$1,000 of original principal. If the S&P 500 Index decreased by 7
percent, he would receive $930 at maturity.

In essence, the investor in a structured note is a general creditor
of the issuing institution. That institution in turn typically secures
its structured notes through a combination of zero-coupon bonds
and derivatives. I would be shocked if many of the purchasers knew
their investment in structured notes could be duplicated through
the use of derivatives. The fees built into the structured notes are
generally higher than the fees would be for purchasing the bonds
and the derivatives to re-create the structured note. Most structured
notes are relatively illiquid, with the exception of exchange-traded
notes, for which an active market exists. The credit risk of the issuer
is another uncertainty often overlooked. Since many of these are
issued by the largest financial institutions, they are thought to be
safe. But what happens if a crisis similar to 2008 were to hit and the
government does not bail out the firms?

Wall Street encourages its customers to invest increasingly higher
percentages of their money in illiquid investments, including private
equity funds and hedge funds. The customers can get their money
out of publicly traded instruments on very short notice, but these

investments lock up their money for much longer. Private-equity investments generally last for years, and each year the managers receive fees. If the management company is affiliated with the brokerage firm, which it often is, then the brokerage firm earns fees for many years and at much higher rates than it would with publicly traded securities. Managers can earn 1½ percent to 2 percent of invested capital every year for five to ten years.

In May 2015, the *New York Times* reported on a recent study by a consulting firm specializing in pension fund performance. The analysis revealed that "more than half of private equity costs charged to United States pension funds were not being disclosed." This study included a review of the $30 billion retirement system for the State of South Carolina, which invested 47 percent of its assets in a combination of hedge funds, real estate, and private equity. Its annual expenses were 1.56 percent of assets, while the national average was 0.57 percent. This extra 1 percent per year of expenses translates into about $300 million more per year, or about $3 billion over a decade. And that's just for one state.

Wall Street's customers desperately need to learn that higher fees almost never lead to greater returns. In July 2013, the *Wall Street Journal* reported on the experience of state pension funds. On average the ten states paying the highest percentage of their assets in money-management fees had lower returns for the five years ending June 30, 2012, than the ten states paying the lowest fees.

The pressure on private-equity firms to reduce their fees has become so great that some of them are either refunding fees or beginning to change their practices going forward. In October 2014, the *Wall Street Journal* reported that the Blackstone Group, which managed about $280 billion, would no longer take consulting fees when selling or taking public companies it owns. Private-equity companies had been getting paid for future services they would never perform, locking in massive fees, come what may, once they raised their initial money. Don't we all wish we could get paid substantial fees for work we never had to do? For example, Blackstone collected more than $20 million in "monitoring fees" from SeaWorld

Enterprises from 2009 through 2013. When the company went public, it paid Blackstone about $46 million in accelerated monitoring fees for future work that was never to be performed. In like manner, Bain, Kohlberg Kravis Roberts, and Merrill Lynch received accelerated monitoring fees of $180 million in 2011 when HCA Holdings went public.

How about deceiving clients into thinking they are earning much more than they actually are? This has become increasingly common in recent years, when interest rates have been so low. Brokers and advisors utilize this technique to trick customers into buying bonds that appear to have better yields but really do not. The broker tells the customer that he is able to get a 5 percent return in a 2 percent world. He does this by going out into the market and purchasing an older bond with a 5 percent coupon. He pays a premium for the bond, so the real rate of return is the same 2 percent as the current market. The broker doesn't tell his customers about the premium, and many of them do not notice or understand what it represents. This enables the broker to claim to be a hero by providing better than market returns while at the same time offering himself the opportunity to earn commissions on the bond purchases.

Let's look at an example using approximate numbers. In a 2 percent world, a bond maturing in five years and bearing interest at 2 percent would sell for $1,000. The owner would get $1,000 at maturity plus $20 of interest every year for five years, for a total of $1,100 of principal and interest. If instead he purchased a bond maturing in five years and bearing interest at 5 percent, he would pay $1,150. The owner would get $1,000 at maturity plus interest of $250 over the five years, for a total of $1,250. But the owner paid a premium of $150, so the net amount returned is the same $1,100. This is just a simple example of the old saying that "if it looks too good to be true, it is."

Until the discount brokers began to take a significant piece of the business, Wall Street's full-service brokerage firms were content to collect their relatively high commissions on equity trades. But as the discount brokers' influence grew, the full-service brokerage firms were under increasing pressure to respond. At the same time, computer systems for managing customers' accounts were vastly improving and made it possible for investment advisors to manage literally thousands of accounts at once.

As these two trends developed, the full service brokerage firms invented "wrap accounts." These accounts wrapped all fees and costs together and enabled the customers to use the services of large and successful asset managers for smaller retail accounts. All of a sudden the brokerage firms could provide their retail customers with access to institutional money managers. The brokerage firms would charge one annual fee for their advisory services in selecting the managers, the services of the managers, and all trades in the account. The brokers would no longer have incentive to churn accounts to generate fees. The wrap accounts work quite well for the brokers in a number of ways. If the money managers selected fail to perform well, that is the money managers' error. The brokerage firms are only too happy to recommend new money managers. Somehow the customers never ask why if the brokerage had selected poor managers the first time it would do any better the next. Surprisingly, there seems to be no accountability. The brokers are able to avoid responsibility for poor performance.

The brokerage firms also benefit from the fees collected on the wrap accounts. For smaller accounts, the annual fee sometimes starts as high as 3 percent of the account value. With the money managers working for less than 1 percent and with trading cost declining with increasing computer automation, this is nothing but a wonderful annuity for the brokers. They no longer have to worry that their incomes will disappear if there is no trading activity. The popularity of wrap accounts has continued to grow despite the high cost of maintaining them. In 2014, in response to abuses, the SEC made wrap accounts an examination priority.

Wall Street has perfected the art of plucking the most feathers from the goose without killing it. Investors can become vigilant and pay only reasonable fees, or they can continue to be tricked or cajoled into paying needlessly high fees. We know that higher fees mean worse performance. Why pay more?

FIVE

# Sky-High Compensation

Today on Wall Street, never has so much money been made by so few for so little contribution to the economy or society. Certainly everyone is entitled to a fair fee for services. But what's fair, and what services are needed? We all believe that fair is what we charge and not one penny more. But are Wall Street's services really needed and beneficial, or are they just generating cost for nothing?

If we look at compensation levels both on Wall Street and in the executive suites of publicly traded corporations, we will see a pattern repeating itself over and over and over again. Certainly many executives are reasonably compensated, but the evidence suggests that far too many are paid far too much for doing far too little. Many of the following examples are from corporate America and not Wall Street, but they feed off each other and share the same problems of excessive stock option grants, lack of fiduciary responsibility, no correlation between performance and pay, gambling with other people's money, and rampant conflicts of interest. Many of Wall Street's top executives serve on the boards of directors of industrial and service companies, and many of the executives of those firms in turn serve on the boards of Wall Street firms. This does not necessarily mean experts are at work.

One quick example. In May 2011, *The New Yorker* ran a major article on the travails of Fred Wilpon, the majority owner of the

New York Mets. Wilpon faced the prospect of being forced to sell the team because of potential liabilities arising from his investments in Bernard Madoff's Ponzi scheme. In an email, Madoff wrote, "Fred was not [at] all stock market savvy." I guess we can't quarrel with that appraisal since Wilpon later acknowledged he did not understand any details of Madoff's scheme. Nonetheless, Wilpon had served for ten years on the board of directors of Bear Stearns, a major Wall Street firm.

These interrelated boards of directors set compensation for each other. What do you think happens when the old boy network is functioning smoothly? Here are some examples of compensation packages that strike me as excessive:

*April 2005.* Three executives of Viacom each receive over $50 million in compensation. The price of company shares fell 18 percent in the preceding year.

*January 2007.* The CEO of Home Depot, Robert Nardelli, quits and receives severance pay of $210 million, which had been "negotiated" when he was hired. During his six-year tenure, Home Depot's share price declined about 10 percent, while the S&P Index increased about 10 percent. His reward for declining shareholder value was about $35 million per year plus his salary, bonuses, and benefits. *Condé Nast Portfolio* named him one of the "worst American CEOs of all time" for this and other work. What would he have been paid for good performance?

*January 2008.* Wall Street's five biggest firms pay a record $39 billion in bonuses for 2007, despite the fact that three of them suffered their worst quarterly losses in history and shareholders lost more than $80 billion in value.

*June 2008.* The CEO of Comcast is entitled to $298 million if he dies while in office; the CEO of Nabors Industries is entitled to $288 million if he dies while employed.

*April 2009.* As part of the government bailout, Citicorp seeks permission from the Treasury Department to pay special retention bonuses to keep the "talent." In 2008 one employee is paid $19 million, another $4.4 million, and a third almost $2 million. All three are gone within a few months of payment.

*April 2009.* In 2008, compensation for the CEO of Countrywide, Angelo Mozilo, falls all the way to $10.8 million from about $51 million in 2007, when he also realized another $121 million from stock options. Seems like a fitting reward for running a company that lost $704 million in 2007. Countrywide was subsequently acquired by Bank of America, which incurred lots of headaches, more losses, and substantial fines for Countrywide's lending practices.

*December 2009.* The CEO of Chesapeake Energy earns $114 million in total compensation as its stock price declines almost 50 percent.

*December 2010.* The median pay of CEOs of S&P 500 companies increases 36 percent from 2009 even as the recession persists.

*July 2011.* Hostess Brands increases the salary of its CEO by 200 percent, and the salaries of nine other executives increase by 35 percent to 80 percent. Four months before these raises were approved, the company had hired lawyers to advise on pending bankruptcy. It filed for bankruptcy protection six months later.

*January 2012.* The *Wall Street Journal* reports that approximately 400 partners at Goldman Sachs will see their 2011 pay cut at least 50 percent from 2010 levels. The *Wall Street Journal* reports that this means a typical Goldman partner will see compensation ranging from $3 million to $6.5 million. In good years these amounts were double. Goldman stock declined about 46 percent in 2011.

*February 2012.* According to the federal audit of the bailout of seven companies, the Treasury Department approves pay packages of

$5 million or more each for 49 executives, even though President Obama promised a $500,000 salary cap.

*May 2012.* JPMorgan Chase announces that the head of its risk management group will leave the firm. She was paid approximately $31 million over the prior two years. Under her watch, the firm incurred losses of $6 billion in unauthorized trading.

*September 2013.* The head of Nokia is to receive approximately $23 million as his firm is acquired by Microsoft. Nokia lost about $23 billion in market value while he was in charge.

*June 2013.* The CEO of SandRidge Energy is fired but gets a $90 million severance package.

*June 2013.* Elon Musk, CEO of Tesla Motors, is paid $78 million for 2012. This is almost 20 percent of the company's gross revenue for the year. It's good pay for an executive of a company receiving all kinds of government assistance and selling an insignificant number of cars.

*December 2013.* Larry Ellison, CEO of Oracle, gets direct annual compensation of about $77 million, his average over the preceding three years. Oracle's stock significantly underperformed the S&P 500 Index during those years.

*March 2014.* The *Wall Street Journal* reports that "bankers hit stock-award jackpot." From 2009 through 2013, employees of the five largest US banks received stock awards totaling $69 billion. This comes right on the heels of the stock market crash of 2008, the bailouts of those very same banks, and the Great Recession that followed.

*March 2014.* Coca-Cola proposes a $13 billion stock compensation plan to cover 6,400 employees. By my math, that's over $2 million on average for each of 6,400 *key* employees. Had this been approved it would have reduced shareholder equity by about 16 percent. (Think about that—a transfer of 1/6 of the value of a massive and established company to employees who are paid reasonable salaries for their work.) Even Warren Buffett, whose company owned about 9 percent of Coca-Cola, said it was excessive—but abstained from voting against the proposal. If Warren Buffett won't rock the boat, then who will?

*March 2014.* McKesson Corporation's fifty-five-year-old chief executive becomes eligible to retire with pension benefits then valued at $159 million. Was this necessary to compensate him for being previously underpaid? He received $51 million in 2013. Such outrage ensued that he agreed to cut his pension benefits to a lump sum of only $114 million.

*January 2015.* The CEO of Time Warner Cable would have received about $80 million if Comcast completed its takeover. Since he became CEO less than two months before the deal was announced, this translates into pay of about $250,000 per hour. Unfortunately for him, the deal was cancelled in April 2015.

It's like Lake Wobegon on Garrison Keillor's show on National Public Radio, where everyone is above average. No company wants to pay its CEO below average, so salaries keep escalating. Of course, what a relatively few employees earn at the large public industrial and non-financial services companies has a relatively small direct effect on the profitability of the companies that overpay, but it often has huge indirect effects on behavior. What the top executives and a large number of the rank and file earn on Wall Street, in contrast, has a significant impact on both the firms' profitability and behavior.

Under their fiduciary duty, the boards of directors are supposed to pay what is required to attract the needed talent, but not more. The directors are obligated to act as if they were spending their own money. But far too many of them abandon their moral and legal duty. For all practical purposes, in large public companies the top executives nominate the members of the board of directors who are then elected (really rubberstamped) by the shareholders. Whose interests do the directors then protect: the shareholders' or the executives'? The directors are hired to represent the shareholders, who are nameless and faceless. But the directors personally know the executives to whom they really owe their positions. I have heard expressed a rather cynical view that the typical board of directors of a large publicly traded company consists of a couple of women, a member of a minority group, and a dozen friends of the CEO.

In contrast, large privately held corporations don't pay massive amounts to their CEOs, who don't get huge stock options. Why not? Because the owners of the companies don't want to be giving away the value of their own companies, and they don't need to in order to attract well-qualified executives. According to *Forbes,* the seven largest privately held companies in the United States would all be among the largest 100 publicly traded companies listed in the Fortune 500. These are all massive companies with annual revenues as high as $135 billion. Some of them are very well known, like Mars, Cargill, and Koch Industries. Since these are private companies, data on compensation is not available to the public. Nevertheless, based on my personal knowledge and that of many colleagues, I think employees who are not controlling shareholders of these massive private companies cannot command huge stock options, enormous severance packages, or sky-high salaries. Yet somehow these companies have continued to grow and prosper for many years and attract the needed talent. In the instances when huge bonuses are paid or massive stock options are granted to management, the executives are usually the owners themselves, and the high pay is to take advantage of the tax law. The directors of these companies are also generally the owners who are protecting their own money and have no reason to give away the store.

How are Wall Street executives and other employees compensated? How are the CEOs and top management of corporate America paid? Different models apply to different players. Let's look at a few.

*Brokers.* Most brokers are paid a commission for products sold. This gives them every incentive to sell as much as possible and to promote products that pay the highest commissions. Commissions put brokers directly in conflict with their customers, who want the lowest commissions and the least expensive products. Who do you think wins this battle?

*Investment managers.* Most independent investment advisors and fund managers are paid a percentage of the assets under their management. Often the percentages decline as the amounts of money under management increase. For example, with an equity account, an investment manager might be paid an annual fee of 1 percent on the first $10 million, ½ percent on the next $10 million, and ¼ percent on additional funds. This can be highly profitable with large accounts since there are economies of scale. For example, managing $40 billion with a fee of ¼ percent results in annual compensation of $100 million. The very top managers make over $200 million every year.

*Traders.* Traders are typically compensated with salary plus bonuses of a percentage of the profits they generate for the year. The good news for traders is that they are not required to pay back prior years' bonuses if they encounter bad years later. A trader responsible for $100 million who earned his firm a 20 percent profit for the year, or $20 million, might well be paid a bonus of 10 percent, or $2 million for that year. Many top traders earn more than that.

*Analysts.* Beginning analysts are salaried employees. As they advance through the ranks, their salaries and bonuses can go through the roof. Ultimately, analysts are compensated by how many right calls they are perceived to have made, how much publicity and recognition they generate for themselves and their firms, and indirectly by how many customers their work brings in. Top analysts used to earn more than $10 million per year, but reforms since the dot-com bust have limited top pay to about $2.5 million.

*Private equity managers.* Most private equity managers receive compensation in at least two distinct ways. Essentially, all private equity firms receive management fees based on the amount of money invested for their clients. Often this is as much as 2 percent per year for a number of years (five to ten years is not unusual). Too many of these firms essentially "double dip" by taking all sorts of fees for related work. This can include fees for financing, commissions on purchases and sales, and additional fees for managing the underlying businesses.

Most private equity deals provide additional compensation in the form of an incentive fee. This pays a portion of the profits (often 20 percent) to the managers. Sometimes the incentive fee kicks in only after the investors have earned a minimum return, or "hurdle."

Here's an example: a private equity firm invests $100 million for its investors and five years later cashes in $250 million. If there is no hurdle, the managers receive $30 million (20 percent of the profit of $150 million). If there is a hurdle of 8 percent per year, then the incentive fee would be $22 million (profit of $150 million less $40 million hurdle or $110 million times 20 percent). For large private equity funds this compensation can be massive. In 2013 nine managers earned $2.6 billion for an average of almost $300 million each, with the range being from a low of about $160 million to a high of about $550 million.

*Hedge fund managers.* Hedge fund managers are generally compensated in two distinct ways. They typically receive an annual management fee of 2 percent of the assets in their funds. In addition, they typically receive 20 percent of accrued profits. (See the details in Chapter 6.)

*Chief executive officers and other top corporate executives.* These employees of large public companies receive compensation in so many ways that sometimes it's hard to keep track. These include salary, cash bonuses, deferred compensation, retirement plans, all manner of perks (e.g., use of private jets, luxury boxes at sporting events, private drivers, etc.), and most important, compensation in company stock or options. In 2014, CEOs of the companies included in the Fortune 500 or the S&P 500 Index had average compensation of about $15 million per year, much of that attributable to non-cash compensation through stock or options.

The granting of stock or options is supposed to align the interests of management and the shareholders. But alas, logic, as history shows, often does not prevail. Compensation in stock or options works so well for CEOs and top management because massive amounts can be paid and usually no one objects. Shareholders would never agree to pay a cash bonus of, let's say, $200 million, but an option worth more than that is often approved for the executives. But when a corporation issues stock for services or when employees exercise stock options at favorable prices, the portion of the company owned by the employees goes up and the portion owned by the shareholders goes down. The dilution is hidden, so the shareholders often do not recognize how they are harmed.

One member of the board of directors of a public utility told me all board meetings really involved three items: (1) complaints about the regulators; (2) concerns over capacity to delivery enough power at peak periods; (3) discussions of "how many stock options we could *get away with.*"

It's one thing to game the system to increase compensation, but far too often the executives cross the line and unlawfully finagle to increase option values. In September 2006, the chairman of the Securities and Exchange Commission indicated that more than 100 US companies were being investigated for backdating stock options. Not content to get stock options for millions of shares, directors and officers of companies arranged to squeeze out a little more by having options backdated to get the lowest price of the month in which they were issued. One study by faculty members at Harvard and Cornell found 1,400 officers and directors at 460 US companies had options issued at the lowest price of the month. Either the employees were incredibly lucky or incredibly arrogant to think they would get away with backdating so often. The probability of options being issued with lowest price for the month is about one in twenty-two. Other studies have suggested the backdating was as high as 30 percent of all option grants in publicly traded companies.

Some actual experience is even more improbable. The CEO of UnitedHealth received stock options in 1997, 1999, 2000, and 2001. In three of those four years they were granted on the date with the year's lowest closing price. The random probability for that was one in 200 million. The *Wall Street Journal* calculated the odds of the favorable prices for options granted between 1996 and 2001 to the CEO of Converse Technology at approximately one in six billion. Similarly, it determined the odds of favorable pricing for stock option grants from 1995 to 2002 to the CEO of Affiliated Computer Services at about one in 300 billion.

CEOs of major corporations owe Michael Eisner and the 1989 board of directors of the Walt Disney Company big time. They set the stage for oversized executive compensation through stock options. Eisner became CEO of Disney in 1984, and in 1989 the Board granted him eight million stock options when Disney stock was selling at about $70 per share. This meant that for every dollar per share increase in the price of Disney stock, Eisner would make $8 million.

Over time there have been, as anyone in the securities industry and in corporate America knows, significant increases in the average value of share prices. At the end of 1988, right before all these options were issued by Disney, the lowest rate of return for the S&P 500 Index for any given number of years—the previous year, 1988; a ten-year period; a fifty-year period—was 9.1 percent. So if over the next ten years Disney's stock merely appreciated like an average S&P 500 company, it would have increased to approximately $165 per share, a gain of about $95 per share. With eight million shares under option, this would produce a profit of about $760 million—not for exceptional performance, just for tracking the S&P average. In fact, in just the three years between 1998 and 2000, Eisner exercised his options and made about $680 million, even though Disney's stock performance was below historical averages.

In 1996, when Eisner's options were already worth at least $360 million, the Disney board members apparently were concerned he was underpaid and needed additional incentive. So what did they do? Grant him an additional 24 million stock options. But he didn't make much on these, for when he left about nine years later, Disney stock was just about the same price as in 1996. Meanwhile, the S&P 500 Index about doubled during that time. After facing much public criticism for Disney's poor performance, Eisner suggested that maybe he received too much credit when things went well and didn't deserve so much blame when results were poor. But then why did the board grant him options for 32 million shares?

In 1994, one of Eisner's hiring decisions only made things worse for Disney's shareholders. When Disney's president unexpectedly died in a helicopter crash, Eisner worked out a deal for his friend Michael Ovitz, the founder of what was then the most powerful talent agency in Hollywood, to become president. Ovitz worked for Disney for only fourteen months, but he left with a severance package of about $38 million in cash and three million stock options worth about $100 million. This means Ovitz, who was seen as a bad fit in the organization, earned his salary plus about $60,000 per hour for his services. Eisner was sued for hiring Ovitz, and the court found that Eisner had failed to act as someone "entrusted with a fiduciary position." But the court ruled that neither Eisner nor the rest of Disney's board had violated the law. Fiduciary duty is for someone else—not the captains of industry.

Years ago a partner of mine met with Ovitz. Our firm represented a who's who of top professional athletes. We knew that many entertainers yearn to be athletes, and many athletes yearn to be entertainers. Unfortunately for entertainers, it's not so easy to become a professional athlete. Fortunately for athletes, they are entertainers to begin with and can perform in other arenas.

Ovitz identified areas where athletes could participate in television and motion pictures. My partner enthusiastically embraced the idea of moving forward with Ovitz on projects as they developed. Ovitz then asked him a simple question. What did he want from this relationship? My partner responded that he was only looking for opportunities for our clients. Ovitz repeated his question. My partner again said that we were not seeking compensation since our clients paid us directly for our work. Ovitz responded that everyone gets paid, and he refused to believe we or anybody else could be different. There's nothing wrong with Ovitz's persistence, but it clearly shows the environment in which he was a major player.

In recent years, corporations have found another way to enrich their top management. Earnings have increasingly been distributed indirectly through share buybacks rather than directly through dividends. Since 2003, dividend distributions have been taxed at the same rate as long-term capital gains, so the tax benefits associated with selling shares rather than receiving dividends has disappeared. But the directors continue with share buybacks, in large part in order to decrease the number of shares outstanding, which would otherwise grow with the exercise of stock options. If the number of shares outstanding were not reduced, then earnings per share, a very important measurement on Wall Street, would decline, adversely affecting the share price—and, of course, their own options. This strategy is just another way to transfer value from the shareholders to the executives who supposedly work for them.

There's an easy way to protect shareholders against this dilution of their ownership. Unfortunately, I have never heard of company directors including it in stock option agreements. If the exercise price of the option was simply increased by the same percentage as the share buyback, there would be no incentive for this behavior.

How overpaid are some of these people? Here's a real easy example, and others abound. The CEO of General Motors made about $9.3 million in 2006 as the company headed into a government bailout and then bankruptcy. Everybody at that time knew that General Motors was floundering. In the year just prior to the bailout, the GM CEO earned more than the CEO of Toyota Motors, the Japanese giant that had become the biggest auto company.

But you say, "So the guy in America made more than the guy in Japan, big deal. We just pay better here in the US." That's true, but the guy in America also made more than the twenty-six highest-paid employees of Toyota combined.

Writing in *Financial Times* in November 2012, Karl Sternberg suggested that Karl Marx would work for a big investment bank if he were seeking employment today. Why? Because for a decade the workers (the top executives and other highly compensated employees) took home everything, while the capital owners were left with nothing but losses. Sternberg observed that the captains of industry had been far more effective than labor unions in destroying shareholder value. And these workers were able to do this by "duping the shareholders that higher pay was essential to retain Talent." But what is the talent worth when shareholder value is rapidly declining over extended periods of time?

As of April 2016, the average stock price for Citigroup, Morgan Stanley, Bank of America, JPMorgan Chase, Goldman Sachs, and Wells Fargo had declined about 10 percent over the last eight years. The S&P 500 Index increased about 48 percent over those same eight years. The shareholders lost billions, but many executives received seven-figure bonuses every year. The average annual compensation of the six CEOs of these firms in 2013 and 2014 was about $18 million each, and that figure increased to about $20 million in 2015.

If your own company were at stake, would you make fabulously rich someone who lost a large percentage of your company's value? Would you pay a departing employee huge amounts that were not required? Would you pay bonuses to retain key employees and not provide for repayment if they failed to stay? Would you lavishly reward employees for average or below average performance?

Pay keeps increasing even though a substantial body of research shows that CEO pay has a low correlation with company performance. Stock options were supposed to tie the interests of management with those of shareholders. In fact, this practice has had just the opposite effect. It has encouraged CEOs to take risks with other people's money and to think and act for short-term benefit rather than the long-term prosperity of their companies. In February 2012, the *Financial Times* reported research from Cambridge University's Judge Business School showing that US companies run by CEOs with large stock incentives had done worse for their shareholders than companies run by those with lower incentives.

It's easy to see why so much of the public is so upset. Fifty years ago the pay of the average chief executive officer was about twenty-five or thirty times that of the average worker. I am not suggesting that is an appropriate figure for today, but 300 times appears excessive for just average performance. Income inequality is necessary in a free society, but it's certainly easier to accept if everyone is participating in economic growth. The public understands increased concentration of wealth when the beneficiaries have contributed to the prosperity of others and not just to themselves. Unfortunately, increasing prosperity for those in the financial sector has not resulted in any gains for the rest of the economy. Just the opposite—it's a drain. The top executives' salaries and Wall Street's take are increasing even when overall economic conditions are lagging.

The amounts paid to CEOs have no effect on the compensation levels of either the lower paid or the rank-and-file employees, which are set by market conditions. Even if the CEO sustained a massive cut in his compensation, the company's other employees would see little, if any, increase in their earnings. In a speech in early 2015 President Obama attacked the CEO of Staples for trying to reduce the number of his company's employees for whom health insurance would be required. The President suggested that the CEO was highly compensated and his high salary would better be applied either to paying the cost of health insurance or to increasing compensation for Staples' employees. But in 2013, Staples employed about 83,000 people, and the CEO's total compensation was about $22 million. If 90 percent of his compensation had been distributed to the lower paid 60 percent of Staples' employees, then each one of them would have received a raise of about $.20 per hour.

The public would view things differently if compensation declined when speculation failed. But what the public sees are government bailouts for the rich and superrich while the middle class gets little or no help. The public now understands that Wall Street has bought itself protection from both accountability and financial loss. Wall Street makes huge campaign contributions, provides other monetary incentives for politicians, and lobbies extensively. All this leads to increased class warfare and either threatened or actual overreaction by the government. More burdensome, more costly, and more ineffective regulations are adopted. Poor solutions are proposed. For example, François Hollande, the president of France, proposed (but failed to achieve) a limit on executive salaries of twenty times that of the lowest-paid employee. If the lowest-paid employee made $30,000 per year, the maximum executive pay would be $600,000 per year. In today's world a limit that low actually would interfere with the ability to attract needed talent.

Switzerland had a national referendum in 2013 on a similar proposal that would have limited top pay to twelve times the pay of the company's lowest earner. That failed at the polls, but the very fact that such a draconian limit was seriously considered and drew a large vote demonstrates how upset many of the Swiss are.

Much of the resentment of sky-high compensation arises from the lack of humility exhibited by too many executives, whether corporate or Wall Street. The Imperial CEO does not play well in our society. (Remember Tyco's former CEO, Dennis Kozlowski, and his $6,000 shower curtain and his $2 million birthday party in Sardinia?) Similarly, the accurate perception that so much of the huge compensation packages on Wall Street are really nothing more than rewards for gambling, overcharging, and shuffling papers does not play well. Most of the American public seems not to resent fortunes made by those who have innovated and made large contributions to the economy or who have demonstrably unique talent and appeal—visionaries such as Apple's Steve Jobs. The public seems to have little resentment of entertainers' earnings. But the public reacts entirely differently when it sees Wall Street executives making lots for doing very little, or worse, even harming the public. Why would anyone support the government bailouts resulting in multimillion-dollar bonuses for Wall Street executives responsible for the unemployment or economic misery of millions of lower-paid people?

In most segments of our economy employees do their jobs without huge potential bonuses. Do we pay bonuses to doctors who save our lives? Do we pay bonuses to members of our military who risk their lives to protect us? Would researchers only find cures for diseases if they had massive stock options? What's so special about the financial sector? In 2014 the average *bonus* for all New York–based employees of the Wall Street firms was about $172,000. How many Americans earn that much in salary every year? In 2015 the average bonus declined to $146,000 but salaries increased so that the average total compensation paid to securities industry employees in New York hit a record $405,000. Something is clearly out of whack when financial folks are the highest paid in our society. In 1997, only two of the wealthiest fifty Americans listed in the Forbes 400 made their money in financial services. And they were father and daughter. In 2014, nine of the top fifty came from finance, as did over 10 percent of the entire list. This is not a good trend if you think financial rewards should go to those who contribute to society by delivering products and services the public wants rather than just transferring wealth.

*Financial Times* publishes a magazine insert every two weeks entitled "How to Spend It." It's filled with stories and advertisements for $20 million houses, limited edition diamond encrusted wristwatches, hotel rooms for at least $1,000 per night, $1,200 shoes, and an unending supply of luxury cars. I shared an issue with my administrative assistant. She commented that it "looks like a rich people's magazine. These are things no normal person can afford." Obviously I couldn't agree more, but I'm sure the advertisers recognize a good market in the financial services industry and their customers. Similarly, once a week the *Wall Street Journal* comes out with its mansion section featuring expensive real estate throughout the world. What better audience?

Sky-high compensation for so little contribution is destroying the fabric of our society and diminishing incentives for work. A nation of paper shufflers will not thrive.

## SIX

# Fees and Sleaze: Welcome to the World of Hedge Funds

How can one person make $4 billion in just one year as compensation for services? You read that correctly—$4 billion. There is but one way in the known universe: run a successful hedge fund.

Most of us think that professional athletes are highly paid (some even think overpaid). The major league basketball, football, hockey, and baseball teams employ about 3,500 athletes in the United States. In 2013, their combined salaries were approximately $10 billion, while in the same year the top *three* hedge fund managers collectively earned approximately $9.8 billion. That's right: three hedge fund managers made as much as *all* of the major league athletes.

That same year the combined compensation of *all* of the CEOs of the S&P 500 companies was less than $7.5 billion, with the top ten making "only" $418 million. The lesson is clear: better to play with other people's money than to operate a huge corporation producing goods and services that people want.

This massive compensation can only be "earned" by investment professionals who are smart enough to call themselves "hedge fund managers" rather than "investment advisors" or "mutual fund managers" or "portfolio managers" or "financial planners" or any other term, for that matter. "What's in a name?" asked Shakespeare. Apparently a lot. Any other financial professional earns much less even when doing exactly the same work. Somehow transforming yourself into a "hedge fund manager" is the key to riches beyond imagination.

So who is qualified to be a hedge fund manager? Anyone who calls himself that and can attract clients. A number of years ago one of my wealthiest clients divided his funds among a group of about ten investment (not hedge fund) managers. After three years he fired the manager who had by far the worst record of the group. A short time later that manager appeared on a list of hedge fund managers being touted for their investment expertise. I still do not know how he earned his place on that list, but he did attract new business in part by agreeing to share his fees with an aggressive marketer. I can only conclude it's better to call yourself a hedge fund manager who shares high fees and has a short-term track record, or no track record at all, than to be an investment advisor who charges much less with a good long-term record.

Let's take a look at the hedge fund industry and see how these staggering sums are "earned." Hedge funds are professionally managed investment vehicles in which investors pool their money (much like mutual funds). The term "hedge fund" is now only a historical reference to the origins of that investment vehicle decades ago. Hedge funds were originally formed to use "hedging" techniques—such as options and futures contracts—to minimize risk in markets or individual investments that could be heading lower. An investor might, for example, buy a "put option" (the right to sell an underlying stock at a given price for a given period of time) as a way of diversifying a portfolio to protect against potential downside risk. Or an investor might lock in a low price for a commodity in the futures market, in anticipation of rising prices.

Today most hedge funds have the goal of maximizing returns, not hedging downside risk. Many are aggressively managed, use risky strategies, own speculative securities (including derivatives), engage in short selling and short-term trading, utilize high leverage, and maintain concentrated positions (rather than diversifying). These speculative practices make investments in hedge funds *riskier* than the overall markets.

Even worse, from the standpoint of investors, is the funds' lack of transparency. Although they resemble mutual funds, most hedge funds are not subject to the Investment Company Act of 1940, which regulates mutual funds. Recent legislation requires investment advisors to hedge funds to report some of their holdings to the Securities and Exchange Commission. However, the hedge funds themselves are not required to report their holdings, there is no requirement to report short positions, and there are significant time lags between date of reporting and the current date. Also, some of the hedge funds have literally thousands of positions so that a review of what the investment advisors control is really of very little help in understanding what the funds themselves own. Since hedge funds are not required to disclose their holdings, many choose not to share their investment activities with their own investors. All the better for the hedge fund managers, who want to claim they have special secrets that result in good performance. If investors have no idea what they own, they cannot evaluate the risks they are taking or the performance of their managers.

Illiquidity (the inability to get your money returned quickly) exposes hedge fund investors to even more risk. Unlike publicly traded stocks and bonds or shares in open-end mutual funds (which can be bought or sold on demand), investors cannot reclaim their money whenever they choose. In turbulent markets this can be crucial. In 2007 and 2008 many hedge fund investors wanted to withdraw their funds as values were rapidly falling. They often couldn't because of lockups (long notice periods), which are standard for hedge funds. As a result, many investors suffered huge losses in 2008 even if they correctly anticipated the financial carnage to come.

Prof. John Cochrane of the University of Chicago Booth School of Business observed that a hedge fund is a compensation structure disguised as an asset class, a completely accurate description. If I call myself anything other than a "hedge fund manager," and if I have massive amounts of money to manage, maybe I can collect a fee of ½ percent per year of the assets I manage. With really large amounts of money I might be able to charge only ¼ percent per year, maybe even less. The fee would depend upon the type of assets I manage, the size of the fund, and what my job entailed. By contrast, hedge fund managers typically get what's called "2 and 20": an annual management fee of 2 percent of the money under management and 20 percent of any profits. This can translate into enormous fees. Suppose I am an "investment advisor" managing $10 billion and my fund has a very good year and goes up 25 percent to $12.5 billion. If my fee is a healthy ½ percent per year, I would be paid $50 million for the year's work. Not bad, but suppose instead I am a "hedge fund manager." My fee is now magically transformed into 2 percent of the assets under management plus a "carried interest" of 20 percent of profits. This produces $200 million as a base fee for managing the money, plus $500 million ($2.5 billion profit times 20 percent) as a performance fee, for a total annual fee of $700 million. I just increased my take fourteen times by changing my title. Never mind that the clients have paid an extra $650 million for what is essentially the same job. These "2 and 20" fees would be illegal if mutual fund managers attempted to charge them, and they contribute to the significantly poor performance that so many hedge fund investors have endured.

Managers who "earn" massive amounts of compensation from hedge funds and land on the list of top earners do not primarily depend on the performance of the fund being managed. Instead, the key is to attract huge amounts of money to manage. (The largest hedge fund complexes manage more than $30 billion, with some reaching as high as $120 billion.) Then, convince your investors to reward you with the "2 and 20" fee, which seems to be the industry standard. Finally, see the value of your fund increase, generally irrespective of how the markets in general are doing.

Let's do some simple arithmetic to show how this works. Suppose you manage a $30 billion hedge fund and have the standard "2 and 20" fee. Further suppose that the S&P 500 Index goes up 32 percent in one year, just as it did in 2013. Lastly, suppose that your fund earned 32 percent, net of the annual 2 percent investment fee, exactly matching the S&P 500 Index for the year. What's your total compensation? Your annual management fee, 2 percent of the $30 billion, would be $600 million.

Most people, myself included, would be happy to stop right there, but that's not how the game is played. With the rise in the market, the fund increased in value for the year by $9.6 billion, of which you are entitled to 20 percent, or $1.92 billion. Add that to the annual management fee of $600 million. Presto, you have earned $2.52 billion. And that's how it's done.

We need to remember, however, that in most cases the 20 percent performance fee is paid even if the manager consistently underperforms the market index. Going back to the last example, let's assume that our $30 billion hedge fund returned only 18 percent for the year, trailing the S&P 500 Index by 14 percent. The manager would still be entitled to his annual management fee of $600 million plus a performance fee of $1.08 billion (20 percent of the $5.4 billion profit). Total compensation for grossly underperforming the market index: $1.68 billion.

Another great deal for the hedge fund managers: even if their performance is erratic, they are paid massive amounts in the years they do well and are not penalized in bad years. Let's compare the compensation of two hedge fund managers—James Simons, the head of Renaissance Technologies, and John Paulson, the head of Paulson & Company. Simons, who made the list of the highest compensated hedge fund managers for five consecutive years, earned between approximately $1.3 billion and approximately $2.5 billion every year from 2009 through 2013, and his total compensation for those five years was approximately $10.6 billion. Paulson, on the other hand, only made the list of the most highly compensated hedge fund managers in three of those five years—2009, 2010, and 2013—but his aggregate compensation for that period was about $9.5 billion, "only" $1.1 billion less than Simons earned. What happened in 2011 and 2012? Some of Paulson's funds got hammered, losing approximately 51 percent of their value in 2011 and another 17 percent in 2012. But even as his funds hemorrhaged money in those two years, he did not have to return to the investors any of the fees he made in the prior years.

And Paulson's horrible performance in 2011 and 2012 was hardly unique. All the studies I have reviewed show that over almost any five-year time period, the average hedge fund's performance has been consistently lower than that of either stocks or bonds. In its cover story of May 24, 2004, *Forbes* magazine observed, "Fakery aside, hedge funds have returned less than stocks and bonds." Similarly, *Bloomberg Businessweek* ran a cover story on July 11, 2013, entitled "The Hedge Fund Myth." *Bloomberg* reported, "One thing hedge funds are supposed to do—generate 'alpha,' a macho term for risk-adjusted returns that surpass the overall market because of the skill of the investor—is slipping further out of reach." The article pointed to the fact that the HFRX Global Hedge Fund Index trailed the S&P 500 Index over eight of the last ten years ending in the middle of 2013. The S&P 500 Index also produced better results in 2014 and 2015.

In 2008 the global hedge fund index substantially beat the S&P 500 Index, but that was the worst year for the S&P 500 Index since the Great Depression. How well over the long haul (2004–2013) did hedge funds protect investors or help them prosper? For the five years 2004 through 2008 (which obviously includes the disastrous 2008) the HFRX Global Hedge Fund Index declined by approximately 1.6 percent per year, whereas the S&P 500 Index declined by approximately 2.2 percent per year (all of the difference attributed to 2008). However, for the next five years the global hedge fund index increased by an average of approximately 3.7 percent per year while the S&P 500 Index increased by approximately 18 percent per year. So we have five years where the hedge fund index was 0.6 percent per year better than the S&P 500 Index, followed by five years where the S&P 500 Index outperformed the hedge fund index by *14.3 percent per year.* The ten-year result: the S&P 500 Index was up approximately 7.4 percent per year and the hedge fund index was up approximately 1.2 percent per year. If you start with $100,000, which would you prefer ten years later—$204,000 or $112,000?

Whether we look at long-term results or short-term results, whether we look back twenty-five years or we look at the present, it doesn't really matter—hedge fund performance has been poor. From 1990 to 2005, the S&P 500 Index increased about 10.5 percent per year. Over that same time period the HFRI hedge fund index increased about 7.3 percent per year. A difference of 3.2 percentage points may seem small, but over 16 years it is substantial—an account of $100,000 would grow to about $500,000 instead of about $300,000.

Let's turn to three recent years. In its May 19, 2014, issue, *Barron's* examined the top 100 hedge funds for 2011 through 2013. Their average annual return was approximately 17 percent, while the S&P 500 Index earned approximately 16 percent per year. So the top 100 funds beat the S&P by about 1 percent per year for three years (on a pre-tax basis). Since index funds sell less frequently than do almost all hedge funds, the taxes paid by the shareholders of the index funds are almost always lower than those paid by the hedge funds' owners. As a result, on an after-tax basis the S&P 500 Index was a better deal. What about the thousands of other hedge funds? The Barclay's hedge fund index, which includes the top 100 funds, showed an average of 4.4 percent per year for those three years. The top 100 funds eked out a small pretax victory while thousands of funds got slaughtered. The conclusion is inescapable: Even with the top 100 funds earning slightly more than the S&P 500 Index, the thousands of others performed so poorly that even with the boost from the top 100 funds, the overall hedge fund returns were about 12 percent per year below the S&P 500 Index. Ouch!

Poor hedge fund performance continued in 2014 when the average hedge fund earned about 3 percent, while the S&P 500 Index returned about 13.5 percent. This was the sixth consecutive year that the S&P 500 Index beat the hedge funds. Through November 2015, as markets were relatively flat, the average hedge fund had lost about 2 percent while the S&P 500 Index increased about 2.5 percent. Even in a flat market, the hedge funds could not make up for the prior years' consistent and substantial underperformance.

Does size matter? Would performance be different if we looked at just the largest hedge funds? Like so much else on Wall Street, big does not mean beautiful for hedge funds—the largest firms are often not the best. In its May 26, 2014, issue, *Barron's* reported recent returns to investors of the twenty biggest hedge funds. Of those, seventeen had been in existence for the five years ending April 2014. The cumulative five-year returns for those largest hedge funds varied from a loss of 4 percent to a gain of 120 percent, with the average being 60 percent. The S&P 500 stock index for that time period returned a total of about 117 percent. Only two of the largest hedge funds had a five-year record that barely beat the S&P, while the other fifteen trailed—some by a lot.

With high fees and poor performance, how has the hedge fund industry managed to grow and grow? In 1990 hedge funds controlled about $100 billion; as of 2014 that had grown to about $3 trillion. We can only conclude that PR and hype trump the truth on Wall Street. Publicly exposing the shortcomings of hedge funds has had no adverse affect. The May 24, 2004, cover of *Forbes* read, "The Sleaziest Show on Earth—How Hedge Funds Are Robbing Investors." Wouldn't you think that would lead investors to ask questions and to rethink their plans? But no, the mystique of the hedge fund has become part of Wall Street pornography.

I think hedge funds have prospered and their managers have been allowed to collect enormous fees for two reasons. First, most money invested in hedge funds is other people's money. Pension funds, endowments, and other managed vehicles are responsible for the majority of hedge fund investments. The representatives of the true investors are not placing their own money at risk and are not particularly concerned with the costs to clients. Second, as *Forbes* put it in 1998 after the collapse of Long-Term Capital Management, a hedge fund that suffered billions in losses in what was believed to pose a threat to many major financial institutions, "Long-Term Capital notwithstanding, hedge funds are here to stay. One reason: they create lots of business for Wall Street." *Forbes* went on to say that hedge funds were the ideal customers for Wall Street, "creating huge volume, frenetic trading, vast debit balances, and lots of short sales." As usual, fees for Wall Street trump good investments for clients.

Gambling, not investing, dominates so much of what hedge funds do. (See Chapter 10.) Hedge fund gambling has resulted in massive transfers of wealth both from one group of investors to another and from investors to Wall Street professionals, but with no net benefit to the economy or society. A case from the subprime mortgage debacle illustrate this well. Bear Stearns, a large investment bank with a long history, was essentially broke in March 2008 when it was acquired by JPMorgan Chase. Just a few months before going out of business, Bear Stearns told its investors that one of its hedge funds that had invested in mortgages had lost all of its value and another of its hedge funds had lost about 91 percent of its value, with losses in excess of $18 billion. But while unfortunate Bear Stearns mortgage investors lost $18 billion, gamblers on the other side of the transactions profited by $18 billion. Those profits then inflated the compensation earned by the hedge fund operators who bet against the mortgage market.

Like almost everyone else on Wall Street, the hedge fund managers utilize PR and hype at every opportunity. Part of the hedge fund mystique arose from claims that from 1990 through 1999 they averaged returns of about 18 percent per year. If true (and I think there are reasons to question the validity of the reported numbers), it sounds good until one realizes that during these same years the S&P 500 Index also increased 18 percent per year. I'm sure that after adjusting for tax consequences, an S&P 500 Index fund was a better deal.

I am constantly amused by the excuses offered for poor performance. It's never that the manager took a chance and lost on his bet, or that the analysis proved wrong. Rather, it's someone or something else's fault. An article in the October 8, 2007, issue of *Barron's* asked why certain hedge funds posted double-digit declines in a matter of weeks. One managing principal of AQR Capital Management was reported as pointing out that "quant [for 'quantitative' investing, the type of mathematical formula-driven strategy involved] investing's core value factors did not fail, but were overcome by mass liquidation." I guess investors felt good knowing that even though they lost lots of money, the black-box formulas would had produced profits if only reality had been different. Similarly, on November 30, 2013, *The Economist* observed, "The main problem is not with the quants' models, practitioners insist, but with the markets themselves." If only we could invest in mathematical models and not be burdened with actual markets, everything would be just fine.

A large portion of the vast compensation hedge fund managers make is attributed to their "carried interest," which is their share of the profits—typically 20 percent—paid to them for advising the fund. It's the share of profits above and beyond what they get for contributing their own money to the fund. Carried interests arose in the private equity and real-estate worlds. Managers would be paid from any profits when investments were sold and the original capital and profits were actually returned to the investors. This has been perverted by the hedge fund industry so that many times huge fees are paid to the managers while the investors ultimately lose.

Suppose you invest in a hedge fund that goes up 20 percent the first year. You pay 20 percent in carried interest, or 4 percent of your investment, to the manager. Your net investment is now 116 percent of the original. Now suppose the next year the fund goes down 20 percent. You might think you are back where you started (+20 − 20 = 0), but that's not how it works. A 20 percent loss on the 116 percent value of your account at the start of the second year results in a loss of 23.2 percent of your original account. This means that you end up with 92.8 percent of your original investment (116 − 23.2 = 92.8). You lost 7.2 percent of your investment but the manager has been paid 20 percent of the "profits." *Forbes* observed that "the 20 percent fee is a ticket to gradual impoverishment." Managers make lots of money while investors lose lots all the time. In just one month— September 2006—Amaranth Advisors lost 70 percent of a $9 billion fund it managed. A short time later the fund closed. Most investors had huge losses, but the managers did not have to return any of the massive fees they earned while the fund had previously gone up. Two years later London-based Peloton Partners Fund became another high-flying hedge fund that crashed hard. During the first part of its short life (the fund opened in June 2005 and closed in February 2008), Peloton was one of the top-performing hedge funds in the world. Unfortunately, in a matter of days in 2008 it managed to lose $17 billion. No fees were ever paid back to investors.

Over time a "2 and 20" fee has a huge impact. The following table shows the growth of an investment earning 10 percent per year both before and after a typical hedge fund fee.

| Annual Return | Original Investment | Value at End Of | | |
|---|---|---|---|---|
| | | 10 Years | 20 Years | 40 Years |
| 10% (Before Fees) | 100,000 | 260,000 | 670,000 | 4,500,000 |
| 10% Less 2/20 Fees (After Fees) | 100,000 | 190,000 | 350,000 | 1,200,000 |

How much better must a hedge fund manager perform year after year for the after-tax and after-fee return to match owning a simple stock index fund? If an index fund earns 10 percent per year, and if that return is in the form of dividends or long-term capital gains, the federal tax rate is at maximum 23.8 percent. The investor keeps a net return of 7.62 percent. If a hedge fund earned 16 percent per year before fees, and if half of the gains were short-term and half were long-term, then net of the "2 and 20" fee and net of taxes the investor keeps approximately 7.6 percent.

Let's think about that. For a hedge fund to beat a passive index fund earning 10 percent per year, the hedge fund manager must beat the index by 6 percentage points per year—that is, perform 60 percent better (.16 − .10 = .06 and .06/.10 = .6 or 60 percent). That's really hard to do. And as we've seen, average hedge fund performance trails the S&P 500 Index significantly.

It may even be worse than that. In August 2014, Forbes.com, not usually very critical of Wall Street, ran an article titled "JP Morgan

Hedge Fund of Funds: Out-of-this-World Fees and Egregious Conflicts." According to Forbes.com, this fund—because of the layers of placement agent fees, asset-based investment management fees, operating expenses, trading costs, and performance-based fees—would have to generate 15 percent annual returns in order to match a 3 percent rate of return on a bond. Good luck with that.

Martin Wolf, a writer for *Financial Times*, summed up hedge funds from the point of view of their managers when he observed, "Since we have made huge profits, our investors have paid handsomely for the near certainty of losing them money."

Many hedge fund managers are not content just to rake in massive amounts of compensation. They also want to continue to pay less income tax than most people (including most high earners) pay on their compensation. They have the audacity (and I use that word advisedly) to fight the closing of the egregious tax loophole allowing them to pay less income tax on their "carried interest." This share of their funds' profits is usually nothing more than a bonus payment for not losing money. However, for income-tax purposes, if the fees based on the carried interest arise from a fund's investment held for more than one year, the fee is transformed into long-term capital gains and the tax rate is approximately 20 percent less than the tax rate on other compensation.

The long-term capital gains rate is intended to encourage investment. But hedge fund managers do not receive their carried interests for risking their own capital. They simply provide services for those interests. Supporters of the lower tax rate for carried interest claim the managers do take risks. In reality, they risk nothing except their time, and for that they routinely receive handsome, sometimes extravagant, annual management fees.

Think of it this way: waiters are paid a base salary and receive tips for good service. Hedge fund managers are paid a management fee and receive carried interest for good service (making profits for others' investments). Why in one case is the reward for good service taxed as ordinary income and in the other as capital gains? The fact that the carried interest gets paid later should not magically transform its tax character. No matter what spin the hedge fund managers try to put on this, carried interests are, pure and simple, a form of compensation for services.

I must admit that I have personally enjoyed this same tax break. All quite legal. Was I happy to save 20 percent in taxes? You bet. Was there any economic or social justification for this windfall? None whatsoever. Should Congress change the law to end this favored tax treatment and raise needed revenue? Absolutely. Here's why:

1. *Inequity.* Wealthy managers may pay federal tax on their compensation at a rate lower than that of their secretaries. A secretary also pays into Medicare. Hedge fund managers making more than $2 billion a year from carried interests pay nothing into Medicare on that income.

2. *Less confidence in tax system.* We have long fostered a progressive tax code—the idea that those who make more can afford to pay more. Is it fair then for the wealthy to pay at a lower rate? Capital-gains taxation at lower rates makes sense for those (including managers) who risk their own capital. The managers have no skin in the game for their carried interest and should not be treated as if they do.

3. *Political deals.* In 2007, the US House of Representatives passed a bill to fix this problem. Senate Democrats, led by Sen. Charles Schumer of New York, came to the rescue of the hedge fund managers and killed the bill. He protected his wealthy constituents (and donors) on Wall Street at the expense of those on Main Street. (Schumer apparently now sees his error and accepts the need to eliminate this tax break.)

4. *No social good.* Our tax code often creates incentives to encourage desired activity. There are deductions for teachers providing classroom materials, benefits to encourage research, and breaks for oil exploration and solar energy. We don't need a special break for carried interest to encourage capital formation or to keep the talent. Does anyone believe hedge fund managers making $2 billion per year would sit on their hands if they could keep

only $1.2 billion after taxes instead of $1.6 billion? If those guys need more incentive, they should ask for a raise, not a handout from taxpayers.

5.  *Substantial lost tax revenue.* In recent years the top twenty-five highest-paid hedge fund managers collectively earned about $25 billion each year. If only half of their compensation were taxed at 20 percent for federal purposes, then the loss in federal tax revenues would be about $2.5 billion per year. Then add in what's lost on their Medicare contributions—about $750 million per year. And that's from just twenty-five lucky winners. It is not a stretch to conclude that the cost of lost income and Medicare taxes from all private equity and hedge fund managers could easily exceed $10 billion each year. Republican or Democrat, rich or poor, all Americans should be outraged that the wealthiest among us get such a needless tax break.

No discussion of modern-day investing would be complete without considering the extraordinary success (albeit fraudulent) of the hedge fund managed by Bernard Madoff, now serving 150 years in prison after pleading guilty to eleven felony charges. For almost eighteen years Madoff operated what he claimed was a hedge fund. Since he was not operating a real fund at all, this investment escapade is an indictment of the entire securities industry, not hedge funds. However, it was much easier for Madoff to pull off his fraud because he claimed he operated a hedge fund. That required many fewer government filings, and investors expected more secrecy. Madoff's funds were in reality a Ponzi scheme that attracted billions of dollars from some of the "most sophisticated investors" in the world. After confessing to his crimes, Madoff himself said the potential losses to his investors could be as much as $50 billion. How did Madoff pull this off over such a long time period when there were numerous red flags and all kinds of evidence that his claimed results were essentially impossible to achieve? How did he survive when federal regulators received explicit warnings? Why did they fail to act?

What is a Ponzi scheme and how was Madoff able to maintain one for so long and on the grandest scale ever? A Ponzi scheme (named after Charles Ponzi, who swindled investors in 1920) is a fraudulent investment plan where funds collected from new investors pay off the old investors. There are no real investments or profits. Let's look at a simple example. The original investors put in $1,000, and later the Ponzi scheme operator claims they have made a profit of $100. The operator has in fact stolen the $1,000. The original investors then ask for their $1,100 (their original investment of $1,000 and their "profit" of $100). The Ponzi scheme operator must now raise $1,100 from new investors to pay off the old investors so that they do not realize their money is gone. As long as the operator can raise enough new money to pay off the older investors who request a return of their funds, the scheme can last indefinitely. However, the whole scheme rapidly falls apart once the operator cannot raise enough new money to pay off the old investors.

Madoff reported high returns to his investors, so they were lulled into complacency, thinking their money was safe and growing with little risk. Many investors were extremely content to leave their funds with Madoff. They thought the money would be reinvested and make even more. From start in 1990 until finish in 2008, Madoff reported a profit every year. For 2000, 2001, and 2002, Madoff had the audacity to report profits of 35 percent despite the fact that the S&P 500 Index declined about 45 percent during those years, its worst performance in twenty-eight years. Similarly, for January through October 2008, he claimed to have earned profits of 4.5 percent while the S&P 500 Index declined 34 percent. Madoff's consistently reporting profits even as markets crashed around him should have been enough for investors to realize that something was really wrong. But that's not what led to the collapse of his firm. Madoff's run ended, as all Ponzi schemes do, when the earlier investors demanded more money back than he could raise from new investors. As markets were falling apart in 2008, his investors started to clamor to get their money out, and very few new investors could afford to put money into Madoff's ventures.

When Madoff couldn't pay the requested withdrawals, he had no choice but to admit that it was all a fraud.

Why would wealthy, presumably sophisticated investors not question claims of unrealistically high returns? Many felt vindicated in the trust they placed in Madoff and their view that they had been smart enough to pick him. Who among us wants to admit that we are suckers for a plan that is too good to be true? Don't we all prefer to think of ourselves as smart (or lucky) and prosperous?

What facts should have alerted Madoff's investors to trouble? Why weren't Madoff's unusual business practices ever questioned? Sure, hindsight is always perfect, but many warnings were in plain sight. Madoff's own fraudulent reports to his clients contained plenty of evidence:

1. Some of the phony trades were reported as occurring on Saturdays, Sundays, or holidays.
2. Thousands of phony trades were reported at prices outside of the trading range for the day (e.g., if a security had traded for a daily low of $10 and a high of $11, a trade might be reported at $11.25).
3. Madoff continued to report that cash was invested in the Spartan U.S. Treasury Money Market Fund for three years after the fund had changed its name.

Other unorthodox practices should have sent out all the needed warnings. The simplest due diligence would have revealed that the outside accounting firm Madoff hired to audit a $50 billion fund had but one active accountant. Why did no one ask the routine question of the identity of the outside auditor?

Madoff claimed his firm was only compensated through normal commissions on trades and that it did not take any fees for its investment management work. We are asked to believe that a hugely successful fund would forego the usual "2 and 20" fee and leave literally billions on the table. Given Madoff's fee structure, fund marketers who just referred clients to Madoff could make substantially more than Madoff himself. Madoff had a nonnegotiable condition that all accounts maintain custody at his firm. There could be no outside parties which could ever control the assets that he claimed his clients owned. This is why, as a general rule, custody of an account should be divorced from its management.

Some respected investment professionals and members of the media gave express warnings that Madoff's fund might not be for real. In its May 7, 2001, edition (about seven years before Madoff was exposed), *Barron's* featured an article entitled "Don't Ask, Don't Tell: Bernie Madoff Is So Secretive He Even Asked His Investors to Keep Mum." *Barron's* did not claim to have exposed the Ponzi scheme, but it did raise significant questions. How remarkable were the reported high annual rates of return and the fact that the fund had never experienced a down year? Why did Madoff, who said he accomplished his results with a proprietary strategy, refuse to give any details of his methods? What should investors think when three strategists for major investment banks told *Barron's* they could not understand how he achieved his reported returns?

The Securities and Exchange Commission (SEC), the federal agency charged with protecting investors, performed miserably. At least twice Harry Markopolos, a seasoned Wall Street professional, wrote lengthy letters to the SEC describing the problems he saw with Madoff's fund. Lest there be any doubt, he was direct. One of those letters was entitled "The world's largest hedge fund is a fraud." The SEC never acted in any meaningful way, even though essentially everything Mr. Markopolos pointed out in great detail was correct.

Madoff did not defraud small and unsophisticated investors. Rather, his investors included some of the largest financial institutions in the world. How did such major institutions as Banco Santander, HSBC, Royal Bank of Scotland, Nomura Securities, AXA, and Société Générale fall prey to such a fraudulent scheme? Were they totally asleep or did they want to participate in a gravy train? I think it was easy for them to believe what Madoff reported. All of these institutions were completely comfortable with Wall Street hype. They may not have been engaged in fraudulent activities, but they could certainly believe claims of high returns with low risk. Apparently "too good to be true" never occurred to them. When a respected member of their own community played the hedge fund game, they could see no reason to pay any particular attention or suspect foul play.

Many of Madoff's largest investors were the so-called "feeder funds"—other investment funds that pooled clients' money and then invested in other opportunities. Feeder funds are often inappropriate investments because they are so expensive. Nevertheless, there may be times when they might make sense if the investments are sound and the fund's structure is fully disclosed to its investors. Unfortunately, once again we saw Wall Street acting in its own selfish interest rather than protecting its clients. The biggest feeder fund abuser in the Madoff case was Fairfield Greenwich Advisors. Fairfield placed about $7.5 billion with Madoff while telling its clients that it was managing the money itself. What was the incentive for that? First, no work is required to manage the money if you pass it on to someone else. Second, you reap the benefits of low overhead—no need for high-priced talent. And third, since Madoff was not charging the standard "2 and 20" fee, a feeder fund could charge an incentive fee and reap huge financial rewards.

J. Ezra Merkin, another investment manager, used Madoff to take advantage of his clients. Like Madoff, Merkin had an impeccable background in the investment industry, having been the chairman of GMAC, the finance company originally affiliated with General Motors. He claimed to manage as part of his own hedge funds about $2.4 billion from universities and other nonprofit organizations that he simply turned over to Madoff. Later Merkin agreed to pay $410 million to settle the charges brought against him by the State of New York. One can only wonder how much he made over the years if he could afford to pay that fine.

Major American institutions stooped to a low level, too. We have only to look at the actions of Bank of New York Mellon. The New York attorney general charged one of its subsidiaries with fraud for deliberately misleading clients about investments with Madoff. The motive: protecting its fee income. In 1998, senior officers of that subsidiary had concluded that client money should not be put into Madoff's funds because he had lied to them and was not investing the money as advertised. Ten years later, when Madoff's fraud was discovered, a dozen New York union pension plans under the subsidiary's umbrella still had funds invested with Madoff, resulting in losses totaling about $227 million.

Madoff pulled off the biggest Ponzi scheme in history because Wall Street wanted to believe. He exemplifies the cult of the Wall Street superstar—someone viewed as having special abilities that only a chosen few possess. For Madoff, it was supposed to be his ability to produce consistent high returns even during the worst market decline since World War II and then again during the worst financial period since the Great Depression. If only it were that easy.

We should look at the hedge funds run by SAC Capital Advisors to learn more of the sleazy side of the hedge fund business. The founder of the firm, Steven A. Cohen, qualified for the list of the top five hedge fund earners every year from 2009 through 2013. According to *Forbes*, his net worth in 2013 was about $9 billion. His firm was so successful that it could charge annual management fees of 3 percent of assets and incentive fees of 50 percent of profits rather than the standard "2 and 20." It's been reported that from 1992 through 2009 he earned for his investors average annual returns of between 25 percent and 30 percent. He qualified as one of the highest compensated hedge fund managers for 2009 through 2013 despite the fact that in 2009 federal prosecutors started arresting some of his employees on charges of insider trading. Eight former employees of SAC Capital Advisors were convicted of crimes arising from their actions at SAC. Their crimes include securities fraud, insider trading, and destroying incriminating evidence.

SAC Capital Advisors employed fifteen people in its compliance department whose job was to make sure no employees violated the law. I guess they were unsuccessful in those endeavors. Although not charged with any crimes himself, Mr. Cohen had previously been censured by the New York Stock Exchange for inflating the price of stocks to increase the value of a portfolio he managed. For that violation Mr. Cohen had agreed to a mere four-week ban from employment with any broker-dealer.

For its securities law violations SAC Capital Advisors agreed to pay fines totaling $1.8 billion. The net result was that SAC Capital Advisors (the firm, not Mr. Cohen) plead guilty to criminal insider trading and paid some fines. As the *Wall Street Journal* pointed out in an editorial on November 5, 2013, "the legal conclusion seems to be that Mr. Cohen is a noncriminal running a criminal enterprise." Early in 2016 Cohen settled potential claims with the SEC. He agreed to a ban from the securities industry for two years. During that time he would be restricted to managing only his own $10 billion fortune. I can hear him laughing in his office in Connecticut from mine in San Francisco.

The overreaching hubris and arrogance of some hedge fund managers, together with the ridiculous compensation many of them enjoy, can be illustrated by the actions of Philip Falcone. In 2009 he earned about $825 million, placing high on the list of top earners. I would be overjoyed to make that much over a number of lifetimes, let alone in only one year. And then I would happily pay my taxes. Apparently Mr. Falcone didn't like that approach. He borrowed about $113 million from his hedge fund to pay his taxes at a time when, because of liquidity concerns, there were restrictions on his investors withdrawing their capital from the fund. Later his fixed-income fund was dissolved, with investors receiving about 45 percent of their money. Since the fund had gone up in earlier years, he had "earned" his compensation and did not have to refund anything when the fund later crashed. But the SEC did charge him with securities fraud, and he agreed to pay $11.5 million of his own money to settle the charges—although the penalty was less than 2 percent of what he earned in 2009.

For all of the spectacular failures of hedge funds and the fraud committed by some top hedge fund managers, Wall Street has decided to ramp up rather than scale back on hedge fund offerings. Why sell only to institutions and wealthy individuals when there are plenty of retail investors to be had? A new group of funds called "liquid alternative funds" has recently started appearing. This is just more bad news for retail investors—more opportunity to pay high fees, take more risks, and earn less. In 2013 the two largest of these funds (one with assets of about $20 billion and the other with about $8 billion) had gains of approximately 17 percent and 8.4 percent respectively, while the S&P 500 Index produced a total return of about 32 percent.

Hedge funds are a bad deal for investors, the economy, and society. They are risky, expensive, and volatile. Their performance has been poor and unpredictable. For investors they are costly vehicles for gambling that fail to deliver their promise. Most hedge funds do not moderate investment risk; instead, they substantially increase it. Performance has been both erratic and poor, as hedge funds have consistently underperformed broad market indices. They hurt individual companies and the economy by focusing on quick results rather than sustained performance. This puts pressure on corporate officers to do what may be in their short-term best interest at the sacrifice of the long-term stability and profitability of the enterprises they operate.

Hedge funds are wonderful vehicles for their managers, who make incredible sums for the privilege of gambling with other people's money. But in the end they are a loser's game for everyone else. Whether you're rich or poor, young or old, liberal or conservative, a high school dropout or holder of a graduate degree, an individual or institution—stay away from hedge funds.

# SECTION III

# Wall Street Pornography

SEVEN

# The Compliant Media
# and the Wall Street Superstar

Wall Street firms and their public relations and advertising departments lure investors into buying their advice and whatever products they are pushing through constant hype, shameless promotion, and hucksterism. Their pronouncements are intended to excite you and entice you with the prospect of imagined riches, easily gained. It's what I call Wall Street pornography (with thanks to Dimensional Fund Advisors for suggesting this term to me). It turns customers on, but they pay dearly for it. Wall Street continually uses terms like "rich," "wealthy," "proprietary information," "secrets," and "special knowledge" to hook customers.

Wall Street pornography is nothing new; it's just becoming more pervasive. The financial shows on the 24/7 cable networks fill their airtime with exhaustive facts and useless analysis. The media should serve as watchdogs and inform the public, but instead they are eager participants, even cheerleaders, and help create traps for investors. What the financial press, the financial departments of the mainstream press, radio, cable television, and now the Internet are really concerned with is how to fill time or space and how to make money doing that. Wall Street presents an endless stream of facts, figures, and analysis and an equally endless pool of Wall Street experts to promote the "opportunities" and often hoodwink the customers.

The coverage reminds me of what can be found on the sports networks. ESPN and other networks devote countless hours analyzing upcoming games. They'll take apart the teams player by player, looking for strengths and weaknesses. They'll compare the coaches, the teams' records, the schedules, the results of prior games, the injury reports, and many other metrics. Professional sports are awash in statistics measuring individual performance: batting averages, field-goal and free-throw percentages, passes completed, yards rushed. When players make an All-Star team, everyone knows exactly how well they've been performing. The analysis is so complete it seems that some experts know what each player eats for breakfast. But tell me, in the two weeks leading up to the 2014 Super Bowl, who predicted that the Seattle Seahawks, led by Russell Wilson, an untested quarterback, would absolutely crush the Denver Broncos, featuring all-time great Peyton Manning? The Seahawks won with the second-largest point spread (thirty-five) in Super Bowl history. Similarly, in 2015, who predicted a Super Bowl that was decided by what turned out to be the worst play selection in the history of professional football?

The analysis of Wall Street may be conducted in different terms, but it is generally just about as useful. We get promises of riches backed by graphs and charts for everything, research prepared by armies of analysts, and interviews with movers and shakers, yet we get surprisingly very little of substance. Wall Street has every incentive to play this game. After all, with all of their alleged expertise, shouldn't the players command high fees, commissions, and other compensation? If Wall Street had nothing special to offer, why would anyone pay them anything?

Your reaction may be, "Well, what's the harm, as long as investors make money?" Here's the problem: if you don't understand whom you are listening to and what you are buying, you can easily be manipulated. (For example, this is exactly what professional bears hope for: bad-mouthing stocks in order to drive down the price, so they can profit from short sales.) You buy risky things that you otherwise wouldn't, and you take advice from the wrong people who put your financial well-being at risk.

Centuries before the first subprime mortgage was ever peddled to an unsuspecting homeowner and then securitized so it could be sold by Wall Street, there was Nathan Mayer Rothschild, the man hailed as the father of modern banking. The shrewd London financier funded both sides of the Napoleonic wars. Legend has it that in 1815, using his network of speedy boats and carrier pigeons, Rothschild got the news of Napoleon's defeat a full day before it was known in London. He grew his family fortune that day by spreading rumors that Napoleon had won the Battle of Waterloo when Rothschild knew he had lost. Rothschild  knew that his false report of Napoleon's victory would drive down the prices of stocks. When that happened,  he gobbled them up at lower prices and made a killing once the true outcome of the battle was known and share prices rapidly increased.

Let's look at a few examples of some of the contemporary problems with misleading advertising or promotional materials about stock-picking and past performance.

*Barron's,* which is in the business of selling its magazine and which touts itself as devoted to stock picking, wants you to believe that its suggestions will make you rich. Its cover story on December 29, 2014, read in large print, "Our 10 Favorite Stocks for 2015." In smaller print at the bottom the cover reported, "Our Top 10 list for 2014 beat the market by more than 15 percent." When I saw this my immediate reaction was: Wow, I want to see what they selected, because the S&P 500 Index was up about 15.7 percent and their portfolio must have increased about 31 percent. You can't imagine my disappointment (but not really my surprise, once I thought about it) when I learned that their portfolio had increased by a total of about 18.1 percent. Yes, their math was accurate: 18.1 percent is 115 percent of 15.7 percent. Their top-ten picks returned an extra 2.4 percent to their investors—not fifteen percentage points, which would have added up to about 31 percent, but 15 percent of 15.7 percent, which is 2.4 percent. When we look at the details, the performance is even less impressive. Seven of the ten stocks returned much less than the S&P 500 Index, and the return on nine of the ten stocks averaged about 5 percent. The only reason for the good overall performance was one lucky pick that went up about 133 percent.

Wall Street can often make itself look good by publishing results that it knows its customers are not likely to understand. On January 6, 1997 (a long time ago but I assure you nothing has changed), Smith Barney sent out its *Portfolio Strategists, A Weekly for Professional Investors*. This issue included the firm's top picks for 1997, indicating that eighty-two analysts had chosen ninety-nine stocks they believed would outperform their peers. The cover also indicated that "in 1996 our analysts' Top Picks produced a total return of 15.8 percent." By historical standards that's strong performance. Only trouble was that in 1996 the S&P 500 Index increased by 23 percent. Let's think about this. This army of well-paid analysts, each choosing stocks in the very narrow industry in which he specialized, picked stocks that significantly underperformed the index. And then Smith Barney proudly proclaimed the results of inferior performance knowing that most of its customers had no clue about just how poor their performance was.

More than a quarter-century later, in 2014, BNY Mellon Wealth Management ran a series of advertisements emphasizing opportunities and risk. One of the ads read in part, "Opportunities are hard to spot in today's volatile markets, even when they're right in front of you. But they exist—as do hidden risks." There's one hidden risk BNY Mellon did not disclose in these ads: the risk that it secretly overcharged its customers. A year later, BNY Mellon agreed to a fine of over $700 million to settle claims that it had for many years charged its clients the highest daily price on currency purchases and gave them the lowest daily price on sales. To illustrate, suppose the Euro traded in a range of $1.25 to $1.26 for the day. Let's further suppose that BNY Mellon executed an actual purchase for a client at $1.253. It then charged the client $1.26 and pocketed the difference. With many transactions over many years this resulted in huge gains for the bank at its clients' expense.

Advertisers can carefully word their claims to be true even though they are confusing or misleading. The *Wall Street Journal*'s mutual fund section of October 8, 2001, contained a two-page ad from Fidelity investments. The year ending September 30, 2001, had been very difficult for investors, as the dot-com bust was underway and the S&P 500 Index had declined about 26 percent. Fidelity highlighted the performance of three of its equity funds, one of which had declined about 13 percent, another of which had declined about 10 percent, and the third of which had actually increased by 10 percent. Given the market, these all represented outstanding performance. But the ad was the result of cherry-picking. The fund that had increased by 10 percent had about $5 billion in assets, while the other two funds had combined assets of about $36 billion. Fidelity was then, as it is today, a massive mutual fund complex. Fidelity actively managed five other equity funds with assets in excess of $20 billion (for a total of $188 billion). These other five funds all realized losses during the same year of between 18 percent and 49 percent. So yes, Fidelity's $5 billion fund did earn 10 percent, but its $22 billion fund lost 49 percent and its $78 billion flagship Magellan Fund lost 28 percent.

Entertainment and sports executives learned long ago that stars sell. That lesson has not been lost on Wall Street as the firms advanced their businesses by developing their version of superstar analysts, strategists, and advisers who are supposed to have an edge over the competition. They are promoted for their special talents, abilities, and track record just as film stars are promoted for their good looks and prior blockbusters.

The cult of the Wall Street superstar is well illustrated by Bill Miller, who managed the Legg Mason Value Fund from 1991 through 2011. During the first fifteen years of that run, he beat the S&P 500 Index every year, an amazing and unmatched record for mutual fund managers. In 1999 he was named manager of the decade for the 1990s by Morningstar, the highly respected mutual fund rating company. The Legg Mason Value Fund grew from about $750 million in net assets in 1991 to over $20 billion in 2006. According to *Forbes*, Miller himself became a billionaire for his work in managing this fund. But alas, his superstar performance did not continue after 2005.

From 2006 through 2011, Miller and the Legg Mason Value Fund lost to the S&P 500 Index in five of those six years, and the difference was massive. The Legg Mason Value Fund's net assets fell from over $20 billion to less than $2 billion through a combination of large investment losses and shareholders withdrawing their funds in response to poor performance. He lost so much that in just six years he gave away almost all the excess performance of the prior fifteen years. For the last five calendar years that Miller managed this fund, one highly respected rating service rated the Legg Mason Value Fund the 857th performer of 858 funds in its universe. Quite a performance for the best manager of the prior decade.

Other rankings were just as bad. For the ten-year period ending November 30, 2011, the Legg Mason Value Fund was the second-worst performer of all equity funds tracked by another rating service. Over the fifteen years ending in 2011 it trailed the S&P 500 Index by 2 percent a year, or a total of about 35 percent. This means almost all the investors who stayed with Miller until he retired would have been better served by an index fund. Many investors lost lots of money because of the terrible collapse of the Fund caused by Miller's misjudgment of the subprime debacle. Just before the great crash of 2008, Miller stated that financial firms' exposure to low-quality mortgages was overestimated by investors. He loaded up on financial firms, including American International Group and Freddie Mac, both of which fell over 96 percent in 2008.

How can a manager go from setting records, receiving unending accolades, and achieving superstar status, to becoming one of the worst fund managers? When he was prospering so fantastically well, was his success the result of keen analysis, luck, or a combination? Had the manager discovered a system that worked well in one market environment and then stubbornly clung to it when market conditions changed?

It's hard to believe that Miller's beating the S&P 500 Index for fifteen consecutive years was attributable solely to luck, and I'm sure analysis played a role in his success. Nevertheless, I think both Wall Street and investors refuse to acknowledge the role that luck plays. In order to understand this, we need to look at probability and the law of large numbers. Suppose Wall Street has 50,000 investment advisors and mutual fund managers. If there is a one in 1,000 probability of an event occurring, and each of these 50,000 professionals made a bet on that event, then random chance would produce on average about fifty winners. If random chance of an experienced investment manager beating the S&P 500 is 50/50 each year (about what history shows), then the random probability of beating the S&P 500 Index for fifteen straight years is about one in 32,000.

Maybe you still are not convinced that random chance is a reasonable or even a possible explanation for long winning streaks for investment returns. We should consider the experiment suggested by Nassim Taleb.

Let's fill Yankee Stadium with 50,000 people and see who wins a contest to predict the results of coin flipping. It goes like this: "Everyone stand up. We are going to flip a coin. If you think it's going to be heads, raise a hand; if you think it's going to be tails, keep your hands at your side." We then flip the coin and announce the results. "Those who got it wrong, please sit down." About 25,000 people take their seats. We repeat the process, and this time about 12,500 folks sit down. This process continues until we get the lucky winner who takes home the prize. With 50,000 people we will probably need fifteen or sixteen coin flips. Now, is our conclusion that the winner is a brilliant predictor of coin flips, or was she just lucky? If we were to repeat the game, how much money would you wager that the first winner will triumph again?

In the real world, no one would credit the winner of the coin-flipping contest as brilliant. But on Wall Street much too much of what is really luck passes itself off as genius. Don't fall victim to the cult of the Wall Street superstar. Don't listen to people who were lucky and then pretended it was brilliance. Vigilance is required to sort out sound analysis from chance and unbridled promotion.

Bill Miller was not the only manager of the decade to crash and burn. Morningstar's successor to Miller was Bruce Berkowitz of the Fairholme Fund, which beat the S&P 500 Index nine times out of 10 from 2001 through 2010. The difference was substantial, averaging almost 10 percent per year. But then things changed, as they so often do. In 2011 the Fairholme Fund trailed the S&P 500 by an incredible 34½ percent and became the worst-performing fund in its category. Things did not improve much after that either. For the five years ending January 31, 2015, the Fairholme Fund had the worst risk-adjusted return of any large diversified US equity fund, according to Bloomberg. During those five years its return was approximately 9 percent per year behind the S&P 500 Index. Apparently what worked well for a number of years was not the path to eternal riches.

Too often great investment performance comes from merely being at the right place at the right time rather than from skill. I refer to this as "surfing." A surfer doesn't create the wave or have any influence over its size, shape, or duration; he just rides it. A good surfer will look terrific on the perfect wave, as long as he doesn't wipe out in the breakers. But what will the surfer look like when the waves are flat?

The Dow Jones Industrial Average (DJIA) hit a peak in 1966. It then declined and did not make a new high until 1982. Many investment managers performed poorly during those years. But then everything changed, and from 1982 through 1999 the stock market soared, with the DJIA moving from about 900 to over 11,500. Almost everyone looked like a genius. The challenge to determine who was really good and who was really surfing became difficult.

The story of Balcor Realty illustrates how surfing works. Balcor successfully syndicated and operated real estate investment funds starting in the 1960s. The firm prospered and its founder, Jerry Reinsdorf, later achieved great fame as the owner of the Chicago Bulls, which featured Michael Jordan and won six NBA titles. Balcor ultimately became a subsidiary of Shearson Lehman Brothers, which in turn was a subsidiary of American Express.

Balcor and its investors prospered in the 1970s and early 1980s as real estate values soared throughout the country. Balcor packaged portfolios of either mortgage loans or real estate equity. Investors believed their money was safe because Balcor owned large and diversified portfolios of mortgages or properties located in many different areas. These diversified portfolios were designed to enable investors to participate in good local real estate markets and to shield them from having too much in any deteriorating markets.

Balcor Pension Investors-VI commenced operation in 1984, raised approximately $345 million, and invested in thirty-one mortgage loans. In its 1992 second-quarter report for this fund, Balcor reported that five of the loans had been paid off, one had been written off (presumably as worthless), and eleven properties had been acquired through foreclosure. In addition, seven other mortgages were then in default. Despite Balcor's expertise and experience, nineteen of this fund's thirty-one mortgages had been in default of one form or another. That is a staggering default rate, significantly higher than the worst default rates on subprime mortgages that led to the Great Recession of 2008. In fairness to Balcor, it did ultimately return the invested capital in this fund to its partners, plus a small profit of about 1 percent per year. But a 60 percent default rate in any market is too high. How did this happen? No waves formed for the surfers to ride.

Balcor Realty Investors 83-Series II raised $70 million and invested approximately $57 million in fourteen properties located in ten different cities. Where had the other $13 million of capital gone? To fees and expenses and to cover losses. Balcor again designed a geographically diversified portfolio to enable its investors to participate in hot markets and to protect them from having too much exposure to poor markets. The Fund's 1991 annual report told investors that six of those properties had been lost to foreclosure and that another four had been sold for amounts approximating the outstanding mortgage balances. Only one property had been sold for an amount in excess of the mortgage, and the three properties that then remained were up for sale. Ten of the fourteen properties had either been sold for the amount of the mortgages or foreclosed. Only 5 percent of the capital had been returned to the investors. Based on the markets for the remaining three properties, at best the Balcor investors received about 15 percent of their money back in what was supposed to be a diversified and relatively safe investment.

Balcor did nothing wrong with its Realty Investors 83-Series II Fund. Rather, this just illustrates the importance of understanding whether prior performance was based on skill or good luck. Was the operator merely surfing and happened to catch a good wave by being at the right place at the right time, or was it able to add value by its experience and expertise?

Balcor raised the vast majority of its money through public funds like the two discussed above—large funds, each with many properties. But sometimes Balcor would raise money from partnerships to invest in one specific property rather than a pool of them. Balcor and other public syndicators were often criticized for this. Many observers thought that the syndicators would save the really good deals for the private market and put the average ones in the public vehicles.

In 1984, a friend who sold private placements approached me with an opportunity to invest in a Balcor private deal. This seemed like the proverbial win-win. My friend would earn his commission, and I would get access to a good investment opportunity. Nevertheless, before I committed my money, I did some personal due diligence to determine my risks and opportunities.

The real estate market was soft throughout the country in 1984. This Balcor deal was located in Orlando, Florida. I attended a lecture by executives of the real estate consulting division of one of the major CPA firms. At that time they considered Florida to be one of only two solid markets in the country. In addition, I had worked with a real estate lawyer in Florida for many years. I asked him to evaluate the location of the property. He told me that the best area in Orlando at that time was at the intersection of two major highways. As luck would have it, this property was about one quarter-mile from each of those highways, or essentially at the ideal location.

I cheerfully made my investment and waited for my profits. Unfortunately, the wave never developed, so neither Balcor nor I could surf it. Balcor sold the property in 1996, and through a combination of returns while the property was owned and the proceeds of sale I received about 23 percent of my original investment. What went wrong? I had invested with the premier operator in the best location available. If markets are bad, only a very special operator will overcome the obstacles. A surfer just cannot perform well when the waves don't form.

Just riding a wave isn't the only way prior performance can be misleading. Consider the fourth-quarter reports for 2007 that Smith Barney sent to its best customers, which featured the following table:

| | | | | | Year of Decade | | | | | |
|---|---|---|---|---|---|---|---|---|---|---|
| Decade | 1st | 2nd | 3rd | 4th | 5th | 6th | 7th | 8th | 9th | 10th |
| 1881-1890 | | | | | | 8.5 | -6.6 | -2.5 | 3.5 | -13.5 |
| 1891-1900 | 17.6 | 1.8 | -20.0 | -2.5 | 0.5 | -2.3 | 12.6 | 18.9 | 6.5 | 14.1 |
| 1901-1910 | 15.7 | 1.3 | -18.4 | 25.6 | 15.6 | 3.1 | -33.2 | 37.4 | 14.1 | -12.1 |
| 1911-1920 | 0.7 | 3.0 | -14.3 | -8.6 | 29.0 | 3.4 | -30.6 | 16.2 | 14.0 | -24.5 |
| 1921-1930 | 7.4 | 20.9 | -1.5 | 18.7 | 21.9 | 5.7 | 30.9 | 37.9 | -11.9 | -28.5 |
| 1931-1940 | -47.1 | -15.1 | 46.6 | -5.9 | 41.4 | 27.9 | -38.6 | 25.2 | -5.5 | -15.3 |
| 1941-1950 | -17.9 | 12.4 | 19.4 | 13.8 | 30.7 | -11.9 | 0.0 | -0.7 | 10.3 | 21.8 |
| 1951-1960 | 16.5 | 11.8 | -6.6 | 45.0 | 26.4 | 2.6 | -14.3 | 38.1 | 8.5 | -3.0 |
| 1961-1970 | 23.1 | -11.8 | 18.9 | 13.0 | 9.1 | -13.1 | 20.1 | 7.7 | -11.4 | 0.1 |
| 1971-1980 | 10.8 | 15.6 | -17.4 | -29.7 | 31.5 | 19.1 | -11.5 | 1.1 | 12.3 | 25.8 |
| 1981-1990 | -9.7 | 14.8 | 17.3 | 1.4 | 26.3 | 14.6 | 2.0 | 12.4 | 27.3 | -6.6 |
| 1991-2000 | 26.3 | 4.5 | 7.1 | -1.5 | 34.1 | 20.3 | 31.0 | 26.7 | 19.5 | -10.1 |
| 2001-2010 | -13.0 | -23.4 | 26.4 | 9.0 | 3.0 | 13.6 | 3.5 | N/A | N/A | N/A |
| Mean | 2.5 | 3.0 | 4.8 | 6.5 | 22.5 | 7.0 | -2.7 | 18.2 | 7.3 | -4.3 |
| Median | 9.1 | 3.7 | 2.8 | 5.2 | 26.4 | 5.7 | 0.0 | 17.6 | 9.4 | -8.3 |
| Total | 30.4 | 35.8 | 57.6 | 78.2 | 269.5 | 91.6 | -34.7 | 218.4 | 87.2 | -51.9 |
| Number of Observations | 12 | 12 | 12 | 12 | 12 | 13 | 13 | 12 | 12 | 12 |

Standard & Poor's 500 Stock Index Gains Per Year (%)
S&P 500 Monthly average prior to 1919 based on estimates from Cowles Commission. Starting 1919 table uses S&P 500 closing prices.

This table shows the annual performance of the S&P 500 Index for every year starting in 1919 and uses a comparable index to take the data all the way back to 1886. I really like having this information in such an easy-to-use form and find it a very valuable tool to this day for referencing history. But Smith Barney had other ideas for using this data, telling its top customers, "The figures above show that the '5th year of decade' has the best returns, averaging about 22.5 percent. The second best years have been the '8th year of the decade' with average gains of about 18 percent. These are the only two years with returns in double digits. Hopefully history will repeat in 2008!

111

Investors of course should keep in mind that past performance is no guarantee of future results."

Wow! Since the year of this report ended in an "8," we should have been hopeful that stock market returns would be great. But the subprime debacle was clearly underway when Smith Barney released this report. The S&P 500 Index had already declined from a high of 1,576 in October 2007 to 1,378 on January 31, 2008. So perhaps Smith Barney should have considered that a sample size of twelve prior readings was too small for statistical accuracy. Shouldn't it have occurred to them that even though we do measure a lot of things on a calendar basis, yearly cut-offs are arbitrary when it comes to stock market performance? Did they notice on their own table that three of the last four years ending in 8 had market returns well below the high averages for all years ending in 8? Did they look at their own chart and notice that 1997 was the fifth-best year in the last sixty-eight years, even though years ending in seven were at that time the worst performers?

Did Smith Barney's customers feel good to get this encouraging suggestion as the world economy was already unraveling? Did any of them buy more stocks in response? Of course we now know that the S&P 500 Index declined 39 percent in 2008, representing the largest single-year loss since 1937, during the Great Depression. (Smith Barney's hope and hype should have made 2015 a great year. According to their chart, years ending in "5" have seen the best returns by far, averaging 22.5 percent. In 2015, the S&P 500 Index decreased about 1 percent, making that year the worst year ever ending in 5—and the only one with a loss.)

This is just an example of "data mining"—searching through past data in the hopes of discovering patterns. It would be useful if past results accurately predicted the future. But often they don't. If past results cannot be explained by a workable model, they should not be relied upon.

The takeaway here seems fairly clear. How can you take someone seriously who suggests that investment returns are influenced by the last digit of the year in which they occur? Numerology, the idea that numbers have significance beyond their arithmetic value, takes on many guises. Examples include lucky 7 and unlucky 13 in Western cultures, lucky 8 in China, and unlucky 4 throughout much of Asia. Meaningless correlations are everywhere. Do you realize that almost everyone in the United States who has developed cancer in the last fifty years drank milk as a child? Or how about the Super Bowl model, which held sway for twenty-seven years? From the first Super Bowl in 1967 through 1993, there was a 100 percent correlation between the National Conference team winning the Super Bowl and the S&P 500 Index increasing for the year. Since that formula worked for so long, would you use it to drive your investment strategy? That correlation came to an end in 1994 and has not been very helpful since. So we're left with the question: When the correlation was high, was it just random chance or did the conference champion influence the stock markets?

But numerology isn't the only trick Wall Street plays with numbers. Too often past performance is measured by arithmetic average returns rather than chained (or geometric) average returns. The difference between the two can be massive. To compute returns using an arithmetic average, you simply add the rates of return for each year and divide by the number of years. For chained results, you multiply the sequence of returns and adjust for the number of years to get annual rates. The following table illustrates the difference in these two approaches for an investment that returns 48 percent in year 1, loses 35 percent in year 2, increases 15 percent in year 3, and declines 12 percent in year 4.

|  | Rate Of Return During Year | Arithmetic Results (Annual Average Rate of Return) | Chained Result (Average Annual Rate of Return) |
|---|---|---|---|
| Year 1 | 48% | 48 | 48 |
| Year 2 | <35%> | 6.5 | <1.9> |
| Year 3 | 15% | 9.3 | 3.5 |
| Year 4 | <12%> | 4 | <0.65> |

If you saw a report showing your account earned an average of 4 percent per year for four years, you would think you were ahead about 16 percent. In fact, as the table above shows, you have lost about 0.65 percent per year, or a total of 2.5 percent.

Whatever Wall Street firms want to pretend, in the real world results are chained. This is one very important reason to avoid large fluctuations in your investment accounts. It's why slow and steady is what you should pursue. What would happen if your investment account went up 50 percent and down 50 percent every other year? You'd be on your way to bankruptcy, as the following table shows:

|        | Investment Results | Value of Account at End of Year (Starting Value = 100) |
|--------|--------------------|-------------------------------------------------------|
| Year 1 | 50                 | 150                                                   |
| Year 2 | <50>               | 75                                                    |
| Year 3 | 50                 | 112.5                                                 |
| Year 4 | <50>               | 56.2                                                  |
| Year 5 | 50                 | 84.4                                                  |
| Year 6 | <50>               | 42.2                                                  |

In its October 28, 2013, issue, *Barron's* published the top picks from the money managers participating in one of its 2013 conferences. *Barron's* invites only All-Star managers to speak at these conferences; no minor leaguers or rookies allowed. The table listing the top picks from seven leading money managers was called "Lining Up Winners." The seven managers each offered between two and four of their favorites, for a total of eighteen selections. Over the next year these winning eighteen selections increased on average by 4.3 percent. If instead a reader had invested an equal amount each of the seven money managers' selections (i.e., one-seventh with each advisor's picks so as not to give more weight to a manager who picked four stocks instead of two), the return would have been reduced to

2.5 percent. Meanwhile, the S&P 500 Index increased 12 percent during that same year.

How did some of the individual advisors do with their picks? Leon Cooperman had been named to *Bloomberg Markets* list of the fifty most influential people on Wall Street. In 2013 and 2014 he was listed in *Forbes* as one of the forty highest-earning hedge fund managers. His own personal net worth was estimated at about $2.5 billion. His two favorite picks were down an average of 39 percent for the year. In 2010, Morningstar named another one of the panelists, David Herro, International Stock Manager of the decade. His selections were down an average of 17 percent for the year. Yet another panelist, Marc Faber, is a prominent Swiss investment advisor. In 2012 he predicted with "100% certainty that a global economic recession would arrive, no later than early 2013." As I write this in spring 2016, we are all still waiting. As of the end of 2014 his favorite picks from *Barron's* conference were down to about an average of 11 percent for that year, while the S&P 500 Index advanced 12 percent.

Picking a good investment manager is extremely difficult. No matter how much experience you have and how many resources at your disposal, you cannot identify great managers until after they have succeeded. By then, it is often too late to benefit from their expertise. Almost nothing can show this better than the history of Fidelity Magellan Fund, which opened its doors in 1963. By 1977 the fund managed assets of about $18 million, and the now-legendary Peter Lynch then began his thirteen-year run as its manager. His performance was absolutely remarkable.

Under Lynch's leadership the Fidelity Magellan Fund averaged returns of about 29 percent per year, while the S&P 500 Index averaged about 13 percent per year. The Fund's assets grew to a then-startling $13 billion when he retired in 1990.

Fidelity then had to find an appropriate successor. Let's think about all the advantages Fidelity had in choosing Lynch's replacement. Any successor would find attractive the opportunity (a) to succeed a legendary manager, (b) to run one of the largest mutual funds in the world, (c) to earn the very high compensation the position would pay, and (d) to bask in the prestige associated with the job. The pool of applicants undoubtedly included a large number of the world's most successful investment advisors and mutual fund managers. Certainly Fidelity would be the most qualified to choose the future head of its own most prized asset. Perhaps Peter Lynch himself offered advice or participated in the selection process.

Let's see how Lynch's successors have done. At first the Fidelity Magellan Fund continued to grow, as stock markets raced up in the 1990s. Lynch's first two successors managed the Fund for a little over six years, and during that time the Fund beat the S&P 500 Index by about 2 percent per year. This is good, but hardly the annual 16 percent advantage Lynch had maintained. As the bull market of the 1990s continued, the assets of the Fidelity Magellan Fund reached an incredible $100 billion by 2000, making it the largest mutual fund in the world. But then things began to change. The Fund underperformed the S&P 500 Index in four of the next five years and seven of the next ten. Assets under management declined because of investment losses and shareholder redemptions, until by 2011 the Fund's assets stood at $13 billion, just where they were when Lynch departed twenty-one years earlier.

By 2012, Morningstar, the respected mutual fund rating service, awarded the Fidelity Magellan Fund one star, meaning its performance was in the lowest 10 percent of all comparable funds. Fidelity Magellan Fund was featured on the cover of *Barron's* on April 5, 2015, as being "Adrift for decades." If Fidelity Investments, with all its experience, resources, and connections, could not for decades successfully choose managers for its hugely successful and highly profitable flagship fund, how could you or I or anyone else?

Of course this didn't stop James Cramer from claiming to know he could identify the next great money manager. Named by *Newsweek* in 1999 as a top buzz maker, Cramer is the host of CNBC's *Mad Money*, the most popular financial show on cable television. As recently as 2008, Cramer was promoting the stock-picking acumen of a most unlikely celebrity: Len Dykstra, a three-time All-Star baseball player who led the New York Mets to a World Series win. He was such a tenacious player that he was known as "Nails," a moniker that suited his reputation as tough and wild on and off the field. Dykstra never cultivated a studious image nor suggested he analyzed matters carefully before jumping into action. In one interview he explained why he didn't read. "You know I never read when I played baseball, I didn't read because I thought it would hurt my eyes. You know what I mean? So it would affect my hitting." Now that's someone you want to secure your financial future.

Nonetheless, Cramer endorsed Dykstra as "a good investment generator and strong contributor" and even hired him to write a stock-picking column for his website, TheStreet.com. In an interview on HBO's *Real Sports*, Cramer said, "Not only is he [Dykstra] sophisticated, he is one of the great ones in this business." Let's stop and think about that. There are thousands upon thousands of highly educated and experienced Wall Street professionals. Dykstra spends his life in baseball and in his spare time becomes one of the greatest?

On TheStreet.com Dykstra bragged that he had picked ninety-six winners against only one loser. Anyone in the financial business knows that is impossible. Good stock picking is a question of batting averages, but no one hits .989. Cramer either was fooled, didn't care, or didn't want to know the truth. Why would any sane person believe that a baseball player could just show up and become a more skillful stock picker than essentially all the professionals who have devoted their lives to investing? What does this say about the investing public when as soon as Dykstra's newsletter had the imprimatur of Cramer and TheStreet.com, $1 million in subscriptions poured in? What does it say about Cramer?

A few years after he started working with Cramer, Dykstra filed for bankruptcy, listing assets of about $25 million and debts of about $37 million, apparently with about 100 creditors. But this soon became the least of Dykstra's problems. He was later indicted for attempted grand theft auto, identity theft, and possession of a controlled substance. He was sentenced to three years in California state prison as a result of a plea deal with the prosecutors.

Cramer himself is another Wall Street luminary whose attractiveness I just don't understand. Why would anybody take advice from someone who's constantly screaming on television? Sure, it makes good theater, but it's your money and future at stake. How about numerous wrong picks? In 2008 Cramer stated, "Bear Stearns is not in trouble." About a week later its total collapse became public. Think about his recommendation in September 2000 that "SUNW [Sun Microsystems] has the best near-term outlook of any company I know." About six months later SUNW had lost about half its value, and within two years was down about 95 percent.

Maybe 2000 was just a bad year for Cramer. In February 2000 he stated, "Enron is certainly for real." It certainly was then, trading for $67 per share on its way to $81 per share a year later. But by November 2001, Enron had been exposed as one of the biggest frauds in history (see Chapter 14), and the stock was trading at 61 cents per share, for a loss of over 99 percent. In August 2000 Cramer told the world, "Global Crossing is a good stock." Less than a year and a half later it too was in bankruptcy.

At least Cramer was trying to help his viewers. The same can't be said of Henry Blodget, Merrill Lynch's superstar analyst during the dot-come bubble. On December 4, 2000, he emailed a colleague, "LFMN [Lifeminders] at $4. I can't believe what a POS [Piece of Sh*t] that thing is." On December 21, 2000, he issued a report to investors which included: "Accumulate…we think LFMN presents an attractive investment."

CNBC should not be supporting entertainment as investment advice. If it's entertainment you want, there's the Game Show Network, the Sci-Fi Network, and the Comedy Channel. In all cases, you'll be better entertained and save money.

But others in the financial media besides Cramer have publicized celebrities with no investment knowledge or experience. In early 2000 José Canseco, a veteran major league baseball star and an MVP award winner, started a financial advisory business. The financial press was only too willing to give his new venture publicity that no one without stardom could ever hope to get. *USA Today* featured a large picture of Canseco holding his laptop and extolled his brilliance: "His hands-on management of his finances is a refreshing change from the days when athletes had an agent or friend handle their fortunes, often with disastrous results."

Canseco said, "I love it. It's like gambling." That comment surely would not give me any peace of mind in trusting him with my financial future. Canseco himself acknowledged that his celebrity status was really what was important, observing, "People think maybe because of who I am, I have access to tips and information, and that's often the case." That approach certainly didn't pay off very well for Martha Stewart, who was sentenced to five months in prison, plus five months of house arrest for insider trading violations.

In March 2000 the NASDAQ Composite Index (an index of stocks weighted extremely heavily toward technology firms) had reached an all-time high of just over 5100. Just two months later, in May 2000, technology stocks had started to crash as the dot-com bubble burst. By the time the glowing article on Canseco appeared in *USA Today*, the NASDAQ Composite Index had collapsed to approximately 3500, a loss of about 30 percent in just two months. Canseco, who said he had invested about 90 percent of his money in technology stocks, indicated he was not concerned because he said the NASDAQ was "going back over 5000 in eight months." Well, it didn't turn out that way. Eight months later the NASDAQ stood at about 2600, an additional decline of about 25 percent. (See the similar predictions of some Wall Street luminaries in Chapter 8.) The NASDAQ stood at about one-half of Canseco's prediction. As I am writing this, about 16 years later, the NASDAQ has finally recovered to 5000 again. It turns out his favorite stock picks didn't fare too well either in the eight months from May 2000 and January 2001. Yahoo fell 80 percent, Microsoft declined 20 percent, Amazon took a 68 percent dive, and Cisco Systems dropped 35 percent, for an average loss of 51 percent.

In 2008 Canseco lost his 7,300-square-foot home in Southern California to foreclosure. In 2012 he filed for bankruptcy, listing his assets at less than $21,000, with debts over $1.7 million. After baseball he did not continue his career as a financial advisor, but rather became a boxer who was paid $30,000 for one losing fight.

All-star status clearly does not mean that money managers will have superior track records for very long. In 2002, Morningstar selected ten members to its Fund Manager Hall of Fame, requiring them to have "a long history of delivering superior results to shareholders." What could be better for a fund manager? Apart from the prestige, lots of assets will flow into your fund. But how good was it for future investors to put money with these advisors?

Since Morningstar emphasized long-term results, I decided to look at the performance of these Hall of Famers' funds over the next ten years. Morningstar rates its mutual funds by awarding them between one and five stars, based upon their investment returns, as summarized in the following table:

| Performance of Fund | Star Rating |
|---|---|
| Top 10% (90% to 100%) | 5* |
| Next 22 ½% (67½% to 90%) | 4* |
| Middle 35% (32½% to 67½%) | 3* |
| Next 22 ½% (10% to 32½%) | 2* |
| Bottom 10% (0% to 10%) | 1* |

Interestingly enough, because of the difference in the criteria for selecting Hall of Fame managers and awarding stars, when elected into the Hall of Fame only three of these managers ran what was at that time a five-star fund. The other seven were rated four stars. For the ten funds, that is an average rating of 4.3 stars. Ten years later, five of these funds maintained a four-star rating, one had a three-star rating, two had dropped to two stars, and two had been relegated to one-star funds (the bottom 10 percent). So the average rating a decade later was 2.9 stars, which is below the average of three stars for the entire universe of funds tracked by Morningstar. Looking back we see that three of the funds tanked almost immediately after their managers were inducted into the Hall of Fame. One of the original five-star funds was in the bottom 25 percent of all funds in its category for five of the next six years. Another Hall of Famer found his fund performing in the lowest 25 percent in four of the next six years. The fund managed by the Hall of Famer who was also named the manager of the decade for the 1990s fell to the bottom 25 percent for three of the next six years and ended with a one-star rating.

Obviously, the requirement of the Securities and Exchange Commission that advertising must include the statement that "past performance is not an indicator of future results" actually makes sense.

I wish I could advertise that my predictions were right all the time, no matter how wrong I actually was. This is easy to accomplish for big Wall Street firms, with the help of the press. What happens if one member of a firm says one thing while another member of the same firm says the opposite? Will the firm be discredited for offering conflicting advice or predictions? Will one member be noted as wrong while the other is honored? No. Whichever one proves right will be lauded for keen analysis and insights, and whichever one is wrong will be ignored.

The March 17, 2014, cover of *Barron's* provides an interesting example of this phenomenon. The cover leads readers to a few of the week's featured articles. One carries the tag "Perilous balancing act for equities," while another has the heading "Jeremy Grantham sees bullish signs." In the first article, Ben Inker, co-head of asset allocation at GMO, "uttered the dreaded 'B' [bubble] word," suggesting that the markets could be headed lower. Problem is that the bullish expert featured in the second article, Jeremy Grantham, is the founder and head of the same firm, GMO. No matter what happens, GMO will get it right.

Sure, each member of a firm is entitled to his own opinion. But what is the investor to do? You'd think that if members of the same firm are going to take opposite positions in public statements, they should be held accountable and required to highlight it in advertising or in other publications. That way all interested parties, including current and future customers and clients, would be kept better informed. Why should we tolerate misleading statements?

How about a Wall Street analyst contradicting himself in back-to-back sentences? In April 2015 Michele Della Vigna, co-head of European research for Goldman Sachs, appeared on CNBC and was asked about future oil prices. He observed, "I think it would be impossible to time it [oil prices] perfectly. We know that the oil price is a very volatile market, but I think we can say with a reasonable certainty that we are seeing a trough of the oil price in the middle of this year." Now help me: it's impossible to time perfectly, but there is a "reasonable *certainty*" that the trough will come within a few months?

I'm not sure why anybody would want to listen to Goldman's predictions on oil prices anyway. In August 2008, when oil was trading at about $125 per barrel, Goldman issued its prediction that in 2009 the price would hit $200 per barrel. By January 2009 the oil price had declined to $47 a barrel, so Goldman revised its prediction and said that it would decline to $30 per barrel in 2009. It finished that year at about $80 per barrel. Obviously, following Goldman's advice would have resulted in significant losses in the oil patch.

Far too often it is advantageous to turn the advice of the experts on its head. For many years *Barron's* has run its semi-annual Big Money Poll, inviting a number of the most prominent money managers to give their prize pick and name their biggest pan (the stock you were advised to avoid). From November 1996 through May 2000, during a time when stock markets soared (the decline in technology stocks was just beginning by May 2000), *Barron's* had eight Big Money Polls. Had you invested an equal amount in each of the stock picks every six months and then sold them six months later and purchased the new picks, you would have gained about 190 percent over the four-year period. That sounds good until you consider that had you purchased the pans, you would have gained about 300 percent.

*Smart Money*, the *Wall Street Journal* magazine, is only too happy to participate in financial hype. Its May 2000 cover included a teaser to a featured article that read: "25% returns! 7 Great Stocks Set to

Soar." This article featured a technique that is used by too many publications, and by too many Wall Street firms, to hoodwink their customers. The technique is called backtesting, which suggests they have succeeded in the past when in fact they have not. It's also used, as in the *Smart Money* article, to entice customers to believing they are following a winning formula when in fact the formula was developed after the fact. Backtesting tests a theory or determines performance by a simulation of a strategy using prior data rather than actually testing going forward. For backtesting to be valid, what happened in the past must be indicative of what will happen in the future. But we know that is often not the case. Backtesting can also be skewed by the time period selected for the analysis.

Suppose you want to find the mutual fund managers with the best record. You would search to see who had done the best. But do you go back three years, five years, or ten years? Do the results of a backtest of a five-year period differ depending upon which five years are selected? Using the returns from the Legg Mason Value Fund discussed earlier, if we had backtested the fund for the years 2000 through 2005, we would have determined that this fund beat the S&P 500 Index every year and was a top performer. But if we had backtested for the years 2006 through 2011, we would have determined that the fund trailed the S&P 500 Index in five of those six years and had been absolutely crushed.

Wall Street firms also use backtesting to make results appear different from what they actually were. Following the great stock market crash in 2008, many of these firms experienced horrible results, and their clients' accounts suffered immensely. How would they be able to explain to prospective clients the value of hiring their firms? The firms mined data to find out which stocks or mutual funds had performed the best during the market crash. These firms had not invested in these mutual funds or stocks prior to the crash. It was only after the fact, with the results of the backtest, that they could identify the best ones to have owned. The firm would reconstruct their clients' portfolios, or their proposals for new clients, to contain the stocks and mutual funds determined after the fact to have been the best performers. They often adjusted the percentages assigned to each category to select the best performers. The speech to the prospective client went something like this: "These are the mutual funds and stocks in our current portfolio. During the market crash of 2008 these investments declined far less than the averages. These performed so well in protecting value during the downturn that we are pleased to own them today." Never mind that they didn't own them during the downturn.

A mutual fund must report actual performance and can't pick and choose which of its stock purchases to report and which to ignore. A mutual fund can trumpet its winners, but it cannot neglect to report its losers. Why then is it both acceptable and legal for brokers, investment advisors, analysts, and other Wall Street professionals to edit out prior poor performance or recommendations? Why can they later pretend their predictions were accurate when they were not?

Backtesting also expressly assumes that what happened in the past will happen in the future. *Smart Money* reported that its backtesting strategy had generated a 25 percent annual return over the past thirty-five years. If that were accurate, then $1,000 invested would have grown to approximately $2,500,000 over the thirty-five years. If that continued for the next thirty-five years, then that original $1,000 would grow to about $6.2 trillion at the end of the seventy years. Think that's accurate?

In fact, there is one stock that has actually increased an average of about 22 percent per year for fifty years, while the annual return for the S&P 500 Index has been about 10 percent. With Warren Buffett at the helm, Berkshire Hathaway has outperformed that index in each of six decades. The media love Buffett because he is the most successful investor of the last fifty years. But his marvelous performance was much greater in the first half of his run than in the second half. During his first twenty-five years at Berkshire Hathaway, he outperformed the S&P 500 Index by about 20 percent per year. The last twenty-five years have seen that drop to about 4 percent per year, though that's still a lot when compounded over twenty-five years.

His incredible success invites those who crave media attention to suggest that his run is over and it's time to cash in your chips with Buffett and move to more progressive managers. The press has been only too happy to publish articles explaining why. In its March/April 1990 edition, *Investment Vision* magazine ran an article titled, "Is the Warren Buffett Era Over?" The subtitle was "Of Demigods and Bull Markets." The unnamed author of the article suggested all sorts of reasons why Berkshire Hathaway was doomed to underperform and suggested that Buffett was just stubborn in not abandoning his approach to investment. The article said he would be better off using shorter-term investment strategies, engaging in market timing, investing in foreign currencies, and a whole lot more. The article suggested it was time for Buffett to move on.

Even much more venerable and highly respected publications have not been afraid to suggest that Buffett had lost his touch and Berkshire Hathaway may have been overvalued. The December 17, 2007, cover of *Barron's* featured a picture of a reflective and seemingly content Buffett. The headline read, "Warren Buffett's Berkshire Hathaway is a great company, but its stock is now overpriced. Better bets: Wells Fargo, American Express [a significant part of which was owned by Berkshire Hathaway], Loew's and AIG." It seems that *Barron's* just could not resist joining the chorus that over the years has warned investors away from Berkshire Hathaway. I suppose that gets people's attention, even if over the long term that continually proves to be poor advice.

So what happened after *Barron's* cover story? By December 31, 2008, about one year later, the US stock markets had experienced their worst results in about seventy-five years and Berkshire Hathaway had dropped 33 percent. Wells Fargo was down 3 percent, American Express had taken a hit of 65 percent, Loew's declined 40 percent, and AIG had all but disappeared, experiencing a catastrophic loss of 97 percent of its stock value (which would have been 100 percent without the government bailout). The average loss of the four "better" bets than Berkshire Hathaway was 51 percent. Since Berkshire Hathaway declined 33 percent in one year, maybe *Barron's* was right in its assessment that it was overpriced, but it turns out that the "better bets" were significantly more overpriced.

Now let's look ahead to 2014 for a long-term view. We would still have been better off with Berkshire Hathaway than *Barron's* four better bets. As of December 31, 2014, just about seven years after the *Barron's* cover story, Berkshire Hathaway had increased in value by 53 percent. The average of the four better bets? A gain of 12 percent.

Still, as good as Buffett has been, let's remember he's not infallible. The difference in the performance of Berkshire Hathaway's stock and that of the CSI Equity Fund, which I managed for thirteen years (1998–2010), shows that it has been possible to outperform Buffett over significant periods of time. Over its thirteen-year life, the CSI Equity Fund earned an average return after all expenses of about 5.2 percent per year, significantly higher than the S&P 500 Index over those same thirteen years. Berkshire Hathaway increased in value about 7.6 percent per year during that same thirteen-year period. But all of Berkshire Hathaway's better performance than the CSI Equity Fund occurred during the first six months of 1998. Berkshire Hathaway returned about 3.5 percent per year for the 12½ years from July 1, 1998, through December 31, 2010, while the total return of the CSI Equity Fund for those 12½ years was approximately 4.2 percent per year. So what did Berkshire Hathaway do in the first six months of 1998 to cause its stock to go up 70 percent? Almost 50 percent of its gains for the year came from issuing shares for acquisitions. That increased the book value and caused the stock to soar. The 1998 annual report for Berkshire Hathaway included Buffett's comment that 1998's performance was "not as good as it looks." I would never suggest that Buffett's approach to the investment process needs to be improved to keep up with the times, and Berkshire Hathaway did outperform the CSI Equity Fund over its thirteen-year life. Maybe it was luck, but I still remain proud that over the last 12½ years we actually did a little better than the Oracle of Omaha.

The financial media are in Wall Street's hip pocket. They promote Wall Street's deceptive practices and aid in its taking advantage of its customers. The media should act as objective reporters and not as cheerleaders promoting superstars, never truly challenging claimed results, and generally giving Wall Street a free pass instead of holding it accountable. Whether advice is offered by the head of a major bank or Wall Street firm, a billionaire, or last decade's greatest winner, consider how luck can affect everything, how cherry-picking and back-testing can mislead, and how averaging rather than chaining results can disguise losses. Remember, hype is the rule of the game. Don't assume something is accurate just because it appears on the pages of the most prestigious publications or is featured on the mainstream electronic media. Whether it's CNN, CNBC, FNN, *Forbes, Fortune, Barron's, Bloomberg,* the *Wall Street Journal,* or countless others, be skeptical.

# EIGHT

# Stupid Predictions and Constant Hype: How to Lose a Fortune

So if you can't trust Wall Street's numbers about actual performance in the past, why should you trust what it says about the future? Let's do something Wall Street rarely does and certainly never wants: examine what its luminaries have predicted. We might, in the words of "Weird Al" Yankovic, "learn a few things we never knew before."

Sure, lots of times the Wall Street experts make accurate predictions, but the fact they can get so much so wrong so often, and by so much, shows they're really guessing. No matter how much analysis and research they do, no matter how many formulas they apply, and no matter whether they are taking conservative or aggressive positions, the Wall Street pundits fail to understand that prediction is fraught with peril. It's just what Yogi Berra said: "It's tough to make predictions, especially about the future."

Major institutional research firms release recommendations to attract business. Poor recommendations made in the past would certainly hurt business if the public knew about them. So simply pretend you never made them. Worse yet, pretend you recommended just the opposite and trust that the investing public is never going to do its homework to discover the truth. It used to be simple to bury mistakes by just ignoring them. Until recently, recommendations were not archived online or kept anywhere else that was easily accessible.

But now, when almost everything is preserved on the Internet, any-one can find past recommendations with a little bit of research.

Take the dot-com bust. The leading gurus of Wall Street were only too happy to make glowing projections at the end of 1999. And why not? From 1982 through 1999, stock markets had relentlessly increased. The S&P 500 Index had increased by an average of about 18.5 percent annually for that entire eighteen-year period. By that measure, those eighteen years were the best in American history.

In December 1999, the Enterprise Group of Funds surveyed fifteen of the nation's leading money managers and issued a press release clearly suggesting that the good times were going to continue. Some of Wall Street's most famous experts were asked their opinion on what was to come. Four very prominent members of the Wall Street fraternity were named in the lead-in to the press release: David Alger, Mario Gabelli, Thomas Marsico, and Ronald Canakaris. Certainly it made sense for them to project that the good times would continue. Optimism always sells on Wall Street, and the wind was howling at their backs. Unfortunately, even though all fifteen of the luminaries interviewed in the press release (who collectively managed over $250 billion) suggested a bullish outlook, 2000 saw the biggest decline in the S&P 500 Index since 1977.

Too many investment professionals are eager to make outlandish and optimistic projections in order to attract attention and gather new business. In its July 6, 1998, issue, *Barron's* ran an article entitled "Seer Speaks. Futurist says Dow could hit 35,000, and he's been right before." The article featured a picture of Harry Dent, holding his new book, *The Roaring 2000s*. The caption under the picture read, "Predicting good times ahead, Harry Dent has gotten rich." The arti-cle pointed out that ten years earlier Dent had predicted the Dow would reach 10,000 by the year 2000, and he was right. In the article, he predicted that the Dow would double again to 21,500 and maybe even quadruple to 35,000 over the next decade. When *Barron's* ran the article the Dow stood at 9025. By December 31, 2008 (10½ years later), the Dow stood at 8776. So over the decade the Dow didn't double or quadruple; it actually went down. I have no idea how rich

Dent got by selling his books and services and by telling us stories, but investors who thought they would be part of the roaring 2000s were severely disappointed.

In late 1999, Charles Kadlec, managing director and investment strategist for J&W Seligman & Co., another respected investment firm dating back to 1864, went out on a limb: "I expect it [the Dow Jones Industrial Average] at 100,000 around 2020." At the time he made that prediction, the Dow stood at approximately 11,500. As of June 2016, about sixteen years later, it was about 18,000. To fulfill Kadlec's prediction, all the Dow must do is increase by about thirteen times more in the next four years than it did in the last sixteen—a compound rate of return of about 53 percent per year (more than any *single* year in history). We must wait until 2020 to see who has the last laugh on this one. As they say in sports betting, I'll take the under.

Morgan Stanley had the leading Internet analyst, Mary Meeker, during the dot-com boom. She was a superstar who reportedly earned $15 million in 1999. But was she a great analyst or a great cheerleader? Meeker appeared on the May 14, 2001, cover of *Fortune* looking rather sad, with *Fortune* asking, "Can we ever trust Wall Street again?" Their story indicated that of the fifteen stocks Meeker was then covering, all but two were "strong buy" or "outperform." Four stocks that she had never downgraded each declined between 85 percent and 97 percent from their peaks. We certainly know the answer to the question *Fortune* posed on its cover. Fourteen years later Wall Street is still hyping stocks with as much vigor as ever and taking in much more revenue. And Meeker herself is now a partner at Kleiner, Perkins, Caulfield and Byers, one of the most prestigious venture capital firms in Silicon Valley.

The July 20, 2000, issue of *Fortune* offered "Top Picks from the Smartest Guys on Wall Street." (A couple of the guys are gals, but no matter.) Then five magic words appear: "Let Them Make You Rich."

These fifteen "*Fortune* All Stars" include one or two analysts from nine top firms—Goldman Sachs, Merrill Lynch, Salomon Smith Barney, Donaldson Lufkin & Jenrette, Credit Suisse First Boston,

Morgan Stanley Dean Witter, Paine Webber, ING Barings, and Robertson Stephens—with no firm having more than two members. Each analyst worked a different sector of the economy—not just the telecommunications, Internet, and software sectors but also traditional sectors such as retailing, multinational banking, regional banking, drugs, household products, and brokerages.

It was widely reported that some of the *Fortune* All Stars selected in 2000 made $20 million that year! Being chosen as an All Star by *Fortune* was much like holding a stock option. If their predictions were right, they would look great. If their predictions were wrong, no one would ever know because there would be no follow-up.

But what about the average investor who might have taken their advice? The fifteen analysts were asked to name their two favorite stocks. One refused to name two stocks. Michael Mayo, the All Star for regional banking, instead proffered the following: "Sell bank stocks." It turns out he was right, but he was later fired.

Each of the remaining fourteen All Stars happily named two favorite stocks. A portfolio of their twenty-eight picks was diversified across fourteen different sectors of the economy. How did they perform from July 2000, when the *Fortune* article appeared, to July 2002, a two-year run? Bear in mind (pun intended), the market had tanked by then. The S&P 500 Index declined approximately 37 percent over that period. Sounds bad until you look at the All-Star portfolio. Investors purchasing equal amounts of the twenty-eight recommended stocks would have lost 63 percent of their money in two years. Four of the All-Star analysts recommended stocks that lost an average of more than 90 percent!

That's the aggregate picture. How did individual All Stars perform? Take a look at the second-best performer on the team. She covered household products, and her two stocks fell an average of only 13 percent for the two-year period. Remarkable, considering the market. But there's more to the story. According to the article, she was resolute in her dislike for Procter & Gamble—which went up 60 percent!

Then there's the media expert. He specifically passed on Disney, although he predicted it would double by 2002. Apparently, he thought his two favorites would do better than that. What happened? His two stocks went down 70 percent on average. Disney did not double as he predicted. It "only" fell by 50 percent.

Let's not overlook the Internet analyst. One of his picks was CMGI, which he had previously suggested was a bargain at $150 per share. By the time the *Fortune* All-Star article hit the newsstands, CMGI was trading at $44 per share. "A screaming buy," he persisted. Meanwhile his persistence and the general hype surrounding CMGI was causing me trouble. A client had purchased some CMGI against my advice some time before then. It did soar to the $150 mark, but then precipitously declined to $50. My client was offended. How could CMGI be valued so "ridiculously low," he asked? Maybe he would follow the All-Star advice and buy more! I succeeded in convincing him otherwise and suggested that it was still grossly overvalued, even at that "low" price. Lucky thing. By July 2002, CMGI was selling at fifty cents a share, down 99 percent.

A very prominent member of *Fortune*'s All Star Team covered the telecommunication sector. He drew lots of media attention both before and after the *Fortune* article. His picks were then well known: WorldCom and Global Crossing. He described them as "dirt cheap" when selling for $45 and $26 per share respectively. Within two years, the companies were broke—each in bankruptcy, among the largest in history. And the two picks of the All Star featured on the cover fell by an average of 88 percent.

Others would argue that it is not fair to look only at the "buy" recommendations without also taking into account the "sells." Certainly these analysts do put out "sell" recommendations on some stocks. However, they did not issue very many—or at least not enough to matter. The *Fortune* article itself pointed out that Wall Street analysts made 33,169 stock recommendations in the prior year. Of those, only 125 were sells. That's 0.34 percent, or about one in three hundred. This is not enough to save investors in a down market or to weed out bad companies in an up market.

Of course, still others argue that it is not fair to play Monday-morning quarterback. After all, throwing passes on Sunday afternoon is not easy. So what about my own two favorite stocks for 2000? That's a question I can't answer. On the basis of such narrow guesswork, I'd end up looking like either a hero or a bum. I don't take this kind of risk with my reputation or, more importantly, with my clients' money. Our firm, CSI Capital Management, would have opted out of the *Fortune* "favorite stock" exercise. We might have picked thirty or forty stocks, but never just two.

A diversified portfolio such as ours didn't make for a bold *Fortune* cover story. But our track record makes for a good story. Between July 2000 and July 2002, the S&P 500 Index declined 37 percent, the All-Star portfolio declined 63 percent, and the CSI Equity Fund declined only 26 percent. The measure of our success in a down market: we cut our investors' losses.

*Fortune* and other publications are never deterred by poor prior recommendations. On June 22, 2009, *Fortune* ran a Special Investor's issue with the cover reading, "Retire Rich (Really!)" The "Rich" was printed in two-inch-high red letters. The story recommended five "smart funds to retire on." Over the next five years those smart funds realized an average cumulative return of about 110 percent. Not bad. The dumb S&P 500 Index returned about 155 percent for the same five years.

Despite how things actually turn out, there is a tremendous bias toward optimism. Wall Street insiders will not offer advice that will adversely affect their own incomes, and their customers don't want to hear bad news. Who's going to buy stocks or other securities after being told that values will decline?

When Wall Street experts make predictions, they can be either optimistic (markets or specific products will go up) or realistic (markets or specific products can go down). After time passes the predictions will turn out to be either right or wrong. The following grid illustrates how Wall Street reacts once predictions meet reality. Here are the possible outcomes:

| Stance | Right | Wrong |
|--------|-------|-------|
| Optimistic | Adulation | Acceptance |
| Realistic | Tolerated | Fired |

Everyone wants to be in the upper left box—optimists who turn out to be right. They will receive both great adulation and rich rewards. But even optimists who make unfortunate predictions are welcomed members of the Wall Street fraternity. Realists who are right are begrudgingly tolerated but had better be right the next time. Realists who are wrong may not need to be concerned, for they are likely to be fired. So if you work on Wall Street, where do you want to position yourself?

Also, because our free enterprise system is so great, optimism is statistically the way to go. Over the last ninety years the S&P 500 Index has increased on average about 9 to 10 percent per year. Stock prices have increased in about 70 percent of those years. With both history and psychology on your side, why wouldn't you always predict that things will be good? And that, too often, is what Wall Street does, regardless of reality. This plays right into the hands of their customers, who are usually optimistic as well. Optimism is often what often drives success. A college teammate of mine and his partner purchased a local company and transformed it into a major national brand, ultimately selling out for a massive profit. In an interview the partner observed that he had never met a rich pessimist. In February 2008 the *Journal of Financial Planning* published the results of a survey of ultra-wealthy investors and their expectations for 2008: 58 percent reported optimistic views and only 4 percent indicated pessimistic views. Of course, 2008 turned out to be the worst year for US stock markets in over seventy years.

Except for the doom and gloom squad, Wall Street's ever-optimistic prognosticators rarely suggest the markets might decline. But not only can't they see or refuse to see when trouble is ahead, they can't see when great times are ahead either. Let's take a look at the *USA Today* article "Investments for the Rest of the Decade," published in early 1995. Ten investment luminaries, including representatives from Salomon Brothers, Dean Witter Reynolds, Janus Group, and Gabelli Funds (Mario Gabelli himself), were asked for their outlook on the financial markets and their projection for the level of the Dow Jones Industrial Average at the end of the decade. At the time of these projections, the Dow Jones Industrial Average stood at approximately 3800 after having increased about 40 percent over the prior five years. The ten experts projected the Dow would increase to anywhere between 4250 and 6750 over the next five years, with the average prediction about 5675. That average called for a total increase of about 48 percent, or just slightly higher than the previous five years, and consistent with long-term experience.

What happened? The Dow Jones Industrial Average closed on December 31, 1999, the last day of the decade, at 11,497, an increase of approximately 197 percent. The closest *guess* of the ten experts was barely half of that. The S&P 500 Index increased even more, as these years saw the best five-year stock market performance in US history. But no one foresaw that—not even the Wall Street superstars. Pessimism may be bad for business, but overly optimistic predictions can look unsupportable, so predictions generally reflect average prior results.

At the end of 1994, *USA Today* asked the year's top fund manager in each of six general stock fund categories what to expect in 1995. 1994 had been a tough year, with the S&P 500 Index showing a total return of only 1.3 percent. One manager said, "Another tough year"; another manager said he was cautious; and a third of the top managers said things were not bright. The fourth manager said things were going to be "frustrating for a while"; one of the managers said he thought there would be interest-rate hikes (which would not be good for stock prices); and the sixth manager expressed concern that interest rate increases would slow the economy and hurt stocks. So what actually happened in 1995? The S&P 500 Index increased by about 37 percent—its largest single-year increase in 37 years.

*USA Today* continued on its winning ways with its 1997 year-end stock market projections for 1998 from representatives from twelve major brokerage firms. Nine of them gave specific projections for the changes in the major indices, and these ranged from a decline of 25 percent to an increase of 16 percent, with the average being an increase of about 1½ percent. Representatives of two of the brokerage firms did not give specific numbers for changes in the market indices, but indicated that 1998 would be difficult. Yet again there was a strong year with the S&P 500 Index returning over 28 percent.

*USA Today* came back a year later for an encore performance. It surveyed fourteen "top strategists" to see what they expected in 1999. The average projection called for an increase in the S&P 500 or the Dow Jones Industrial Average of about 3 percent. By year end the S&P 500 Index had increased about 21 percent.

In early 2000, Larry Kudlow, who for many years has hosted a financial show on CNBC, said, "This correction [downturn in the market] will run its course until the middle of the year, then things will pick up again." By the middle of the year the S&P 500 Index had indeed recovered, but then declined about 10 percent over the next six months. Then over the next two and a half years, through December 2002, the S&P 500 Index declined an additional 38 percent. The results for the NASDAQ Composite Index were even more dramatic, increasing about 25 percent from January through mid-March 2000 but then crashing 40 percent in just three months. It then declined an additional 60 percent over the next two years. So maybe Kudlow was right that the market correction would run its course until the middle of the year. The only question is, which year?

In April 2000, Myron Kandel of CNN said, "Before the end of the year, the NASDAQ and the Dow will be at new highs." When he made this great prediction, the high for the NASDAQ had been 5,132, and the Dow high had been 11,750. By the end of the year, the NASDAQ stood at 2,470 and the Dow at 10,787. Through December 2014 the NASDAQ had still not reached a new high, and the Dow did not reach a new high until October 2006, only to crash again in 2008 to 8,118.

What did Louis Rukeyser, the star of the long-running and highly respected PBS show *Wall $treet Week*, have to say at the time? In November 2000 he told us with confidence, "Over the next year or two" the stock market "will be higher, and I *know* [emphasis added] over the next 5 to 10 years it will be higher." The S&P 500 stood at 1,314 at the end of November 2000 and then declined to 936 by the end of November 2002. And what about his long-term certainty that in five to ten years it would be higher? Five years later, at the end of 2005, the S&P 500 stood at 1,248, while ten years later at the end of 2010 it had rebounded to 1,257, still lower than five or ten years earlier. Yet he *knew* the market would increase. To be fair to Rukeyser, the S&P did rise in 2007 to a high of 1,569 before crashing in 2008 and 2009 to 683.

In January 2001, after the NASDAQ composite had declined about 30 percent in 2000, Suze Orman offered this advice: "In the low 60s here, I think the QQQ [an exchange traded stock which tracks the NASDAQ Composite Index], they're a buy." By the end of 2002, QQQ was trading at 61 percent less than when Orman made her recommendation.

Goldman Sachs and its renowned Abby Joseph Cohen were also part of the chorus singing of good times ahead. In 2000, the *Wall Street Journal* quoted her as maintaining her "resolute optimism." In September 2000, when the S&P 500 Index stood at about 1430, she predicted a 10 percent increase to 1575 by December 31, 2000. The actual year-end figure for the S&P 500 Index was 1320, or a decline of about 8 percent. The decline in the S&P 500 Index did not deter Cohen from her continual optimism.

In April 2001, she observed, "The time to be nervous was a year ago. The S&P was then overvalued; it's now undervalued." Not so fast, Ms. Cohen. At that time (April 2000) that index stood at 1500. Just three months before, as a participant in the annual *Barron's* Roundtable, you had predicted that the S&P would rise in 2000. But I thought you said in 2001 it was overvalued in early 2000—so why did you say in 2000 that it would rise? The S&P 500 finished 2001 at 1148, a decline of 7 percent from the date of another rather aggressive and optimistic projection. You were off by *only* 41 percent on a ten-month projection. Each year from 2000 through 2002 you predicted that the S&P would increase, while in fact it declined in each of those years, and the overall decline was the largest in twenty-eight years.

Since Cohen represents Goldman Sachs, her opinions are sought after whether she's been right or wrong previously. The press is only too happy to feature her. But if I were relying on a strategist for advice, I would not want one who had remained overly optimistic and missed the major turning points in the market after attempting to predict them. The financial press doesn't seem to share my concern.

Remember how in March 2001, Cohen told the *Wall Street Journal* that the S&P 500 Index would reach 1650 by the end of 2001? Because of 9/11 and the fact that the stock markets had continued to slide before then, Cohen revised her projection for year-end 2002 to a range of 1300 to 1425, or an increase of about 25 percent. Cohen was not alone in her optimistic forecast. In *Barron's* after 9/11, stars at Lehman Brothers, J.P. Morgan, Credit Suisse First Boston, UBS Warburg, and Bank of America assured us that the S&P 500 Index would go up by December 2002, with their average projection calling for an increase of 27 percent. In fact, the market declined 15 percent more by the end 2002, winding up at 880, from 1145 in April 2001, when Cohen had said the S&P was "undervalued."

Cohen has no shame when her predictions turn out wrong. For years she was known for beginning almost all of her media interviews and conference calls with the words "as I predicted." This reminds me of the song from the musical *Fiddler on the Roof*. The lead character, who struggles to eke out a living, wishes he were a rich man. He says if he were a rich man, people would come to him for advice and he would gladly give it, saying: "And it won't make one bit of difference if I answer right or wrong. When you're rich, they think you really know."

Still, Wall Street does have a doom and gloom squad that perpetually predicts financial ruin and other disasters lying just ahead. Many of them are just distributors of Wall Street pornography, trying to peddle whatever they have for sale—just to a different audience. Since they survive through scare tactics, their recommendations usually cover more than just investments. They often recommend buying gold and silver coins, stocking your house with large stores of food, fuel, and other supplies, and preparing yourself for social unrest. Some of these pessimists have made a very good living for a very long time selling their advice and publications. Fortunately for the rest of us, so far they have been nothing but wrong and have had little impact on financial markets.

And of course there are the "short sellers," who have a financial stake in seeing particular stocks go down—and can often be heard expressing their bearish views in order to create a self-fulfilling prophecy. (More about selling short can be found in Chapter 12.)

But for the most part, prominent brokerage firms, banks, investment advisors, mutual fund managers, hedge fund operators, chief economists, and other strategists are constantly making overly optimistic or even clearly ridiculous forecasts without any adverse effects on their status.

Ben Stein has been a Wall Street megastar for many years, and he knows the value of being highly confident in his projections. During a panel discussion on Fox News in August 2007, Stein was asked about the effects subprime mortgages would have on the markets. He said they were a "tiny problem." He went on to say that any concerns of a credit crunch were overblown and that the stocks of financial companies were "cheap" and "being given away." One member of the panel suggested the financial stocks were about to crash and this led Stein to be even more vociferous in his recommendations to buy financials. Citibank, Wells Fargo Bank, JPMorgan Chase, and Bank of America were by far the largest banks in the country at that time. Over the next sixteen months their average stock price declined about 47 percent. Goldman Sachs, Morgan Stanley, and AIG were also among the financial giants. Over the same sixteen months the average price of their stocks declined about 74 percent. But that wasn't the bottom of the market. By February 28, 2009, the average stock price of those seven financial companies, which according to Stein had been "cheap," had declined 73 percent in the one and a half years since he made his strong buy recommendation. And just in case you think that his recommendation was good over the long term, more than eight years after he told us how cheap the financials were (as I write this in spring 2016), the average stock price of those seven companies is still down about 20 percent. Of course, making foolish statements never hurts your stardom once it's established. Stein was featured as a "Wealth Wizard" in *Forbes*'s 2013 Investment Guide.

Or consider the January 4, 2011, prognostications of Laszlo Birinyi, a revered Wall Street advisor. Birinyi had been head of equity market analysis at Salomon Brothers, a major firm before its merger with Smith Barney, another giant firm. He was a frequent guest on *Wall $treet Week* (the highly rated and long-running PBS show), CNBC, and Bloomberg TV. For his great work, he was inducted into the *Wall $treet Week* Hall of Fame.

On January 4, 2011, the S&P 500 Index stood at 1271. InvestmentNews.com featured an article titled, "Birinyi's S&P 500 prediction a jaw-dropper." He stated that the S&P 500 Index would reach 2854 on September 4, 2013. Before we see what actually happened, let's consider what Birinyi said. We are asked to suspend disbelief and think that anyone can make such a specific projection almost three years out. Wouldn't it be next to impossible to predict that the index would rise to, say, 2800 during the third quarter of 2013? How could anyone select such a precise date and such an exact number for an index that can easily fluctuate 1 or 2 percent daily?

How did Birinyi's jaw-dropping prediction pan out? Between January 4, 2011, and September 4, 2013, the S&P 500 Index increased from 1271 to 1653, or about 30 percent. Birinyi's prediction called for a total increase of 125 percent, or an annualized appreciation of 35 percent for 2⅔ years. By way of comparison, the best three-year performance for the S&P 500 Index is about 31 percent per year. Birinyi was projecting a three-year record-breaking performance, but instead he got just average results.

Why would Birinyi make such an outlandish prediction? My guess: he knew he had nothing to lose and everything to gain by making headline-grabbing news. If the prediction eventually proved wrong or even ridiculous (as it ultimately was), Wall Street firms, the financial press, Internet services, investors, and television pundits would not hold him accountable. He could proceed with his reputation completely intact. Birinyi had every reason to believe his prediction would stand out not only from those taking a cautious approach, but even from those taking an aggressive stance. If his "jaw-dropper" turned out to be even close to accurate, Wall Street almost certainly would have hailed him as brilliant. Regardless, Birinyi's services and opinions are as much in demand today as ever.

Wall Street strategists have a knack for consistently failing in their stock market projections. This is particularly true when markets decline. In the middle of 2014, Birinyi Associates (the firm founded by Laszlo Birinyi) released its study of the average annual forecast for 2000 through 2013 of about eighteen strategists it tracked. The results are illustrative, but hardly shocking. Every year, for all fourteen years, the strategists predicted an increase in the S&P 500 Index. Turns out that 2000, 2001, and 2002 saw the S&P 500 Index decline, and the overall decline was the largest cumulative decline in twenty-eight years (about 44 percent).The difference between the annual projections and reality was significant. The projections were about 30 percent higher than the actual performance in both 2001 and 2002. Then six years later, in 2008, came the massive decline in the S&P 500 Index, ushering in the Great Recession. The index declined by approximately 37 percent, for the largest single-year decline since the Great Depression about seventy years earlier. The average projection for 2008 by the prominent firms tracked by Birinyi associates? An increase of 10 percent.

The projections were off base in the good years, too. In 2013, the S&P 500 Index increased about 32 percent, for its largest increase since 1997. Unfortunately, the strategists tracked by Birinyi saw a modest 8 percent to 9 percent coming.

Mario Gabelli has been a super-successful and revered Wall Street money manager for forty years. As of December 2014, his company managed over $47 billion. He has certainly made many good calls and has built his reputation as a great stock picker. He's had a string of poor picks too, but somehow those have not tarnished his status at all.

At the end of 1991, *Fortune* published a special issue: *1992 Investor's Guide.* Included on the cover was the caption, "Mario Gabelli and other top pros create a winning portfolio for you." The year 1991 had been a fabulous year for the stock markets, with the S&P 500 Index returning over 30 percent. Beginning in 1982 and extending through 1991, the S&P 500 Index had increased by an average of over 17 percent per year, for one of its best ten-year runs. In *Fortune*, Gabelli stated his goal of achieving 28 percent per year for his clients. That's a great goal, but what basis in reality does it have? Gabelli himself may have earned that for a few years, but can anyone sustain 28 percent per year over the long run?

History and mathematics strongly suggest that 28 percent per year is not realistic over the long term. Let's take an extreme example from the world of professional sports. In 1950, the owner of the Boston Celtics offered to sell one-half the team for $5,000. Today one-half of the Celtics would be worth at least $850,000,000. That's a mammoth increase, but it's nowhere near 28 percent per year—it's an annual compounded rate of return of approximately 20 percent. Had the investment in the Celtics increased by 28 percent per year, the value of one-half of the team would now be about $46 billion. Even for pro sports franchises, that's too good to be true. (Maybe the whole league is worth that, but not one-half of one team.)

Let's return to the real world and take a look at Gabelli's goal of 28 percent per year in the stock market. Since Gabelli stated his goal in 1991, the S&P 500 Index has increased slightly more than 9 percent per year. Warren Buffett's renowned Berkshire Hathaway has increased by approximately 15 percent per year since 1991. So Gabelli is trying to convince eager readers of *Fortune* that he can create a winning portfolio that can almost double the return generated by Warren Buffett and Berkshire Hathaway. Gabelli's firm manages over twenty mutual funds. None of them has generated long-term returns even approaching 28 percent.

What had Gabelli actually accomplished for his clients when he announced his lofty goal of 28 percent per year in 1991? A client of my law firm hired Gabelli and his firm to manage an equity portfolio. Gabelli's new client placed only one restriction on the account: that it be fully invested in equities at all times. In other words, Gabelli and his firm were hired to choose what they thought were the best stocks. The client opened his account with Gabelli early in 1989. The stock markets continued their strong runs and by September 30, 1991, the S&P 500 Index had increased an average of approximately 17 percent per year for those two and three-quarter years. My client's account with Gabelli earned about 3 percent per year. This massive difference in performance has substantial impact. Each $100,000 my client invested with Gabelli grew to about $109,000, while just matching the S&P 500 Index would have resulted in each $100,000 growing to about $154,000.

Ken Fisher is another Wall Street luminary who is never shy about making predictions. Fisher, who according to the Forbes 400 list of the wealthiest people in America is a multi-billionaire himself, operates a large money management firm and has written for *Forbes* for over twenty-five years. In 2007, Fisher was among many on Wall Street who believed financial markets would continue their upward trajectory and that any problems with the mortgage markets would be relatively unimportant. In the July 18, 2007, issue of *Financial Times,* Fisher observed, "Fact is, subprime is a relatively small part of the overall debt market and the talk is much ado about little. . . . We have been hammered with subprime headlines. . . . So bring on the hype and the headlines. The more there are, the more bullish it is." He then concluded, "I remain very bullish for the remainder of 2007." Remaining very bullish in July was consistent with his position in March 2007, when he told *Bloomberg News,* "I'm on the wildly optimistic side of things." After his July 2007 very bullish stance, the S&P 500 Index proceeded to decline about 10 percent by the end of the year. The following year saw an additional decline of about 37 percent, the worst single year in seventy years. Fisher, like so many others on Wall Street, knows that it is smart to predict good times ahead. Whether it is smart for you to listen is another matter.

Fisher's column in *Forbes* of June 24, 2013, was very bullish on the prospects for Canadian stocks and carried the headline, "Oh, Canada! You're a Buy." From the date of publication through April 2015, the Canadian markets did improve substantially, as the Toronto Stock Exchange Composite Index rose about 29 percent. So Canada was a buy, but the Standard & Poor's 500 Index over that same time period increased about 32 percent. More interesting, however, was the performance over that time of the five Canadian stocks Fisher recommended. On average, his five Canadian stock picks were just about unchanged, significantly underperforming the Toronto Stock Exchange Composite Index. Good idea to buy Canada, but better not to have purchased the expert's stocks.

Always ready for good times, in August 2014 Fisher said in his *Forbes* column the fourth quarter was postured for a "big volatile melt-up," and in September 2014 he again said the stock market was headed for a fourth quarter "melt-up." From the start of the fourth quarter through December 16, 2014, the S&P 500 Index was dead even. The S&P increased over the next two weeks to finish the fourth quarter up about 4 percent. At the end of the first quarter of 2015, the index increased an additional 0.4 percent. I leave it to you to determine if that qualifies as a "melt-up." Fisher is on record saying 2015 would be "another year to thrive" and to expect an increase in 2015 in the S&P 500 Index of "15% plus." In fact, for 2015 the index decreased about 1 percent, for its worst year since 2008.

Fisher has, of course, made many accurate predictions. But he has missed a lot too. In its June 18, 2007, issue, *Barron's* reported, "Gurus have emerged to tell the masses what they want to hear. . . . Money manager and *Forbes* columnist Ken Fisher insists he invests by 'knowing what others don't.'" Really? There are thousands upon thousands of highly educated and experienced investment advisors, analysts, mutual fund managers, and other Wall Street professionals, yet he knows something that others don't? He knows it's smart to keep in the limelight, provide predictions on market movement, stay optimistic, and tout individual stocks. I can only assume that the people who follow him do believe that he does have something special to offer. All I can say is that when it comes to making predictions about specific market movements, you don't know, I don't know, and the Wall Street luminaries don't know either.

In early January 2009, Bloomberg turned for advice to investment strategist Russell Napier, named by *Institutional Investor* as the top-ranked Asia strategist from 1997 to 1999. Napier thought that the great global stock market crash in 2008 (the largest since the Great Depression) was likely to continue. He based this projection in large part on the Q ratio (developed by Nobel prize-winning economist James Tobin), which compares the market value of companies to the cost of their constituent parts. Napier stated that the S&P 500 Index might continue its precipitous decline (from about 1500 in 2007) and reach a bottom of 400 by 2014. At the time he made this pessimistic prognostication, the S&P 500 Index stood at about 900. He was projecting a 55 percent decline over the next five or six years. Fortunately, he was really wrong. By December 2014, the S&P 500 Index had advanced to an all-time high of 2,085, an increase of about 130 percent. Has this hurt Napier's reputation on Wall Street or his business? Not that I know.

Tom DeMark is another often-quoted Wall Street advisor. He has consulted with many of the most famous and wealthiest hedge fund operators, including George Soros, Leon Cooperman, and Steven Cohen. He is renowned as the creator of indicators to predict turning points in the level of investment markets. In May 2014, when the Dow Jones Industrial Average was about 16,700, DeMark told *Bloomberg* that the Dow would start "declining if the following pattern occurs: one daily close above 16,581, accompanied by an intraday high exceeding 16,661." Well, that happened, but the Dow continued to advance, and by December 2014 had climbed past 18,000. Never mind that DeMark was wrong, and never mind what his formula was—I'm puzzled and amused by how anyone can take seriously a prediction that is so precise. Sure, the numbers he used must have been generated by a computer program, but would

DeMark's thoughts have been different if the daily close had been above, say, 16,500 instead of 16,581?

Since no one really knows what to make of so much financial news, the Wall Street experts and press are only too happy to publicize completely contradictory analysis. It's the old cliché: "You pay your money and you take your pick." On April 13, 2012, JPMorgan Chase and Wells Fargo reported their quarterly revenues and earnings. The headline on the *Wall Street Journal* article the next day read "Bank Earnings Dismay Investors." The same day the headline on the *New York Times* article read "Solid Results at 2 Banks Bode Well for Industry."

We're always getting vastly different projections from highly respected experts. Unfortunately, we have to figure out whose advice to follow. In January 21, 2013, *Forbes* published, just two pages apart, the expert opinions of Gary Shilling and Ken Fisher. Shilling predicted the S&P 500 Index would decline about 42 percent, while Fisher said he expected stocks to shine in 2013. Fisher gets the prize here, as the S&P 500 Index increased about 30 percent. But we should remember that Shilling correctly called the housing and stock market collapses in 2007–2008, while Fisher missed them.

In *Financial Times* on September 3, 2013, two highly renowned and respected academics expressed diametrically opposite views on the stock market. Robert Shiller of Yale University thought that the US stock market was 62 percent overvalued, while Jeremy Siegel of the Wharton School of Business at the University of Pennsylvania suggested that the US equity market was cheap. At the time this is being written about two and a half years later, the S&P 500 Index has moved up approximately 17 percent since those views were published. Siegel has the early lead on this one.

In its November 10, 2014 issue, *Barron's* ran an article entitled "The Favorite Picks of Top-Performing Hedge Funds." Does this sound like another great opportunity? In an unusual moment of candor, *Barron's* itself acknowledged that the year before the nineteen selections of its top-performing managers declined an average of 7 percent while the S&P 500 increased by 17 percent.

How can the best and the brightest be so far off so often? Could it be they are just playing to their audiences, knowing full well that almost no one is out there checking the accuracy of their predictions? If their predictions pan out, they themselves will remind us, and public accolades and honors will surely follow. If their predictions are wrong, you will be forced to do a lot of research to discover the truth.

Advice that sounds authoritative is worthless when attempting to predict the unpredictable, which the future is. And as we have seen, it doesn't matter how impressive someone's track record is—or appears to be. Even if their performance hasn't been enhanced by backtesting or cherry-picking or random luck, always remember: "Past performance is no guarantee of future results." So I'm going to ask you to do, with respect to Wall Street, what the rap group Public Enemy said in a different context: "Don't believe the hype."

# NINE

# Not Present at the Creation: IPOs

inancial news is filled with stories of actual or anticipated initial public offerings (IPOs). What are IPOs, and why has the investing public become so infatuated with them?

An IPO is the first time a private company sells stock to the general public. The shares in the company can then be traded among owners over established securities exchanges. An IPO changes the company in many ways. It must register with state and federal governments and become subject to numerous laws and regulations, including many reporting requirements. The number of shareholders typically increases vastly, from a relatively few insiders and employees to as many as millions. Companies generally go public either to raise capital for operations or expansion or to provide liquidity to the earlier investors or founders who want to take some of their risk off the table.

IPO shares are sold to the public at a price determined by the company's management in consultation with its investment bankers and other advisors. Prior to the IPO the investment bankers are able to explore the public's interest in the company and use their experience to determine what the initial offering price will be. Typically, company management and the investment bankers have "road shows" both to gauge potential interest in the IPO and to promote its sale.

IPOs draw lots of attention in large part because of the price increases that are often realized in the very first day of trading. The financial press is only too happy to assist in the pre-offering hype and later publicize the first-day results. The company or the selling shareholders receive the IPO price for the shares they sell to the public. Any increase in the value of the shares after they are in the public's hands accrues to the benefit of later buyers and sellers, not to either the company itself or the initial selling shareholders.

Investment banks and brokerage firms are always looking for new companies to take public because of the fees generated, which can be as high as 7 percent of the amount raised, although they are often significantly lower. It was reported that Facebook paid "only" about 1 percent for its IPO, but since it raised $18 billion, that amounted to $180 million in fees. When trading in the company's shares starts, the brokers earn commissions for buying and selling those shares. With a popular ("hot") offering, the sales volume and commissions can be significant.

There is so much good press around IPOs that many investors clamor to get shares. But how realistic is that, given how shares are allocated to customers of the underwriting firms? Strange but true, the Securities and Exchange Commission, which has jurisdiction over public companies, does not regulate the allocation of IPO shares, having ceded that to FINRA. For hot IPOs, the shares are typically allocated to the best customers of the investment banking firms underwriting the deal. Obviously this means that wealthy investors, large institutions, and mutual funds get most of the shares. If the share value then increases from the initial offering price, these favored customers, not small investors, get the profits. Furthermore, the large entities participate in all of the hot IPOs, while smaller individuals only get allocations some of the time.

Part of the frenzy surrounding many IPOs arises from investors' belief that they will be able to buy the next Google or Microsoft. Google went public in 2004 and in 2015 its shares were valued at about fifteen times the price at IPO. In 2015 Microsoft, which went public in 1986 (in what was an entirely different financial era), was valued at more than 400 times its IPO price. These are the one in 1,000 cases, but just the thought of them entices buyers to lust after gains.

Quite frequently Wall Street can orchestrate a first-day feeding frenzy, which produces a significant increase in the stock's price over its original issue price. The first-day pop for an IPO then leads to increased interest in the next one. In April 2015, *Financial Times* reported that the average one-day pop for US-listed IPOs was 13 percent in 2014 and about 14 percent in the first three and a half months of 2015. During the heyday of the dot-com bubble in 1997 and 1998, the average first-day price increased about 19 percent. The feeding frenzy is often fueled by the Wall Street analysts who work for the very same firms underwriting the IPO. They issue favorable reports because they are rewarded for assisting investment banking deals. It is so prevalent that *Barron's* has referred to it as a technique "employed by bankers everywhere."

Wall Street's hype of companies that have little history and no earnings became exaggerated during the technology bubble of the late 1990s. One strategist for Solomon Smith Barney recommended buying shares only in companies that were losing money. Why would he say that? You would think it would be better to own companies that actually made money. His reasoning was clear. If the company had any earnings, then investors could apply a price-to-earnings ratio and see how that compared with other firms in the market. But if there were no earnings, there was no price-to-earnings ratio. Pie in the sky was the limit. Like so much other terrible advice given by Wall Street, this worked very well until it didn't, and then those who followed it lost a lot.

Far too often the issuing companies, heeding the advice of their investment bankers and other advisors, purposely set the IPO price below the market for the shares, knowing there is demand at a higher price. A feeding frenzy will follow, driving up the price of the stock. Creating a hot IPO is generally viewed by the Wall Street community as a positive development instead of what it is: a transfer of wealth in which the difference between the IPO price and the first sale price goes not to the company issuing the shares but to the first shareholders—often big financial institutions that simply flip the stock. Large customers rewarded with a significant allocation of shares in a hot

IPO are often pressured to increase business with the brokerage firm that provided the shares. In the *New York Times* of March 10, 2013, Joe Nocera reported that it was not unusual for investment firms "to ask that 30 to 50% of the first-day profits be returned." Nocera went on to note, "To this day, an I.P.O. with a first-day jump is considered a success, even though the company is being short-shrifted." So here we have yet another example of Wall Street breaching its fiduciary duty.

The day after Facebook's IPO in May 2012, the *Wall Street Journal's* headline read: "Investors Pummel Facebook." Elsewhere the Facebook stock issuance was referred to as a "failed IPO." What was so terrible? Facebook went public at $38 per share. It then jumped to $45 per share before ending the first day's trading at $38.23 per share. So a stock that ends up trading just slightly higher than its IPO price is one that got "pummeled." Wall Street's expectation seems to be that the IPO price will be set below what the market will bear so that the speculators who buy the stock at IPO can flip it and make a lot of money. It seems to me that Facebook's underwriters valued the stock properly, so that the company realized the maximum value from the IPO rather than passing a significant portion of that value to the speculators.

Facebook's stock declined after the IPO. About five months later the price had bounced off a low of about $18 per share and recovered to about $23 per share. Then it was time for *Barron's* to run a cover story declaring that Facebook's stock was "Still Too Pricey" with "Next stop: $15." It didn't quite happen that way. During the next year Facebook gradually increased to $50 per share, and in the year following that advanced to $79 per share. As of April 2016, Facebook was trading at over $117 per share. So which is better: an IPO with a large first-day jump in the stock's price followed by poor performance both by the company and its stock, or a properly priced IPO with no first-day pop but a healthy company later producing massive increases in shareholder value?

Once the first-day frenzy subsides, the performance of most of IPOs has not been good. In its October 14, 2014, issue, *Financial*

*Times* ran an article entitled "The proof is in the pudding for hyped-up IPOs." There were sixty-four IPOs underwritten in the first nine months of 2014 by seven of the largest European and US investment banking companies. These IPOs were each worth over $200 million. On the first day of trading their average stock price had increased over the offering price, but by the end of the third quarter the average stock price had declined.

Groupon, a company that provides discount coupons online, was hyped by Wall Street before its IPO in November 2011. The investment bankers had no problem pushing the stock on the public with an IPO price of $20 per share, which gave the company a market capitalization of $13 billion. The stock price jumped to $28 on the first public trade after the IPO, increasing the market capitalization to about $18 billion. It seemed not to matter to anyone that Groupon had lost over $450 million the year before and was still not profitable. During the first day of trading Groupon's shares hit a high of $31 and closed at $26. But that was as good as it ever got. The stock proceeded down almost immediately, and one year later had declined almost 85 percent to $4.15 per share. As of December 2015, its price stood at $2.87, so those who were caught up in the hot IPO hype were burned.

Twitter, the very popular social media messaging firm, had its IPO in November 2013, selling 70 million shares at $26 per share, for a total of about $1.8 billion. The stock hit a high of $50.09 during the first day of trading before closing at $44.90. By my calculation, this means Twitter could have realized an additional $1.3 billion of capital for itself had it and its underwriters priced the shares properly at around $45 instead of at $26, in order to avoid the IPO feeding frenzy and the first-day price jump. Where did that $1.3 billion of value go? It was transferred to those who got the shares at the IPO price of $26. And who were these lucky winners? Almost all were the best customers of the underwriting firms.

LinkedIn, a social media company designed to connect members of the business community, had its IPO in May 2011 at a price of $45 per share. This was another red-hot IPO, with the first trade after

IPO at $83 per share. It then soared to $122 per share before closing on the first day at $94.25 per share, or an increase of 109 percent from the IPO price. Again, this seems to indicate that LinkedIn took in only about half of what it could have as about $300 million was transferred from LinkedIn to the underwriters' best customers.

Etsy, an online marketplace for handmade and vintage goods, made its stock market debut on April 16, 2015, with an IPO price of $16 per share. Its first trade after IPO was at $31 per share, and it closed the first day at $30. Just five days later the shares were trading at $25.75. According to the April 16, 2015, edition of the *Wall Street Journal*, about 85 percent of the 16.7 million shares available at IPO were sold to institutional investors. This would leave about 2.5 million shares for smaller investors. The *Wall Street Journal* reported that Etsy had set up a program for small investors to buy as much as $2,500 of the stock at IPO, allowing them to be part of frenzy. Were these long-term investors or were they able to flip their shares and make about $2,500? Those small investors who did not flip their shares have not done well in the first few months following the IPO. In December 2015, Etsy was trading at $9.30 per share, or about $7 below its IPO price.

How high were the expectations in 2015 for IPOs and the companies' founders? The headline of an April 24, 2015, article in the *Wall Street Journal* that read: "Rich, But Not Silicon Valley Rich" gives us a clue. The story told of the IPO of Box Inc., an online file storage company, with a January 2015 IPO price of $14 per share and a first day closing price of $23.23 per share. The next day the stock hit a high of $24.39 and then drifted down until it was trading at $18.28 by the end of April. The two founders of the firm were described as having a combined net worth at the time of the IPO of *only* about $100 million after spending ten long years developing the company. At the time of the IPO, Box had never made money, and its cumulative losses exceeded $500 million. We'll have to wait to see how this works out in the long term for the investors at IPO.

The IPO for Priceline, the online seller of travel services, and its history over the next fifteen years show us a lot about Wall Street's culture and the difference between long-term and short-term results. Priceline's IPO was one of the most anticipated during the dot-com boom of the late 1990s. In March 1999, Priceline set its IPO price at $16 per share. At the end of the first day of trading the price had soared to $82 per share. This was an incredible jump even during the peak of the frenzy for online companies in the 1990s. And it only got better: a month later Priceline was selling for $162 per share. But then reality set in and its trajectory began to spiral down.

The September 6, 1999, issue of *Fortune* had a lengthy article on Priceline with the title: "The Hype Is Big, Really Big, at Priceline." By then the stock had declined from that high of $162 per share to $70 per share, and the company was hemorrhaging money. The article detailed what its author thought was wrong with Priceline's business model. Over the next year, Priceline's stock crashed to $5 per share, seemingly validating *Fortune*'s view. In November 2000, *Fortune* ran an article on Jay Walker, Priceline's CEO: "Inside Jay Walker's House of Cards." *Fortune* observed that Priceline stock had "deflated from $162 to $5." This article again outlined the multitude of problems with Priceline's business. *Fortune*'s analysis certainly appeared solid at the time. Within six weeks of that publication, Priceline further declined to a low of $1.06 per share. Priceline seemed to be on its way out of business.

As Priceline declined from a peak of $165 per share in 1999 to a low of just over $1 per share in 2000, what did some of the Wall Street folks say? With Priceline trading at $87 per share, First Union Securities upgraded it to a "buy," indicating it had strong business momentum. As the stock price hit $44, AG Edwards upgraded its recommendation to "accumulate," indicating that it was attractively valued. When the stock price further slid to $39, CS First Boston initiated a "buy" rating. After Priceline fell to $4.72, Merrill Lynch downgraded their recommendation to "accumulate," indicating, "We think the model can eventually work." When Priceline traded at $2.63, Merrill Lynch downgraded its recommendation to "neutral."

How we evaluate these recommendations may depend upon the time frame. Whether you bought it $87 per share, or $44, or even

$4.72, you suffered substantial losses as Priceline continued its rapid slide to $1.06. Priceline's stock did not recover quickly, and two years later, at the end of 2002, it was trading at $1.60. But then Priceline's fortunes gradually changed, and six years later, in December 2008, the price had increased to $12 per share. By then Priceline had established itself in the marketplace and its revenues and profits continued to grow. By March 2011, twelve years after the IPO, its reverse split-adjusted stock price had finally returned to the level of the close of its first day of trading. Now that's a long road back! Since then, Priceline has continued to grow, and by April 2016 was trading at about $225 per share on the reverse split-adjusted basis and by 2015 had become the third-most-profitable Internet company, earning about $2 billion and trailing only Google and Facebook.

Hot IPOs are not limited to technology companies. Between October 2013 and January 2015, six popular casual restaurants went public (El Polo Loco, Habit Restaurants, Shake Shack, Noodles & Co., Potbelly, and Zoe's Kitchen). All six saw substantial jumps from their IPO price on the first day of trading, with an average increase of 81 percent. Since then progress has been slow. From their opening prices on the day of the IPO through April 2015, the average price of the six companies had increased about 2.7 percent. This represents below-average performance, as the S&P 500 Index had increased significantly during the time these companies had been publicly traded. This contrasts to the experience of Chipotle Mexican Grill, which came public in 2006 at a price of $22 and saw an opening trade at $45. The price in April 2015: $640. A year later that had declined to $420. Everyone thinks they're going to own the next Chipotle and not the average performers or the losers. If you're lucky enough to get the one Chipotle, and if you hold on long enough, it will make up for a lot of losses on other IPOs. Two big "ifs" there. Dare I say, it might be feast or famine.

Both Wall Street professionals and investors like to talk only about their winners, never the losers. The IPO game has not been a winner for most investors, unless they have been lucky enough to get in on the Googles, Amazons, and eBays. But whether we look back to the dot-com era of the late 1990s or take a much longer perspective, the results are the same. The cover story in *Fortune* of May 21, 2001, suggested that the credibility gap between investment banks and their clients had never been wider. "Why? Just look at the IPO con game." The ensuing article noted that three quarters of the almost 800 IPOs from the prior two years were trading at below their offering prices. In September 2014, *Barron's* ran an article after Alibaba's IPO, the largest ever. *Barron's* observed that the "typical IPO delivers a negative return to investors over its first four years." Alibaba had its IPO in September 2014 at $68 per share. A year later it was trading at $60 after reaching a high of $120.

I think the days may be over for making massive profits by buying at IPO. A company can go public, grow its business, and see its stock price increase. But future gains by purchasing at IPO may be more limited. The massive valuations of many private companies before they come public, or the large market caps (the total value of all a company's stock) when they do become public, make the experiences of the past almost irrelevant. Everyone is hoping to find the next Microsoft or Walmart, but given market caps at IPOs these days, it just cannot happen. When Microsoft issued its shares at IPO in 1986, its market cap was about $800 million. In April 2016, that market cap was about 475 times greater, at more than $380 billion. Similarly, Walmart's market cap at IPO was a relatively modest $21 million. An investment at IPO has grown about 11,000 times.

Let's compare those experiences with that of Facebook, which came public in May 2012 and had a market cap of about $100 billion. If this increases ten times (as of April 2016 it had already tripled) the market cap would be $1 trillion, which is more than any company today. Apple, as of April 2016, has the largest market cap in the world, at approximately $525 billion, and the biggest Internet company by far is Google, at about $485 billion. In order to increase as much as Microsoft has from its IPO, Facebook would have to be worth about $47 trillion, significantly more than the combined value of all publicly traded stocks in the United States in 2016.

When companies like Uber, the ride-sharing company replacing taxis, come public, we can only imagine what the market cap will be. As of December 2015, Uber was seeking additional funding based on a value of $62 billion, and the previous round of private financing had valued Uber at about $41 billion. That may be inflated because of protections given the investors, but the market cap at IPO is likely to exceed that amount. How much room will there be for investors to profit?

We need a constant flow of new companies in order to keep our economy vital and growing. But what we don't need is Wall Street foisting on us companies that are too early in their life cycles to be anything but speculative. Wall Street has every incentive to push as many IPOs as it can, for it earns consulting fees and sales commissions from the IPOs and commissions on further trades. We know that investors in most IPOs eventually lose. It ultimately comes down to whether you want to play the ponies. Sometimes the long shots come in and those ticketholders win big. Occasionally you hit the trifecta and really score. But most of the time you tear up losing tickets. You have to decide how often to go to the racetrack.

# SECTION IV

# The Ultimate Con Job

TEN

# The Casino: Wall Street's Gambling Problem

Wall Street has been able to successfully masquerade gambling as investing, and we are all paying for this. Sure, many of Wall Street's gambling opportunities are sanctioned by the government and papered with disclosures prepared by lots of lawyers. But massive legal documentation does not change the substance of a transaction.

When you own a stock, you own a piece of an enterprise. With a true investment, both parties to a transaction can ultimately profit. If a company is growing, I can buy a stock today and sell it to you later at a higher price. You in turn can sell it for even more in the future if growth continues. The only limit on the profits from our transaction together is the health of the enterprise.

So on Wall Street, stocks, bonds, and most mutual funds can be true investment vehicles. But short sales, options, futures contracts, other derivatives, most hedge funds, and a lot of short-term trading strategies are generally vehicles for gambling, which is a zero-sum game—one party wins and the other party loses the exact same amount. The parties think they can outsmart one another. There is no possibility for overall growth. Actually, Wall Street has created a negative-sum game. The players are betting against each other, but fees and commissions come out to pay the Wall Street community. It's akin to the casinos in Las Vegas raking the poker pot with every hand played.

Wall Street and the financial media continually use gambling terminology in describing numerous activities. And there's a very good reason for that. The transactions are in fact wagers and accurately described as bets. Let's take a look at just a miniscule sample of the financial press's use of gambling vocabulary to see the many types of transactions to which it is applied.

1. *Financial Times*: "Moody's 'did not understand' $6.3 bn MF Global *bet* on European debt."
2. *Wall Street Journal*: "Global Central-Bank Policy Moves Are Creating More Opportunities to *Wager*."
3. *Wall Street Journal*: "Hedge Funds Use Insurance-Like Contracts to Amplify *Wagers* on Weak Firms."
4. *Wall Street Journal*: "Hedge Funds Hawk *Single-Bet* Deals."
5. *Financial Times* reports that Ray Dalio, founder of Bridgewater Associates, a $165 billion hedge-fund operator, said in a note to clients that he is "avoiding large *bets* on the financial markets."
6. *The Economist*, reporting on what went wrong leading to the first phase of the stock market crash in 2008, reported that "Their [bankers and fund managers] *gambling* has been fed by the knowledge that, if disaster struck, someone else—borrowers, investors, taxpayers—would end up bearing at least some of the losses."

Why is no one saying that gambling is not good for the economy, let alone for those engaging in it? Why can Wall Street firms and their customers gamble with literally billions, while a five-dollar bet on three-card Monte is a crime? New York cleared out those operators from Times Square, but not the big boys on Wall Street.

Gambling makes markets more volatile, increasing everyone's risks. J. Bradford DeLong, professor of economics at the University of California at Berkeley, thinks that "There are two sustainable ways to make money in finance: find people with the risks that need to be carried and match them with people with unused risk-bearing capacity, or find people with such risks and match them with people who are clueless but who have money." He goes on to observe that "America's financial system is less a device for efficiently sharing risk and more a device for separating rich people from their money."

But traders welcome more volatility, which increases everyone's risk, so they can exploit it. In January 2015, the *Wall Street Journal* reported that a number of "traders complained that several years of low volatility had made it difficult to make money buying and selling oil." In a similar tone, *Financial Times* reported in February 2013 that hedge funds had made billions betting on the Japanese yen in the periods during which it was unstable, and that the managers of those funds were hopeful for a return to volatility. If someone can explain to me how it helps anyone, other than the traders, if oil or currency markets are volatile rather than more orderly, I certainly want to learn.

Gambling is at odds with investors achieving long-term success. Investors should strive for more consistent returns, which can be realized through investing, rather than volatile returns, which are much more often the result of gambling. If you had a choice of the following two investment results over a 10-year period, which would you prefer?

| Year | Investment 1 Return in Percent | Investment 2 Return in Percent |
|------|-------------------------------|-------------------------------|
| 1 | +20 | +6 |
| 2 | +21 | +10 |
| 3 | +10 | +6 |
| 4 | −16 | +10 |
| 5 | +12 | +6 |
| 6 | −2 | +10 |
| 7 | +22 | +6 |
| 8 | −6 | +10 |
| 9 | +11 | +6 |
| 10 | +15 | +10 |

Investment 1, the riskier investment, outperformed investment 2 in seven of the ten years, but the ending values of the two funds are essentially identical. In essence, you must choose between gambling and all the risk that entails or investing for long-term growth.

Management's control over their own firms' gambling activities is increasingly difficult as investment techniques become more complex and opaque. A trading scandal hit Union Bank of Switzerland in 2011 with a resulting $2 billion loss. *Financial Times* reported that the head of one brokerage commented on these transactions by saying: "If you sat down with CEOs and asked them to please explain what happens they would try but they couldn't give you an accurate answer because they don't understand." Investing is not quantum mechanics. If it can't be explained in simple language, then something is wrong. Shouldn't a CEO adopt a policy that he won't authorize a strategy he does not understand?

Please don't let Wall Street convince you that 2008 was an aberration when it comes to gambling. Sure, it was the largest stock market crash in seventy years, but the gambling practices that led to it were and remain commonplace. The losses suffered by the investors in Enron and Long-Term Capital Management prior to 2008, by customers of MF Global in 2011, and by the spillover into the general community can be laid at the feet of gambling. A more recent example: In January 2015, the Swiss government, in an unannounced and surprise move, removed the cap on its currency's value against the Euro. This led to a 20 percent increase in the value of the Swiss franc in just one day and resulted in Citigroup losing more than $150 million almost instantly. The company owning one of the largest foreign-exchange trading platforms for individual investors in the United States announced that the surge in the Swiss francs value had led to $225 million in customer losses, which might put the company in breach of its capital requirements.

In January 2012, *Financial Times* reported the breakdown of 2010 revenues for the eighteen largest investment banks. Corporate finance, debt capital markets, and equity capital markets combined for 20 percent of the revenues, while secondary market trading was responsible for 80 percent of the revenues. If the vast majority of these companies' revenue comes from trading, they have every reason to encourage more needless activity.

The volume of foreign-exchange trading rose about 23,000 percent between 1977 and 2010. Certainly times were different in 1977 when international trade and globalization were much less developed than today, but that much growth in trading currencies is not attributable to the need for funds in commerce. In November 2010, the *Wall Street Journal* reported that "Currency Trading Soars" to a daily volume of $4 trillion, about double what it was just six years before. That's about $1 quadrillion per year, which is many multiples of the world's entire GDP. Today the daily volume is about $5 trillion.

Outstanding margin debt has increased in the last decade from about $250 billion in 2005 to about $450 billion in 2015. The same trend holds for the notional value (the face amount of the underlying securities) of derivatives, which increased from about $220 trillion in 2004 to about $700 trillion in 2014. Hedge funds, which utilize so many gambling techniques, have seen their assets grow from about $1.1 trillion in 2005 to about $3 trillion by the end of 2014.

A discussion I had recently with a long-standing client shows Wall Street's great success with the ultimate con job. Against my advice, my client had purchased an interest in an entity that owned a number of hedge funds (a "fund of funds"). Over the next few years this investment performed poorly, and he decided to liquidate one half of it. I asked why he chose not to liquidate the entire account. He responded that he was worried that as a trustee for a client's wealth he could be criticized for not owning hedge funds as part of a large portfolio. Wall Street and the hedge fund industry should be proud of themselves for being able to get customers to accept such baloney. I am happy to report that a little while later he liquidated the rest of his hedge fund holdings.

Since I support free markets and free enterprise, people often ask me what's wrong with a culture of gambling and who gets hurt. Shuffling money from losers to winners does not increase our wealth.

Every time we celebrate the winners we conveniently forget to mourn for the losers. Gambling destroys thrift and the work ethic. If investors believe they can get rich quick with no work, why would they want to make strenuous efforts to succeed? Large gambling losses have significant long-term implications. When pension plans, IRAs, and 401(k) plans gamble and lose, retirement incomes diminish. In some cases, the government gets to pick up the tab.

The more gambling gains acceptance on Wall Street, the more many members of our society come to distrust Wall Street, and more importantly to question the very efficacy of capitalism. Ultimately, all this gambling may prove to be Wall Street's undoing. The longer it goes on, the more Wall Street invites increased regulation and interference with free markets. And the more our economy becomes socialized, the poorer we will all become. When the public associates investing with gambling, it has every reason to be suspicious of what it is being told the free enterprise system represents. The stock market crash of 2008 and the ensuing Great Recession has caused too many people to equate the hijacked free enterprise system with the real thing.

The Wall Street apologists either don't care or don't understand that for every gambling dollar won, the same dollar is lost by someone else. In 2008, Lehman went under, Iceland suffered immensely, AIG was history except for the government bailout, pension funds lost billions, and large unemployment followed. Why should we foster a system that allows this when we have nothing to gain from it?

## ELEVEN

# Myopia: Short-Term Trading

yopia, a medical term also called nearsightedness, denotes
defective vision of distant objects. As the son of an ophthal-
mologist and someone who has had to wear corrective lenses
for most of my life, I am all too familiar with its physical aspects. But
myopia has also come to mean a lack of foresight. Throughout my
career, I have seen Wall Street focusing too much attention on short-
term actions and not enough on long-term results.

There is no question that over the past twenty-five years Wall
Street's time horizon has shortened. The daily trading volume on
the established exchanges has increased significantly, even after
adjusting for the fact that more companies are listed today. The large
increase is made possible by more efficient computers and the massive decline in trading costs associated with computerized trading
and record-keeping.

Before deregulation in 1975 and the advent of the firms originally
called "discount brokers," commissions were fixed and very high by
today's standards. An investor could expect to pay a commission of
1½ to 2 percent of the cost of acquiring or selling shares. A $25,000
purchase of 500 shares of a $50 stock, for example, could earn the
broker a commission of $500. These high commissions discour-
aged short-term trading because the cost would substantially reduce
or eliminate the gains. "Churning" was the term used to describe

stockbrokers' frequent and illegal trades in clients' accounts in order to earn commissions. This could result in customers making little or losing while brokers made significant sums.

With the appearance of the discount brokers, trading costs diminished significantly and became much less important in determining clients' ultimate gains or losses. Today stocks can be purchased at retail for $8.95 per trade or less. Some firms trade equities for no cost if the customer maintains a large enough account balance. Commission rates have declined by 98 percent since the fixed-commission era.

Lower commissions were clearly a positive development in many ways. The whole concept of churning vanished. But as trading became easier and faster and cheaper, a very unexpected effect was a much greater focus on short-term performance. Market forces that saved customers lots of money also had a negative impact by converting customers from long-term investors into short-term traders. Day trading became acceptable and later encouraged by Wall Street. The idea that stocks should be purchased as a long-term investment found increasingly less support.

Wall Street provides its customers many different opportunities to deploy their capital. We can categorize them very broadly as (1) investment—the purchase of an asset with the anticipation that it will provide income, appreciation, or both and be sold at a higher price later; (2) speculation—the purchase of a riskier asset in anticipation of realizing higher gains, while possibly losing a much higher percentage of the original capital than through investment; (3) gambling—trading in assets that must result in offsetting gains and losses for the parties to the transaction (meaning that whatever one party to the transaction makes, the other party loses the same amount).

Our financial system cannot function well without adequate investment, and in appropriate circumstances can be enhanced by speculation, but it is ill-served by gambling. Unfortunately for all of us, Wall Street has a gambling problem, which involves (among other things) what I call the "right now syndrome."

History shows beyond any doubt that the shorter the time horizon, the more random the performance becomes. This is true for so many things—whether it's flipping coins, the on-the-field success of a major league baseball team, or investing on Wall Street. I think we would all agree that if we flip a coin one million times, the proportion of heads to tails will be very close to 50–50. But what if we flip it just once? How much would you risk on a single coin flip? Or suppose we flip the coin four times? We could get four heads in a row, although we know that streak will not continue for very long. On Wall Street, day trading is equivalent to one flip, short-term speculation comparable to four flips, and long-term investing analogous to one million flips.

How does long-term investing differ from gambling? If you invest in an index fund, the odds are good that you'll make money over time. Since it debuted in 1926, the S&P 500 Index has increased on average about 10 percent per year. But stocks don't just automatically increase each year. The S&P has increased in about 70 percent of the years and correspondingly decreased in about 30 percent of the years. And even in the up years there are lots of down months and down days. So anything could happen if you bet on a single stock on a single given day, or even on an index fund for a single day.

For another perspective on this, consider baseball history. In every year from 1993 to 2012, the New York Yankees had a better season record than the Pittsburgh Pirates. The Yankees won fourteen division championships and placed second five other times, winning 60 percent of their total games. The Pirates managed just one second-place finish in their division during those twenty years, winning only 43 percent of their total games. Based on those numbers, a bet during those years that the Yankees would have a better season record than the Pirates was reasonably safe. But what would have happened if we had narrowed the time frame? How safe would you have felt if you had to bet that the Yankees would have a better week than the Pirates? How about a better day? The shorter we make the time frame, the more random the outcome becomes. Betting on the Yankees over the Pirates on a single day is akin to day trading, while betting on their performance for the season is more like investing. But we must remember that even long-term investing can go awry: in 2013 and 2014 the Pirates won more games than the Yankees did.

IRS statistics from income tax returns show that long-term investing is more profitable than short-term trading. In 2007, the S&P 500 Index increased about 3.5 percent. How did the traders do? IRS reports show short-term capital gains and losses by monthly holding periods. For periods of less than seven months, there were net gains reported in four of the monthly periods and losses in three. Some of those losses may have been realized for tax savings, but clearly not all of them. Once the holding periods were seven months or longer, aggregate net gains were realized regardless of how long assets had been held.

In *Financial Times* of March 29, 2014, Tim Harford reported on what he called the "Investor's Tragedy: that the typical investor doesn't do nearly as well as a typical investment." He cited a survey from 2000 that looked at the trading performance during the 1990s, when markets were soaring, of 65,000 retail investors with accounts at a large discount broker. They concluded that while the US stock market returned about 18 percent per year, the investors who traded the most actively earned about 11 percent per year.

The performance of Apple's stock provides an interesting example of how fortunes and perceptions can radically change and that initial or short-term performance may not indicate what is to come. In 1980, Apple's stock issuance was one of the first hot IPOs of the technology boom. Its IPO was the largest since Ford Motor Company's in 1956, was wildly anticipated, and was priced at $22 per share. Apple's stock opened trading at $28.75 per share and closed the day at $34.13 per share. Although Apple did become a big part of supplying computers to schools, it initially made little headway in the business world, and its stock price reflected this. In August 1985, almost five years after the IPO, Apple's stock was selling at $14.50 per share, significantly below the IPO price. A full twenty years after the stock came public it was trading at a price that represented an annual return of about 2.3 percent from its close on its first day of trading. Meanwhile, the S&P

500 Index had increased about 18 percent per year during that same twenty-year time period. That's right: for twenty years Apple's stock hardly appreciated, even in the best of financial times. An investment of $1,000 in Apple on the first day of trading grew in twenty years to about $1,600, while the same investment in the S&P 500 Index grew to about $27,000. But then things began to change, and over the next five years Apple's stock increased about tenfold. If you were a trader setting a target price and realized a gain any time during those five years, you probably made a tidy profit. But what did you lose by not continuing to own Apple? Over the next ten years Apple increased another thirteen times. As I write this Apple has the largest market cap in the world, but for its first twenty years as a public company it had a significantly underperforming stock.

Despite all the evidence that short-term trading is not as profitable as long-term investing, Wall Street keeps coming out with exciting innovations to enrich itself by encouraging its customers to gamble more often. Apparently it's not enough to have stock options expiring quarterly or annually. Wall Street recently introduced weekly options so its customers could bet on the volatility of stocks. Are daily options on the way? This could be as much fun as daily betting on fantasy baseball teams.

Why has Wall Street invested so much in promoting short-term thinking instead of adopting a longer-term and safer approach? Because it's in their financial interest to do so. The more turnover they can generate, the more commissions and markups they can earn. The more product they can sell, the greater the opportunity to collect more. A shorter time horizon also requires their customers to look to them for advice and expertise much more frequently. Fast and furious—rather than slow and steady, which is so much less exciting—fits easily into today's culture of shorter attention spans. It's get rich quick by speculation or gambling rather than get rich slowly through hard work and savings.

Enron and Global Crossing, two of Wall Street's biggest darlings during the late 1990s and early 2000s, illustrate so well the problems with this short-term focus. In 2001, rather than developing real customers for their businesses, the two companies discussed a deal in which Global Crossing would pay Enron $650 million for its fiber-optic network, while Enron in turn would pay Global Crossing the same amount for use of the network. The idea was that both companies would then book $650 million in revenue even though there was nothing really being exchanged. Yes, this may well have been fraudulent, but it shows how far firms and their accountants were willing to go to provide the appearance of short-term profitability.

We have also seen short-term thinking for a long time in the private equity world. It has not been unusual for a private equity firm to take over a public company, incur a lot of debt and costs to boost short-term returns, and then sell the company back to the public for a quick and substantial gain.

High-frequency trading (HFT) takes the "right now syndrome" to the extreme. HFT has attracted lots of attention in recent years as it becomes more and more prevalent and adds to Wall Street's success in stripping money from its customers. HFT is computer-driven algorithmic trading using market data to take advantage of short-term opportunities at ultrafast speed. The market data can be an announcement of a company's fundamentals, such as sales and earnings, or it can be the supply and demand in the marketplace for the shares of a particular company. When we say fast, we mean really fast. A *Wall Street Journal* article in February 2014 cited market data and transmission information from Bloomberg, Dow Jones, and Thomson Reuters showing that a high-frequency trader was able to sell shares in a company within fifty milliseconds (that's 1/20 of a second) of an electronic announcement of earnings. This was about 1/10 of a second before the first publication to a wider audience. High-frequency traders can act on news before other investors even know of it, let alone are able to act on it.

Wall Street firms are spending hundreds of millions of dollars in order to get an infinitesimal yet important advantage over competitors. The *Wall Street Journal* reported in 2012 that one firm had spent about $300 million in order to cut the time of communications between Chicago and New York by 3/1,000 of a second. This would enable the firm's trades to be placed more rapidly. But does this make any sense? Yes, I understand in today's system how that small difference in time does produce an advantage. But should we have a system where computers, not humans, are making decisions and where we use our resources to try to squeeze out the last millisecond so that one party can get information before others? The essence of free markets is equally well-informed parties making voluntary decisions in their own self-interest. Is it healthy to have a system where one party can gain an advantage by knowing what other parties to the transaction do not? In 2015, Richard Grasso, former head of the New York Stock Exchange and a critic of high frequency trading, observed, "A fast market is not necessarily a fair market."

HFT also arises in another entirely different context: traders (actually computers) trying to exploit price differences in separate markets, or the spreads between the bid and ask quotes on securities. Proponents of HFT claim it provides liquidity and makes for more efficient markets. What really happens may be quite different. HFT has turned quickly into what's known as "front running"—knowing what someone else is buying or selling and taking advantage of the information to trade before they do. Front running has been illegal for years, and the SEC's regulatory efforts against it have been significant. But the SEC doesn't seem concerned if it is done through HFT. In fact, the SEC says HFT is designed to "protect investors, maintain fair, orderly, and efficient markets."

Let's look at an example of traditional front running. Suppose you work for an investment firm and are advising your clients to buy a particular stock. Before they make their purchases, you personally go into the market and buy shares in the same company. Then your clients buy a substantially larger block. Presumably the increase in demand will drive up the price. You can then sell your shares for a profit or hold them for future appreciation, having been able to purchase them for less than your clients paid for their shares. HFT can do the same thing, but in a less personal manner and at vastly greater speeds. HFT may only involve squeezing out a fraction of a penny on each share, but when billions of shares change hands every day this adds up. *Financial Times* reported that HFT is costing investors as much as $10 billion to $22 billion per year. One study found that investors who interacted with high-frequency traders saw adverse pricing of about one third of 1 percent. In 2014 Virtu, a high-frequency trading company, had its IPO. Its registration statement revealed that it had lost money during only one trading day in nearly five years, and its net profit margin was about 25 percent. I'd say that's a profitable enterprise.

HFT displays another characteristic tendency on Wall Street: the willingness to push to the borderline of what's legal or even to step across that line. Not content merely to be able to front run their customers, many of the high-frequency trading firms try to game the system. Sometimes this takes the form of illegally acting as both buyer and seller in the same offering. Another popular technique is called "spoofing." This is the practice of entering and almost immediately canceling orders to trick others into making trades, thinking there is demand in the market that really isn't there. Charles Schwab himself wrote in April 2014 that more than 95 percent of high-frequency trade orders in 2013 were canceled. He indicated that HFT was a "technological arms race designed to pick the pockets of legitimate market participants." He then suggested a simple solution: just impose a cancellation fee. That makes sense, but I'm not sure what to make of Schwab's position on HFT. Four days after he issued that statement, the *Wall Street Journal* reported on its website that some analysts estimated Charles Schwab and Company was paid about $100 million annually for selling orders for its customers to middlemen who used high-frequency strategies. Apparently Schwab saw the error of its ways here and later stopped this practice.

I keep asking myself what high-frequency trading has to do with the real economy or liquidity for investors. One study estimated that in 1999, about 1,000 quotes per second were registered on US exchanges. By 2013 that number had increased to approximately 2,000,000. Is this really needed or helpful? Since most of the orders are cancelled, what liquidity is provided? In 1999, I never noticed any liquidity problems with 1/2,000 of today's volume of quotes. Maybe an increase of ten times would be appropriate, but not 2,000 times! I'm afraid we have Wall Street using the call for liquidity as its excuse for further dipping into our pockets. Fidelity is now guaranteeing that stock trades at the market will be filled within one second. Do we really need quicker execution?

HFT caused two very famous stock market incidents in recent years. The first occurred in May 2010 and has been enshrined in Wall Street literature as the "flash crash." A trader using the "spoofing" technique made and quickly cancelled large bids on futures contracts tied to the S&P 500. When other computers reacted, stock prices plunged, and in less than twenty minutes the Dow Jones Industrial Average fell 9.2 percent, temporarily wiping out over $1 trillion of market value. About an hour after the flash crash, markets rebounded. That did not restore the substantial losses many innocent investors incurred when their stocks were sold at artificially low prices. American Electric Power and NextEra, two huge utility companies, both saw their stock prices fall more than 50 percent before rebounding. At the very extreme Apple, which was trading at about $250 per share, had one trade at $100,000 per share, and Accenture's price temporarily dropped from $50 to $0.01.

What does that say about a system if one relatively small trader can trigger a massive decline in the entire market? How can we allow $1 trillion in value to disappear, even temporarily, when nothing has changed in the real world? Is HFT really serving us? Where are the regulators? Why are we fostering a system that takes money from us, provides little or no benefit, and increases the risk of market instability?

In 2012, a computer glitch caused Knight Capital, then the largest trader in US equities, to lose $440 million in less than an hour. Almost immediately after the error was discovered, Knight Capital asked the government for relief, since the trades were not intended. As big as Knight Capital was, it was not big enough for a government favor. A few months later the company was forced to merge with another financial firm in order to stay in business. But when Goldman Sachs later made a large series of trading errors it was able to get the transactions reversed.

Strange but true, there seems to be a quick and easy fix that would eliminate a lot of the mischief caused by HFT. According to many experts, if the high-frequency trades had to remain open for just one second, the problem would go away. Why don't we give that a try? If one second won't solve the problem, then we can explore really long time periods. How about five seconds? In the meantime, if the current system continues in place we will all keep paying our small tolls and allowing more money to be lifted from our pockets and deposited into Wall Street's accounts.

# TWELVE

# Don't Get Caught Short

Wall Street enthusiastically encourages the increasingly popular, yet risky, investment technique of short selling. Short selling means selling stocks or other securities that you currently do not own (hence you are "short") and later purchasing them to close out the trade. If the price declines from the time of your sale until the time of your purchase, you make a profit.

A simple example will show how short sellers can profit. Suppose a company's stock is trading at $50 per share. The short seller borrows 1,000 shares and then sells them, collecting $50,000. Time passes and now the shares are selling at $34 each. The short seller goes into the market, purchases 1,000 shares for a total of $34,000, and returns 1,000 shares to his lender. The short seller's profit is $16,000, the difference between the $50,000 he originally collected and the $34,000 he later paid.

I have never shorted any stock, although I have been severely tempted to do so. One time I saw a company that I thought was destined to be a loser, and another time I saw a vastly overpriced stock. Both were ideal candidates to short, but even though I was so certain I was right, I just couldn't pull the trigger. My fear of high stakes gambling with potentially no limit on my losses stopped me.

The first case involved Integrated Resources, a publicly traded firm that sponsored numerous high-profile investments known as "tax shelters." These enabled investors to avoid taxation on real income by taking deductions for what were often either accounting losses or even phony losses. For the wealthy in the 1970s and early 1980s, investment in tax shelters had all the characteristics of a mania. Many otherwise-astute investors checked their brains at the door and put their money into them. Unfortunately for too many of those investors, the losses claimed for tax deductions turned out to be bogus. Many times their money disappeared too, resulting in real losses.

As a tax lawyer in the heyday of tax shelters, I was often asked to advise clients who were tempted to invest. I reviewed quite a number of Integrated Resources' tax-shelter offerings and every time concluded that the projected tax benefits were highly likely to be disallowed if challenged by the IRS, which would defeat the whole purpose of investing in them. In all of those cases I reviewed, the economics of the investments were shaky at best. Fortunately, I succeeded in keeping my clients away from Integrated Resources.

While Integrated Resources' tax-shelter business was still rapidly growing, I was invited to attend a presentation by James Chanos, regarded now as one of the premier short sellers of this generation. When I saw him he was just getting started and trying to show the investment community how he determined which companies had poor prospects and were good candidates to short. During his presentation he described his two "flaming shorts." One of these was Integrated Resources. He described how its financial statements made no sense, how debts were lurking, how its business model was flawed, and how it was only a matter of time until the whole company collapsed.

Chanos described at the corporate level almost exactly what I had observed in its tax-shelter offerings. We both thought the collapse of Integrated Resources was a matter of when and not if. In fact, just a little time later Integrated Resources filed for bankruptcy, and its stock became worthless. The IRS ultimately successfully brought cases against many of its investors, and their actual losses were substantial. (In 1986 Congress revamped the Internal Revenue Code and eliminated the income-tax advantages of most tax shelters.)

Nevertheless, I was unable to muster the courage to go against my convictions and short the stock. I would have made a 100 percent profit on my investment if only I had acted. But I don't regret not acting, and my second case explains why.

During the dot-com boom of the late 1990s, the stock prices of Internet companies soared to unsustainable levels. Investors acted like every company with a ".com" in its name was entitled to a high valuation regardless of its business model, its lack of significant sales, or its profitability. Even companies losing huge amounts of money and unable to forecast profits in the foreseeable future were pumped up. One company that had nothing to do with the Internet simply added ".com" to its name. It made no change whatsoever in its business, but the next day its stock jumped significantly.

In early 2000, just before the collapse of the boom, I wrote a paper explaining in great detail why Yahoo was overpriced at $500 per share. Anyone who even remotely agreed with my analysis and who had any interest in shorting stocks would have immediately jumped into action. Over the next twenty-one months Yahoo stock fell to a split-adjusted $16 dollars per share. If I had been willing to sell short and held off buying until the bottom, I would have made a profit of about 97 percent on my investment. Even if I had pulled out earlier, say at $50 per share, I still would have made a profit of about 90 percent on my investment (sold short at $500 and bought back at $50). As of December 2015, Yahoo stock sat at a split-adjusted $160 per share, down about 33 percent for the year and down about 68 percent since my evaluation.

So what does my inability to short Yahoo at $500 per share or Integrated Resources while it was on its way to bankruptcy tell us about investing? Let's look at what would really have been required for an investor to have shorted Yahoo successfully. In June 1999, when Yahoo was selling for $150 per share, a speculator who believed the company was overvalued (as it was, and as I believed) could have shorted 1,000 shares then and pocketed $150,000. Unfortunately for him, the stock price continued to increase. But to make his bet pay off, he would have had to stick to his belief that it would eventually decline below his cost of $150 per share. By January 2000, when Yahoo was trading at $500 per share, the short seller who had sold Yahoo at $150 per share probably couldn't bear the pain of not knowing if the price would ever fall again back to that level—which was required for him just to break even. But closing his short position in January 2000 would cost him $500,000—i.e., he would have had to buy the shares at a much higher price to replace the shares he had borrowed and sold at a much lower price—thus realizing a loss of $350,000, or $2\frac{1}{3}$ times what he invested.

But in spring 2000 the technology bubble burst and, by September 2001, Yahoo's shares declined to a split-adjusted low of about $16. If the short seller who bought at $150 per share been able to hold steady during the Internet bubble, he would have made a substantial gain of about $134,000. In hindsight, he would have been proved right that Yahoo was overvalued when it was selling at $150 per share. But his timing was wrong. And very few people seeing the relentless increase in Yahoo's stock price during 1999—from $150 to over $500 per share—would have been able to withstand either the financial or the psychological pressure to maintain a short position and wait for the eventual decline.

The point is that hindsight is always 20/20. I'm reminded of one of my favorite Snoopy cartoons. He is on the tennis court holding a racket and looking very dejected. He then says something like, "If only we were playing 'should of's' I'd be winning now." The problem with shorting stocks is we just can't know for certain that a stock is going down in price, and even if we are very confident that it is, we can't know when to sell and when to buy. And almost all of us lack the nerve to hold on during wild stock-market gyrations. Short selling is less a true investment opportunity than yet another excuse to gamble.

Sometimes I start my analysis of a Wall Street product by asking a simple question: would it be legal under state law if it were a transaction between two private parties—say, you and me? I can sell you a stock or bond in a private transaction. Yes, sometimes there are regulatory issues, but there is nothing inherently illegal about the sale.

But we can't make a $100 bet where I say a stock is going to go down six months from now and you say it's going to go up—loser pays. That's illegal under state law, but it's almost exactly how a short sale works. It's perfectly legal for me to make a $100 million short sale on the stock market, but not to make a $100 bet in a private transaction.

Short selling is very risky because of the potential for unlimited losses. A short seller does not own anything other than the obligation to close his short position at some future time and return the borrowed shares to his lender. So his potential losses can go far beyond the amount of the original transaction, as we saw in the Yahoo example.

Potentially even worse for investors, the increasingly widespread use of short selling adds to Wall Street's ever-growing conflicts of interest. Unbeknownst to their customers, Wall Street firms have used short sales as a way to profit at their customers' expense or to favor one group of customers over others. For example, they can accomplish this by selling products they think will decline to one group of customers while having their favored customers sell short those very same investments.

Facebook's IPO and short sales created more conflicts of interest for Wall Street firms. Most of the IPOs of leading tech companies have resulted in the proverbial "feeding frenzy" on the first day of trading. But Facebook was unusual. On the first day of trading its share price did not increase, and a week later the price actually had declined about 28 percent. As Facebook's shares started this decline, some of the managers of the IPO were attempting to keep the price up, while others (sometimes even in the very same firm) were helping short sellers who wanted to bet the shares would fall further.

In its second day as a public company, about 25 percent of Facebook's trading volume was attributable to short selling. Not exactly how one builds for the future, but it seems neither Wall Street nor many investors care. Facebook may not have experienced a first day pop in its stock price, but as of this writing it has not had a long-run decline, which has so often been the case with the hot IPOs. About 2½ years after its IPO, Facebook's stock is selling at about 2½ times the initial offering price, but first it hit a low well below that price. So the short sellers who covered early won and those who held on for the long term lost big. The Wall Street firms, of course, earned their fees whether the stock price went up or down.

On Wall Street the herd instinct often leads to substantial losses. We can see this with short selling when we compare the short interest in a stock with its subsequent price performance. Short interest is the percentage of a company's outstanding shares that have been sold short. The higher the short interest, the less the investing public thinks of the company's prospects. For example, if a company has 750,000 shares sold short and 5,000,000 shares outstanding, the short interest is 15 percent. Since the short interest is published daily, we can evaluate investor sentiment in the stock and compare it to future performance.

Let's look at Facebook again, which came public at $38 per share and over the next four months declined in value, reaching a low of about $18 per share in September 2012. The short interest peaked at just about that time. The short seller's timing was completely wrong, and over the next 2½ years the stock increased to about $80 per share, causing substantial losses for the short sellers. It just did not pay to join the stampede to bet against the largest social media company in the world.

Netflix provides yet another illustration of the risks of short sales and the herding mentality. In late 2012 Netflix stock was trading at about $55 per share, down from about $270 per share just 1½ years earlier. Short interest then peaked at about 23 percent. Over the next two and one-half years Netflix soared to a split adjusted price of about $900 per share, an increase of about 1,600 percent. Short sellers who gambled on future declines incurred significant losses.

Wall Street's advice on which stocks to buy has time and again proved worthless, and the same holds true for advice on which stocks to sell short. In June 2009, *Barron's* published its "short list" of "excellent candidates for shorting." A year later only one of them had declined (and that one by only 3 percent). The average price for the five companies had increased by about 15 percent, virtually identical to the increase in the S&P 500 Index during that period. An investor who followed *Barron's* advice and shorted the five "excellent candidates" would have lost 15 percent over the next year.

The investing public continues to make poor decisions when choosing which stocks to sell short. In 2013, a division of Standard & Poor's conducted a study of short selling the stocks in the Russell 3000 Index (an index of the stocks of the 3,000 largest companies in the United States). This study compared the performance of the 100 most heavily shorted stocks with the index itself. The most heavily shorted stocks (the ones investors thought had the worst prospects and were betting would decline the most) increased in share price an average of about 34 percent from January 1 through August 16, 2013. This, while the index itself was up about 18 percent. So the least favorite stocks returned substantially more than average, and the short sellers got killed yet again.

Short selling is nothing more than gambling. The short seller does not own anything other than his bet that the price of the share he is shorting will decline. A short seller thinks (or at least is willing to bet) that everyone else in the market is wrong and he knows better. Even worse, some short sellers try to game the system. They will short a stock and then generate negative publicity about the company, whether accurate or not. Sometimes short sellers are successful in driving down the price of stock this way for no reason other than their greed.

Hedge fund manager Bill Ackman, founder of the $11 billion hedge fund company Pershing Square Capital Management, engaged in the most highly publicized attempt in recent years by a short seller to manipulate the price of a stock. He accused Herbalife of being a "pyramid scheme." In December 2012, CNBC reported that he said Herbalife was the most compelling case for a short sale that he had ever seen. Herbalife's stock price started December 2012 at $46.19 per share and ended the year at $32.94 per share. But Ackman was unable to get the government to agree Herbalife operated a pyramid scheme, and its stock increased significantly in 2013, ending the year at $78.70 per share. As of December 2015 it had declined to $58 per share, but that was still significantly above the price about three years earlier when he claimed it was his most compelling short ever. His efforts to drive down the price of the stock in order to profit from his short position failed.

Substantial costs make short selling far from free. The brokers earn their commissions on the sales, and a short seller must maintain collateral with the broker in order to insure that he has the funds to make the needed purchase later to close his position. In addition, if the short sale moves against the seller, he will be required to post additional collateral, or the broker will unilaterally close the short and a loss will result. This can put substantial strain on a short seller's resources and can force the short seller to liquidate a position when he would rather not. Often the collateral accounts are tied to margin accounts (accounts in which the investor borrows from the brokerage firm; see a more complete discussion in Chapter 13). This increases the risk and cost for the short seller while it generates additional interest income for the broker. Since the gains on short sales are taxed as short-term capital gains, short sellers incur higher income-tax costs than on other investments. The government collects about double the federal income tax on short sales than on long-term capital gains (39.6 percent instead of 20 percent, not including the medical care tax).

The Wall Street apologists offer many excuses for short sales. They claim short selling exposes fraud or poorly run companies, pressuring corporate executives to do the right thing or punishing them if they do not. Even if that were true, it does not mean that short selling is a solution to the problem of corporate fraud or mismanagement. A shareholder who has lost confidence in the management of a company can simply sell his stock. If he wants to share his concern with others, in today's world he can post his findings on the Internet. He does not need to gamble and try to take advantage of someone who he thinks is not as well informed as he is.

Over the years I have discussed my views on short selling with many Wall Street professionals. To those who support short selling I ask a simple question, which so far no one has been able to answer satisfactorily. Why is there a market for selling short United States Treasury Bonds? What's worse, why can an investor (gambler?) borrow funds and then hope to make double or triple the movement in the actual price? If one wants to gamble that interest rates will go up, then shorting US Treasury Bonds makes sense. Interest rate increases will cause the value of the bonds to fall and a short sale of those bonds will result in profits. But what does that have to do with fraud or poor management? Is the idea that we are somehow punishing the United States government for borrowing money at a lower interest rate than we think it should or will be paying? These short sales certainly will have no impact on government policy.

There is evidence that short sales can decrease market volatility, but unfortunately they often increase that volatility, especially during times of market stress. The ability to short subprime mortgages certainly contributed to the 2008 stock market crashes throughout the world. As part of its effort to put rules in place to protect against future financial crises, the European Securities and Markets Authority was given the power to ban short selling in emergencies. But if short selling is good for markets, why would we want to ban it just because markets were declining? If the benefits from short selling were real, as proponents claim, we would not want to shut it down just when it might come to the rescue. To me, the reason seems abundantly clear: short selling just adds to speculative tendencies in markets.

Short selling is yet another invitation to lose money so Wall Street can make more. It is just another technique to get investors to gamble rather than invest for the future. To the extent that short sales are part of hedge fund strategies, they are further diminishing our wealth. To preserve and increase your wealth, invest in things of value for the long term. Short selling is a loser's game. Don't get caught short.

# THIRTEEN

# Leveraging Yourself to Death

The Wall Street firms encourage you to swing for the fences by borrowing from them to increase the amounts you invest. This is called buying on "margin." For you it's risky, but for them it's a sure winner. They are protected by having your account as security for your loan. Regulation T of the Federal Reserve Board allows you to borrow up to 50 percent of the purchase price of your stocks, but also requires you to maintain at all times at least 25 percent of the market value of your securities in your margin account.

Here's an illustration. You start with $10,000 in your account, borrow $10,000 from your broker, and purchase $20,000 of stocks. If the market value of those stocks falls to $12,000, then the equity in your account will fall to $2,000 ($12,000 minus the $10,000 loan), which is less than the required $3,000 (25 percent of the market value of $12,000). You would then have to deposit into your account additional cash or securities to bring the equity in your account back above $3,000. If you fail to respond almost immediately to this "margin call," the brokerage firm has the right to sell your securities without any further notification to you. This can result in significant losses, and margin calls have ruined many investors.

By 2014, total margin debt with Wall Street firms had more than doubled during the previous five years, standing at an all-time record. Of course, no modern economy can function efficiently without reasonably available credit. But even if debt is maintained at appropriate levels, good debt must be distinguished from bad debt. Good debt is incurred for productive purposes—e.g., to build worthwhile projects, acquire needed facilities and equipment, provide funds for short-term liquidity needs, and finance business operations. Good debt also requires a clearly identifiable and reliable source of repayment. This can be returns from the project for which the borrowed funds were used, profits from a business, or another secure source of funds (e.g., your salary to pay your mortgage). In addition, good debt is limited in amount so that a default will not lead to bankruptcy.

But then there is bad debt. This is debt used for nonproductive purposes—e.g., gambling or consumption. It is debt for which there is no clear source of repayment; only a hope and a prayer exist that the loan will ever be paid back. Credit-card debt is the perfect example of bad debt. It is expensive, and many of the borrowers have no clear path to repayment. They only pay the minimum each month and watch as their balances grow. I am not a psychologist, but my guess is that the angst of looking at the credit card bill every month and having to make significant payments is greater than the pleasure experienced with most of those purchases. Which is better: a week's vacation in Hawaii on the credit card with the debt staring at you for a long, long time, or a week's vacation at the local resort paid with cash?

Unpayable debt caused the subprime crisis of 2008. Responding to the political and legal pressures from the US government, the banks and mortgage companies had been extending mortgages to many borrowers who had no realistic chance of repaying their loans. Wall Street firms then bought these subprime mortgages and created collateralized debt obligations (CDOs—a form of asset-backed security). The rating agencies, in order to increase their own profits, were only too happy to rate this high-risk ("junk") debt as AAA (the safest rating). So the Wall Street firms could pretend these were high-quality investments and pawned them off to unwitting investors. In many cases the Wall Street firms then sold credit-default swaps (contracts to pay in the event of default) on the CDOs. Speculators (like AIG) then made oversized bets that subprime loans borrowers would not default.

The Wall Street firms' employees were only too happy to play this game and risk other people's money—that of the shareholders and the companies for which they worked and were obligated to protect. Changes in the law allowed many firms to borrow more than thirty times the amount of their equity and put themselves at great risk. At a debt-to-equity ratio of thirty to one, a small decline of only 3 percent in the value of their assets would bankrupt a company. This is yet another clear example of Wall Street firms' breach of their fiduciary duty. No one in his right mind would leverage his own assets thirty to one. Think about it. Would you buy a stock for $30 per share and risk bankruptcy if the stock price fell only $1, to $29 per share? I certainly don't know anyone who would.

Why did the Wall Street firms incur so much debt? Because the executives' and traders' compensation would greatly increase if they borrowed money and made successful bets. And if their wagers failed, they ran no personal risk. Let's look at a simple illustration:

Suppose I work on Wall Street and my employment contract provides me a bonus of 10 percent of the profits I generate through my trades. Suppose I manage (speculate with) a $1 million account, have an incredibly great year, and generate a 50 percent profit, or $500,000. At 10 percent I would be entitled to a bonus of $50,000. Everyone should be happy. My firm has a $450,000 profit, and I get $50,000.

But everyone is not happy. I got a bonus of only $50,000. How could I get a lot more? Easy, my firm could borrow $29 million. Now I have $30 million to manage. Fifty percent profit for the year generates $15 million and my bonus is $1,500,000. I'm making real money and the firm is extremely happy with its net, $13,500,000, after deducting my bonus.

What happens if things don't work out so well and I have a down year? Let's say I lose only 3 percent of the account. With no leverage, I started the year with $1 million and end with $970,000. I may get no bonus that year, but my firm loses only $30,000.

But what happens if the firm borrowed twenty-nine times the equity? My $30 million account loses 3 percent, or $900,000. After repaying the loan of $29 million, my firm has $100,000 of equity remaining. Now 90 percent of the firm's equity is gone. Do I have to pay back any part of the $1.5 million bonus from the prior year? Of course not. That's the beauty of the system. Heads I win, tails you lose. And if there's any talk about a discretionary bonus (which is probable), I am likely to get a hefty one. After all, I made the firm so much money in the prior year, how could they afford to let me get away?

The meteoric rise and the subsequent crash of Long-Term Capital Management (LTCM) shows the appeal that leverage has for Wall Street and the risk it entails for speculators—and for all of us when government bails out failing firms. It's a story that began a little while ago, but all of its lessons apply today. LTCM was a hedge fund founded in 1994 by John Meriwether, who had been the head of bond trading at Salomon Brothers, an old and highly respected Wall Street firm. LTCM's board of directors included Robert Merton and Myron Scholes, who would win the 1997 Nobel Prize in economics for their work in valuing derivatives. In addition, the board of LTCM included five members with PhD degrees from the Massachusetts Institute of Technology. Could the pedigree possibly be any better?

With its incredible roster of heavy hitters, LTCM was able to quickly raise significant capital, most from the Wall Street community itself. LTCM employed many different, highly leveraged derivative strategies, with the largest segment of its business in swaps. The initial results were spectacular, averaging nearly 40 percent per year its first three years. LTCM's strategy was to run exhaustive computer studies to determine the correlation between the prices of various bonds. Its computers would then search through the current market prices. If it discovered a discrepancy in the market between the prices of two bonds and what their historical difference was, then LTCM would buy huge amounts of the bonds the computers indicated were underpriced and sell short huge amounts of the bonds its computers indicated were overpriced. Once the market prices returned to the normal difference,

LTCM would sell the two positions and reap its profits. It also used derivatives to achieve the same results. Because the discrepancies that LTCM's computers found were typically very small, earning significant profits required huge amounts of leverage on large quantities of bonds. A small profit percentage on a massive amount could then be significant. LTCM's activities involved such socially advantageous behavior as discovering, for example, the differences in the prices of two bonds that were identical, except one had a twenty-five-year maturity and another had a twenty-five-and-one-half-year maturity.

By 1998, just four years after its founding, LTCM was riding high, and its equity had increased from about $1 billion in 1994 to almost $5 billion. Since LTCM had been so successful and since its business model depended upon large amounts of borrowing, its debts stood at about $125 billion, or a debt-to-equity ratio of about twenty-five to one. This means that a decline in value of just 4 percent of its assets would result in bankruptcy. In 1997, a financial crisis arose in East Asia, and in 1998 Russia was in severe economic distress and threatening to default on its bonds. Turmoil reigned throughout the world, and many of the historic correlations among bond prices no longer held. As someone so aptly put it: everything was perfectly correlated until one day it was not. As a result, LTCM's bets resulted in massive losses, and its equity rapidly dried up. By September 1998 its capital had declined about 90 percent in just nine months to about $500 million, but it still had liabilities of about $100 billion.

The Federal Reserve Bank of New York became concerned that a total collapse of LTCM could have serious systemic effects. So what did it do? Did it leave creditors who were foolish enough to loan LTCM $100 billion to figure out how best to salvage the situation and let them deal with their losses? Did it suggest those creditors take any haircut? Well, of course not. That's what happens when you or I make poor investments, but not if you are a large Wall Street firm, which usually gets government protection when it speculates and loses. Since LTCM's debt was so large, the Federal Reserve thought it necessary to organize a $3.6 billion bailout with the creditors of LTCM.

As for the founder of LTCM, John Meriwether's engineering of his firm's spectacular crash and burn seems not to have tarnished his reputation in the circles that matter. Even before LTCM was completely liquidated, he raised about one-quarter billion dollars and launched a new fund that would continue to use strategies similar to LTCM's.

High debt-to-equity ratios for the Wall Street firms themselves and highly leveraged investments for their clients were all too common in the years leading up to the market crash of 2008. Bear Stearns and one of its hedge funds provide a good example. One of those funds raised about $600 million from investors and borrowed at least $6 billion more to invest in subprime mortgages. When the value of those mortgages declined by just 10 percent, their investors' money was gone, and ultimately so was Bear Stearns itself.

But the rest of us are not likely to be rescued by the Federal Reserve or Wall Street or anyone else if we go into debt. The Wall Street firms are only too happy to jump on the debt bandwagon and encourage their wealthier clients to use as much debt as possible for their investments. Every dollar you borrow to invest results in more money drained from your accounts into theirs. When you borrow to purchase more stocks, bonds, mutual funds, or other products, Wall Street makes more commissions, markups, or fees. In addition, the more you borrow, the more likely you will purchase products with higher fees and commissions. When the Wall Street firms extend credit to their customers, they are making what is essentially a risk-free loan. The firms hold the customers' investments as security for repayment, and the interest charged to customers increases as the firms' borrowing costs go up. The Wall Street firms' employees who push credit on their customers don't care that the risk is greatly increased. They are making more. If things go well, customers will be happy and even more bonded to the firm. If things go badly, the firm may offer all kinds of excuses, and many clients fall for those maneuvers.

A simple example will show the lure of borrowing to purchase investments. You invest $1,000 and very successfully earn a 40 percent profit. Your portfolio now has a value of $1,400, for a profit of

$400. But suppose instead you borrowed $1,000 and invested $2,000 (your original $1,000 plus the $1,000 borrowed) into the same opportunity and earned the same 40 percent profit. Now the portfolio has a value of $2,800. You then pay back the loan of $1,000 plus interest of say 5 percent or $50, leaving a net profit of $750, or 75 percent. Looks great. Who wouldn't prefer a 75 percent profit to a 40 percent profit? What's the danger?

Let's run the numbers again, but this time we'll assume a bad experience and the investment declines in value by 40 percent. Without the use of credit, the $1,000 investment loses $400 and declines in value to $600. The $2,000 investment made with borrowed funds loses $800 and declines in value to $1,200. Then you pay back the principal of $1,000 and the interest of $50, leaving you with only $150. If the investment declines, the all-cash investor is left with $600 and the investor who borrowed is left with $150. Would you prefer a loss of 40 percent or 85 percent?

The following table shows the results of the same investment made with and without borrowing:

| Investment Results | WITHOUT BORROWING | WITH BORROWING |
|---|---|---|
| | $1,000 cash<br>Ending Account Value | $1,000 cash/$1,000 debt<br>Ending Account Value |
| 40% Increase | $1,400<br>+ 40% | $1,750<br>+75% |
| 40% Decrease | $600<br><40%> | $150<br><85%> |

Moreover—and this may surprise you—if your investments decline in value, leveraging them can result in losses even if they later recover to their original value. Common sense says that returning to the original value should mean breaking even. But as the famous song from the opera Porgy and Bess reminds us, "it ain't necessarily so." Let's take a look.

You purchase an index fund for $10,000 and it declines 10 percent to $9,000. It then rebounds by 11.111 percent to go back to $10,000. You did not use any leverage and you broke even. Now let's see what happens if you purchased an ultra fund (one that uses borrowed funds to invest for increases in prices of the underlying assets) from your friendly Wall Street broker. An ultra fund is designed to give investors twice the return of the index in which they invest, by borrowing an amount equal to the equity invested and maintaining a 50/50 ratio of debt to equity each day. The following table shows how an ultra fund works. In this table we use the same facts as before, with the underlying index returning to its original level. The only difference will be the added feature of borrowing. Here's the math:

**ULTRA FUND**

| | | |
|---|---|---|
| Invest Equity | 10,000 | |
| Borrow | 10,000 | |
| Value of Account | 20,000 | (10,000 Equity; 10,000 Debt) |
| Index Declines 10% | <2,000> | |
| Value of Account | 18,000 | (8,000 Equity; 10,000 Debt) |
| Pay Down Debt | <2,000> | |
| Value of Account | 16,000 | (8,000 Equity; 8,000 Debt) |
| Market Increase 11.111% | 1,780 | |
| Value of Account | 17,780 | (9,780 Equity; 8,000 Debt) |
| Pay off Debt | <8,000> | |
| Value of Equity | 9,780 | |
| Loss | 220 | |

Now, even stranger but true, had you purchased the ultra *short* fund (one that uses borrowed funds to invest for decreases in prices of the underlying assets) at the same time that you bought the ultra fund, you would have lost money on that one, too. Yes, with the index fluctuating but returning to its original value, the investor with no leverage would be even. But an investor going either double long or double short the index would lose. Here's the math for the ultra short fund:

## ULTRA SHORT FUND

| | | |
|---|---|---|
| Invest Equity | 10,000 | |
| Borrow | 10,000 | |
| Value of Account | 20,000 | (10,000 Equity; 10,000 Debt) |
| Index Declines 10% (Ultra Fund increases since short) | 2,000 | |
| Value of Account | 22,000 | (12,000 Equity; 10,000 Debt) |
| Borrow Additional | 2,000 | |
| Value of Account | 24,000 | (12,000 Equity; 12,000 Debt) |
| Market Increase 11.111% (Ultra Fund decreases since short) | <2,670> | |
| Value of Account | 21,330 | (9,330 Equity; 12,000 Debt) |
| Pay off Debt | <12,000> | |
| Value of Equity | 9,330 | |
| Loss | 670 | |

If we cannot win by going either long or short in an ultra fund, what should we do? Fortunately, there is an easy answer. Don't borrow to make investments. Many of your underlying investments already have significant amounts of debt. Corporations use debt to finance their operations, and real estate firms have mortgages on their properties. In the words of the blackjack players, there's no need to double down. But the Wall Street firms keep encouraging us to borrow more and ratchet up our risks. They recently introduced exchange traded notes (ETNs), which are leveraging foreign currencies three times. Those fearless investors are making huge bets on currencies and at the same time becoming unsecured creditors of the issuing banks. Good luck.

If the key to prosperity were borrowing more, I'd be fighting my way to the front of the line. But in reality, the more that you borrow, the more exposure you have. I guarantee that if you use debt in the securities markets, you'll eventually get hammered when unexpected downturns come along. You can "go for it" and risk a lot, or you can be more conservative and strive for consistency. I'm the tortoise here, who usually wins, but occasionally the hare has an upset victory. Which do you want to be?

FOURTEEN

# Options, Derivatives, and Other Great Ways to Lose Money

all Street's gambling problem and its never-ending quest to raise its own income at its customers' expense cannot be better illustrated than by its increasing sales of derivatives. We learned a lot about derivatives over the last decade because they were the leading cause of the market crash of 2008 and the Great Recession that followed.

Derivatives are contracts that derive their value from changes in the value of an underlying asset or changes in an interest rate or a financial index. In essence, their value depends on something you do not own. There are numerous types of derivatives, but the most common are options, futures, and swaps. Occasionally derivatives are used for hedging against price movements that can directly affect the user. But all too often today they are used to gamble on changes in the price of assets or interest rates or market indices in which the buyer has no direct stake.

Derivatives are contracts between two parties, each of which has a right to collect from the other depending upon the outcome of future events. They are just a means for two parties to gamble against each other, with no possibility for both of them to profit from the transaction. This is the quintessential zero-sum game. Whatever one party wins, the other party loses.

Only a portion of the face amount ("national value") of a derivative is truly at risk. Nevertheless, even a small percentage of a massive number can be huge. At the end of 2014, five US banks held in total about $270 trillion in derivatives. Despite all the evidence that derivates are really only working for Wall Street, their use seems only to be growing. In 2000, the national value of the world's derivative contracts was estimated to be about $100 trillion, and by 2014 the total market for derivatives had increased to about $700 trillion. I cannot even start to tell you how scary that is.

Derivatives are designed to shift risks to companies better able to evaluate those risks and price them appropriately. They are supposed to insure investors in corporate or government bonds against changes in interest rates. They are meant to protect commodity users against future price increases—for example, owners of corporate bonds insuring against default, banks locking in favorable interest rates on their loans, or airlines worried about rising fuel prices. Legitimate business reasons can support using derivatives in these ways.

However, most of the volume in derivative trading on Wall Street has nothing to do with that kind of risk management. Instead, it is speculation by gamblers who have no financial stake in the underlying assets, interest rates, or market indices of the derivative contracts. Let's look at how some of these derivatives work in the real world and how Wall Street greatly benefits from them, whether or not their customers do.

Publicly traded stock options are now deeply embedded in Wall Street's array of "investment opportunities," but they are so relatively new they didn't exist when I started my professional career. We need to distinguish between stock options granted to top executives and other corporate employees and publicly traded stock options. In both cases, an option is a contract that gives the owner the right, but not the obligation, to buy an underlying asset (stock in an executive's own company, for example) at a set price on or before a set expiration date (this is known as a "call" option). On Wall Street, publicly traded options can also give the owner the right, but not the obligation, to sell an asset (a "put" option).

But there are huge differences between employee stock options and publicly traded stock options. A typical employee stock option is granted by a corporate employer either as a reward for past service or as an incentive for future service. These options are often exercisable over a long term and in most cases have a "strike price" (the amount that must be paid for the underlying stock at the time of purchase) of at least the fair market value of the stock on the date of issuance. They are not standardized (i.e., each one has its own terms rather than having a customary form) nor are they tradable. Publicly traded stock options, in contrast, have standardized terms. Typically, they expire in two years or less. In the United States they are traded almost exclusively through the Chicago Board Options Exchange.

For example, on March 31, 2015, when Procter & Gamble was selling for $82.44 per share, you would have paid $600 for the right to buy 500 shares at a price of $90 on or before January 15, 2016. Until maturity, the call's value will fluctuate with the price movements of Procter & Gamble shares. If on January 15, 2016, Procter & Gamble is selling for less than $90 per share, you would allow the option to expire because you would not want to pay $90 per share to purchase a stock that you could buy for less on the open market. Your loss on this transaction would be the premium you paid to purchase the option plus the commissions ($13), or a total of $613. If, on the other hand, Procter & Gamble is selling for more than $90 per share on January 15, 2016 (let's use $97 per share), you would exercise your option and your profit would be $7 per share ($97 minus $90). Your overall profit would be $2,887 (500 shares x $7 per share – $613). Wall Street would emphasize the huge percentage gain you made on this transaction. For an investment of $613, you would have realized a profit of $2,887, or 371 percent on your investment in just about nine months.

Wall Street hypes options as a way to magnify your gains and to limit your losses. Seems too good to be true. It certainly is true that the percentage gains realized from successful option trading exceeds those from trading the same underlying stock. But there is a catch. Losses that might be limited in actual dollar amounts may be significantly higher as a percentage of capital invested. Let's go back to our Procter & Gamble example. Let's assume that Procter & Gamble shares have declined to $75 when the option expires. Although the stock has declined $7.44 per share (or a total of $3,720), the premium you paid for the option was $1.20 per share (or a total of $600). Your loss on this transaction (not including commissions) is $600. So Wall Street is right: The option limited your loss to only $600, while had you purchased the stock the loss would have been $7.44 per share, on a total of $3,720. However, with the stock ownership your loss is about 9 percent of your investment (7.44/82.44), whereas with the option your loss is 100 percent of what you had in the game. If the stock price moves down even moderately, as in our example, one way you lose 9 percent and the other way 100 percent. On the upside the leverage associated with options works in your favor. It really comes down to a choice of whether you'd rather risk everything in order to try for a home run.

Wall Street pushes options because they increase commissions. As of March 2016, Charles Schwab and Company charged $8.95 for an online stock trade and $8.95 plus $.75 per contract (100 shares) on option trades. In our example, the commission would be $8.95 to purchase 500 shares of Procter & Gamble stock at $85 per share, a total transaction of $42,500, whereas the commission would be $12.70 ($8.95 plus (5 x .75)) to purchase five option contracts (covering 500 shares), a total transaction of $600. So in dollar terms, the commission for the option trade is more than 40 percent greater than for the stock trade ($12.70 vs. $8.95). Expressed as a percentage of the total transaction, the difference is even greater: the commission on this stock trade would be .02 percent of the total ($8.95/42,500), whereas the commission for the option trade would be 2 percent of the total ($12.70/600). In other words, as a percentage of the order, the commission would be *100 times greater* for the option trade than for the stock trade.

In addition, options expire regularly. If a customer bought and held 500 shares for three years, there would be a one-time commission of $8.95. If, however, he purchased option contracts covering the same number of shares for each of those three years, the total commissions would be $38.10.

Many Wall Street brokers convince their customers to engage in a strategy of selling "covered calls" in which the seller owns the securities underlying the options. Wall Street accurately points out that sellers of "covered calls" cannot directly lose. If the price of the stock stays below the strike price, the buyer of the call will let it expire unexercised. If the price of the stock increases, the buyer will exercise and then the seller of the call can deliver his own shares to satisfy the call. The seller keeps the premium as his profit. So what is missing?

The problem is that for the small premium the sellers get for the call option, they may be forced to sell a stock rather than continuing to hold it for significant additional gains. For example, if Apple is now selling for $125 per share and I sell a call (which covers 100 shares) at a strike price of $130 for $6.70 per share exercisable over the next 9½ months, I would collect a premium of $670. Let's say that Apple rises to $150 per share. With no covered call, I would still own Apple, and my gain would be $25 per share, or a total appreciation of $2,500. With the covered call, I would have to sell the stock at $130 per share (for a gain of $5 per share), plus the option premium of $6.70 per share, for a profit of $11.70 per share, or a total of $1,170—less than half of what I would have made if I had simply held the shares. Not a good move to have sold the option.

While options may limit potential losses for buyers, they don't always limit them for sellers, who can suffer unlimited losses if they do not own the underlying shares. If the price of the stock rises significantly, the seller would either be forced to buy it at a much higher price in order to close the transaction or buy options to cancel out his options. For example, suppose a stock is selling for $10 per share, and a call is sold for $12 per share. If the stock is trading at $100 per share when the call is exercised, then the seller would have a loss of $88 per share.

Most investors in publicly traded stock options can avoid one significant risk associated with most derivates: counterparty risk, which is so prevalent and which contributed so much to the market crash in 2008. This is the risk that the party with whom you are contracting will be unable to deliver a security or to transfer funds. This can leave the other party with a legally enforceable contract right but the inability to get paid. Even if funds can eventually be recovered in a bankruptcy proceeding, this may be of little consolation if funds are tied up for years.

Futures contracts are derivatives in use for many years. These are contracts between two parties to buy or sell an asset for a price agreed upon at the time the contract is entered into and for which both the delivery of the asset and the payment are to be made at a later date. Futures contracts typically involve commodities, and their use arose from a desire of both buyer and seller to protect themselves against future price changes. For example, a farmer wanting price stability for his wheat crop could enter into a futures contract with a flour manufacturer specifying the price and the delivery date. Both parties then know in advance the price of the wheat and can plan accordingly.

Today, futures contracts are available on a huge assortment of commodities and financial instruments, including currencies, interest rates, oil, grains, metals, sugar, and cattle. When futures contracts are used by actual users and producers of the commodities in question, they can in fact serve as a way to moderate risk. But when they are bought and sold by investors who do not utilize the commodities (as most traders in futures contracts today), they are a means of speculation by those who want to gamble on movements in the prices of the underlying commodities.

Here are a couple of examples of typical futures contracts in early 2015:

- **July 2015:** wheat at $504¼/100 bushels. Contract size: 5,000 bushels. Contract value: $25,212. Initial margin required: $1,612. (Leverage approximately 15:1)
- **August 2015:** gold at $1,179.50/ounce. Contract size: 100 ounces. Contract value: $117,950. Initial margin required: $4,125. (Leverage approximately 28:1)

There is no limit to the amount of gain or loss that can be realized on futures contracts. If prices were to soar, so could the losses for the party required to deliver the commodity. As a result, the futures exchanges require the parties to maintain margin (keep adequate security in an account) throughout the life of the contract. As with any margin requirements, margin calls (requests for more assets for security) will be made if the value of the account drops below required minimums.

Incredibly, Wall Street now offers options on futures. So we now have more derivatives on derivatives and have further magnified the potential for both gain and loss. All the better either to strike it rich on Wall Street or to end up in the poorhouse.

Over the last two decades the volume of trades in swaps has vastly increased. Again, as with so many other Wall Street innovations, there can be legitimate uses of swaps as a means of providing financial stability. Unfortunately, as with so much on Wall Street, swaps have been used to increase leverage and to provide new ways to gamble. Warren Buffett has referred to them as "financial weapons of mass destruction."

A swap is an agreement to exchange future cash flows based on the changes in underlying prices. Today these are usually based on interest rates, foreign exchange rates, and stock-market indices, but they can be applied to other things, too. Swaps can be used to mitigate risk if the party to the contract has a direct economic interest in the subject matter of the contract. For example, a corporation issues ten-year bonds with a variable interest rate of LIBOR (London Interbank Offered Rate—an interest rate banks charge each other for short-term loans) plus 2 percent, adjusted semiannually. At a time when LIBOR is low, the corporation may want to lock in the interest rate on its bonds at the correspondingly low rate of LIBOR plus 2 percent. It can do this by entering into a swap agreement in which it agrees to pay a fixed rate over the remaining life of the bonds, and the other party to the swap (the investor) agrees to pay it LIBOR plus 2 percent. The corporation would do this to protect itself against rising rates, while the investor would do this if it thought rates would decline.

The swap becomes a speculative investment, really a gamble, when used by investors who have no direct interest in the underlying rates or indices. If you have not issued or bought bonds, then you have no direct exposure to swings in interest rates. You are merely speculating that your view of interest rate movements will prove correct. If you eventually win this bet your profits can be huge, since many swaps last for years. Unfortunately, the other party to the swap incurs a loss equal to your gain. As a result, there is no net economic gain, just a shifting of wealth from one party to another.

Derivatives have too often been used as a tool for deceit. In late 2001, Enron Corporation filed for the largest bankruptcy in US history, and one of the greatest financial scandals so far this century emerged. Enron was a derivatives trading firm that grew rapidly in the 1990s until it ranked number seven on the Fortune 500 list, with annual revenues exceeding $100 billion. Its market capitalization soared to about $185 billion, and for six years running it was named by *Fortune* as "America's most innovative company." Enron was a pioneer in the use of derivatives called prepaid forward contracts. With help from its accountants at one of the largest accounting firms in the world, Enron used derivatives to hide a portion of its losses and debt and make its cash flow seem better. JPMorgan Chase and Citibank were accused of using these derivatives to make disguised loans to Enron. One JPMorgan Chase executive told a US Senate hearing in 2002 that "the prepaid forwards were undoubtedly financing, as all contracts are that involve prepayment features, but every financing is not a loan." That certainly was an interesting way to parse words. The banks collected nice fees from Enron for the financings, which Enron then did not disclose in its books. Shortly thereafter Enron imploded, wiping out not only its shareholders' equity but the retirement plans of many of its employees. In a most unusual development, some of the top executives of Enron actually served jail time, and the compliant accounting firm was forced out of business.

Some derivates are so complex and have such long maturity dates that they are very difficult to value, and sometimes owners and their accountants make this worse by using different valuation methods. This leads to some interesting problems and opportunities.

Derivatives are either assets or liabilities and must be included in the financial statements of their owners. In some instances it's possible for both parties to book a profit on the same derivative contract at the same time, even though in reality whatever one gains, the other must lose. The day of reckoning is postponed until the maturity date. In the meantime, one party or the other, or even both, may be issuing misleading financial statements.

Credit default swaps are an example of complex derivatives. They were rightfully blamed for accelerating, if not causing, the 2008 financial crisis. Wall Street sold these instruments as if they were insurance for the buyers and a low risk (or no risk) way to collect additional income for the sellers. According to Wall Street, owners of bonds and other debt instruments could protect themselves against default like this: you pay me $3 and I will pay you up to $1,000 for each bond of General Electric if it defaults within the next three years. If you actually own General Electric bonds, this might protect you. However, if you do not own General Electric bonds, you are merely speculating that General Electric will default. You can't be insuring something you don't own. As a third-party seller of the credit default swap in this example, I am speculating that General Electric will not default. But if I am not a true insurance company, how I am pooling my risks?

If you insure your home for its value, then you are lowering potential losses. But if six strangers insure your home for a total of six times its value, they are just gambling you will have a fire. Comparing the total amount of credit default swaps to the total amount of bonds and other debt that supposedly are "insured" through those swaps shows how they are just another means of speculation.

For example, when Delphi Automotive filed for bankruptcy in 2005, the notional (face amount) amount of the derivatives outstanding was about $20 billion, or ten times the amount of Delphi's outstanding bonds. Recent estimates show that bonds with a face amount of about $2 trillion are subject to credit default swaps. However, the notional value of bonds subject to credit-default swaps is about $10 trillion. If credit default swaps were really insurance, this would mean that the bonds have been insured five times over. Obviously no owner truly has insurance for five times his potential loss. But one of the great beauties of credit default swaps for Wall Street is that while only a limited number of bonds can be sold, there is no limit on the amount of credit default swaps that can be issued against the same bonds.

During 2007 and 2008, outstanding contracts in the credit default swap market amounted to about $60 trillion. As of November 2014, that had been reduced to about $20 trillion. By 2014, the US economy had substantially recovered from the bottom of the Great Recession of 2007–2009, and the S&P 500 Index has increased to 2058 on December 31, 2014, from 903 on December 31, 2008. If credit default swaps were so important to the functioning of our credit markets and our prosperity, then why did the disappearance of nearly $40 trillion of credit default swaps make no difference to the bond markets or the economy? Could it be that gambling in credit default swaps really had no positive effect whatsoever on the economy or the financial markets?

Trading volume on individual corporate credit default swaps was estimated in September 2012 to be down about 23 percent for the year, compared to the prior year. In a fight to save their revenue, some of the Wall Street firms decided to revamp an index that tracks the price of credit default swaps. The reason for the revamp? There were too few actively traded corporate names to make up the hundred-company index. Not a problem for Wall Street. The index provider just added three new companies to its index. In the words of an Everly Brothers song (a very popular singing group from my youth), "Only trouble is, gee whiz," no bank then offered a credit default swap for any of the three new companies. That's right, the index provider added three companies for which no credit default swaps existed. The derivative traders were hoping this would force the banks to offer credit default swaps for those companies. Talk about creating a product for which there seems to be neither need nor demand.

Wall Street continued on its quest to encourage gambling by inventing even riskier instruments: synthetic CDOs. A CDO is an asset-backed security. The issuer of a CDO creates a pool of debt instruments (e.g., mortgages, car loans, or credit card debt) and then issues securities against them. The investors then share in a large pool of debts rather than owning just a single one. Originally CDOs were backed by pools of corporate debt, but their use quickly spread to include mortgages. CDOs played a huge role in the financial collapse of 2007–2009. Like so many other Wall Street innovations that began as a good idea, they soon became subject to all sorts of abuse. Wall Street, never content with just a simple product, sliced and diced CDOs into tranches with different risks to increase the number of securities that could be sold. The owners of the upper tranche would be paid first and then the owners of the mezzanine tranches would get paid in their descending order of priority. Finally, the owners of the lowest, or equity, tranche would be the last to be paid. Investors would pay more for the upper tranche and less for the lower tranches to account for the levels of risk. This theoretically allowed the more conservative investors to buy the upper tranches and the more speculative investors to pay less for the lower tranches.

In a synthetic CDO, investment pools are collateralized by credit default swaps or other derivatives instead of the actual debt obligations. Leading up to the crash of 2008, these CDOs used derivatives on subprime mortgages. This investment was really a bet backed by derivatives on the performances of risky mortgages. Think about how much risk that entails. But these synthetic CDOs enabled Wall Street to aid its customers who wanted to bet either for or against subprime mortgages by creating a limitless supply of them in the form of derivatives. There was a finite amount of subprime mortgages, but there was no limit on the amount of derivatives. One estimate put the bets on subprime mortgages made in this fashion at about 75 times the face amount of the underlying mortgages.

History shows that the CDOs were not the world's path to prosperity. As reported in *Financial Times*, about $68 billion of CDOs were issued in 2000. The amounts issued each year gradually increased through 2004 and then began to explode, increasing to about $250 billion in 2005 and about $500 billion each year in 2006 and 2007. This increase contributed greatly to the numerous causes of the financial crash. As financial conditions deteriorated in 2008, the amount of new CDOs declined to about $62 billion and in 2009 all but disappeared ($4 billion issued). It sure looks like the buildup of CDOs set the stage for their collapse and then the downward spiral in the world's economies.

Because of the subprime debacle, Wall Street cannot now market CDOs backed by subprime mortgages. Not a problem—just create new CDOs backed by other assets. Recent "opportunities" now for sale include synthetic CDOs on high-yield (junk) bonds. And the beat goes on. Wall Street's abusing CDOs has only made markets less stable, all of us less secure, and ultimately the economy less likely to grow.

Wall Street has been only too happy to work in tandem with the techies to create derivatives for Bitcoin. For those who have the courage to use it, Bitcoin functions like currency, although it has been referred to as "crypto-currency." It uses computer-driven cryptography to control the creation of computer-generated "assets," which are exchanged between users like money.

Whether you think Bitcoins are a good idea or not, you must be a brave soul to speculate on their value. So Wall Street is now "insuring" crypto-currency by offering derivatives based on Bitcoins themselves. Given that there is no long-term history with this type of currency, how can anyone reasonably set a cost of "insurance"? As long as the counterparty to the Bitcoin derivative contract remains solvent, then I guess the Bitcoin users can protect themselves against loss in extreme circumstances. For those who don't own Bitcoins and thus have nothing to protect, buying derivatives is risky gambling and nothing else.

Bringing reform to the derivative markets will be very difficult since the Wall Street establishment has so much at stake. Derivatives are a significant source of fee income for the Wall Street firms, and their traders can make them even more. Just one example: Puerto Rico paid an estimated $690 million to various Wall Street firms to cancel derivative contracts that were supposed to lower borrowing costs.

On May 20, 2009, *Financial Times* offered its analysis on the role of derivatives in an article entitled "Let Battle Commence." The subtitle: "**Derivatives**. As the US administration tackles what it sees as a main cause of the crisis, an arcane and unruly industry is seeking to defend its *lucrative turf*" (emphasis added).

The lack of moral hazard only encourages Wall Street executives to keep aggressively using derivatives. They continue to believe, and probably correctly, that if anything goes seriously wrong, the taxpayers will rescue them yet again. This only encourages more gambling and less concern with the consequences. In 2012, Mike Kobida, executive director of collateral services at CME (Chicago Mercantile Exchange), showed his great confidence that the government would protect the derivative market and its traders when he stated: "We know that if there was an event where we needed liquidity tomorrow, the Fed would be there." So the high-stakes gambling will continue despite all of our experience demonstrating that derivatives destabilize our system rather than moderate risk. They just won't disappear.

In 1998, just before the Federal Reserve bailout of Long-Term Capital Management (see the previous chapter), LTCM tried to raise private money on its own. One offer came from a consortium that included Berkshire Hathaway. I am fascinated that Berkshire Hathaway, led by Warren Buffett, would participate in such an offer. Four years later, Buffett negatively referred to the LTCM bailout in Berkshire Hathaway's annual report and also called derivatives "time bombs" that create "daisy-chain risk." By the middle of 2012, Berkshire Hathaway itself owned credit default swaps, interest-rate derivatives on foreign currency, and equity-index put options valued at about $4 billion, with a notional value of over $60 billion. On average these expire in 2020, so we'll have to wait to see how this bit of speculation plays out for the Berkshire Hathaway shareholders.

Paul Volcker, former chief of the Federal Reserve, also thinks that the products Wall Street has developed to increase systemic gambling are of no use. In 2009, speaking at a meeting sponsored by the *Wall Street Journal*, Volcker observed, "I wish somebody would give me some shred of evidence linking financial innovation with a benefit to the economy." What, in Volcker's view, was the only financial innovation that the banks had made over the past twenty-five years that had lasting value and really helped consumers? The ATM.

# SECTION V

# An End to Business as Usual?

# FIFTEEN

# Enforcement: Missing in Action

US securities law consists of thousands upon thousands of pages of statutes, rules, and regulations. Federal and state governments require the registration of both securities offerings and financial firms. The enforcement agencies can impose civil and criminal penalties for violations. Private industry associations also set policies and standards and have their own enforcement mechanisms. We might think this massive system would curtail, if not substantially eliminate, major and systemic abuses; but sadly, meaningful enforcement is missing in action.

Why? The government has large bureaucracies, but its agents seem much more concerned with checking boxes on forms and protecting their own jobs than in pursuing real problems. Too many bureaucrats enforce the letter of the law in cases of technical violations that cause no harm but do too little pursuing real wrongdoers. A few of my personal war stories when dealing with the Securities and Exchange Commission or the California Department of Corporations sadly illustrate their agents' approach.

Years ago a government auditor came into our office unannounced, as is their policy when examining investment advisory firms. After he properly identified himself, we sat down in my conference room to discuss what he planned to do during his review. He was obviously an experienced auditor and said to me, "Well, you know how this is going to go." I responded something to the effect of "I'm not sure; please tell me." He replied, "I'm going to poke around here for a few days and will find a technical violation or two. There are so many little rules, and some of them are very arcane. I am essentially certain to find something. Then I'm going to write you a letter and explain what your problems are. Then either you or your lawyer will write me a letter saying 'Gee, we're sorry, and we're going to fix that.' Our investigation will then end." And then he added, "After all, we know that the guys who are really cheating don't register, so I can't audit them."

Another time an SEC auditor wanted to make sure we were complying with all the rules regarding custody of clients' accounts. At that time, we had only one client for whom we were maintaining a bank account. The auditor asked to see copies of the quarterly account reconciliations we sent to the client. We provided copies of our monthly account reconciliations, which contained all the required disclosures and data. The auditor was not satisfied because he wanted the quarterly reports the regulations called for, and he proceeded to write us up for a violation. We fixed this problem by continuing our practice of sending the monthly reports, but also at the end of each quarter including a copy of the prior two months' statements. A stapler got us out of that brush with the law.

A few years later another SEC auditor showed up to investigate our compliance with a hot-button regulatory issue: advertising. The SEC claims to be vigilant in policing advertising so the public is not misled. We were well aware of the importance of this issue to the SEC and never used advertising materials without first getting approval from our securities lawyer. The piece in question was a reprint of a front-page article that had appeared in *Investment News*, a highly respected securities industry publication. The reporter had interviewed me, a couple of my All-Star sports clients, and the mother of one of those clients. My client's mother was not your typical sports mom, as she later served as a justice of the Supreme Court in her home state. The reporter asked her to describe her decision-making process when choosing to retain my firm. She said she really liked the fact that I did not appear fancy because I wore the same sweater to two meetings a day apart.

The auditor sent a letter advising us that our use of this article to solicit clients violated the rules prohibiting client endorsements for investment services. Needless to say, both my lawyer and I were astonished. The auditor said that my client's mother's statement that she "liked" me for reasons having nothing to do with investments constituted a client endorsement. I had three choices: stop using the article, remove the mother's comments from the article since the rest of it was all right, or face enforcement action from the SEC. I assured the government that we would choose one of the first two options. Fortunately, that was the end of that matter. The investing public was safe for another day.

The enforcement agencies waste incredible amounts of time and resources addressing theoretical rather than real problems. This pulls them away from investigating activities that actually cause significant losses, where they could help the investing public. The enforcement agencies need to understand one size does not necessarily fit all and that both regulation and enforcement require flexibility and sometimes exceptions to the general rules.

For example, the government has rightfully been trying to prevent front running. (See Chapter 11.) A meticulous set of rules and record-keeping requirements now apply, regardless of how insignificant an advisor's transaction. Investment advisory firms must keep voluminous records of their employees' personal securities trades. Burdensome notification and approval processes are also imposed. But these rules make no sense with small trades in massive enterprises. We had to establish elaborate procedures and maintain records so we could purchase for our personal accounts 100 shares of Procter & Gamble, which has an average daily trading volume of about 7 million shares.

Wouldn't it be so much smarter for the regulations to state that transactions of perhaps less than 1/10 of 1 percent of the average daily trading volume of a company with a market cap in excess of $10 billion are exempt from obtaining prior approval? This would save huge amounts of time and money for investment firms, result in no harm to the firms' clients, and allow the SEC to look into more real problems with stocks of small companies.

We have all heard about another problem: "too big to fail." We are told that we just can't allow major financial institutions to fail, or they will bring all of us down with them. It seems they are also "too big to jail." Eric Holder, when serving as US Attorney General, said that he was wary of "negative impact" if the Justice Department prosecuted large financial institutions. The message is clear: if you're big enough we won't bother you.

So much of the difficulty in passing effective legislation, adopting workable regulations, and meaningfully enforcing the law is attributable to the great political influence of the major financial firms. In its July 15, 2013, issue, the *New Republic* reported on a study tracking political donations and reached the conclusions that "the financial sector is far and away the largest source of campaign contributions to federal candidates and parties." Obviously that buys support. This reminds me of a rare moment of candor in testimony before a congressional committee investigating campaign contributions. A major donor was asked if he thought he was buying influence. He responded something to the effect of "well, of course."

In 2011, MF Global (discussed in Chapter 2) illegally transferred customer money to its own accounts, which the *Wall Street Journal* reported was "violating a cardinal rule of the financial industry." At the time, Jon Corzine was the chief executive of MF Global, previously having served as the chairman of Goldman Sachs and as a Democratic senator from New Jersey. Do you think he was financially and politically connected? Despite the fact that about $1.4 billion of customer money went missing, no criminal case was ever brought against Corzine or any other member of his firm. Now I don't know whether Corzine himself knew enough to be personally responsible, but someone in MF Global authorized the $1.4 billion to be transferred, and he is walking.

Were the government bailouts of the major financial institutions in 2007–2008 done for the benefit of the public, or were they personally and politically motivated? Key officials in the US government debated whether to provide a massive bailout of AIG and eventually approved $85 billion. The head of the US Treasury Department, Henry Paulson, who was formerly the chairman and CEO of Goldman Sachs, met with Lloyd Blankfein, who was then the chairman and CEO of Goldman Sachs, the day before the AIG bailout was approved. It was widely reported that Blankfein argued that Goldman would lose $20 billion and possibly fail unless AIG was rescued.

Wall Street will continue to loot its customers' accounts, inappropriately gamble with its shareholders' money, and raid the public coffers until penalties for wrongdoing are (1) significant, (2) probable, and (3) paid by the bad actors themselves. Currently a company and its representatives can break the law, violate regulations, commit fraud, and deceive clients yet continue to profit at the expense of its customers, shareholders, and the public. This bad behavior will continue until the personal risks to the bad actors outweigh the potential gains. Just as with other crimes, whether petty or violent, penalties do not deter action unless the criminals believe they are personally at risk of real punishment.

In November 2014, Citigroup agreed to pay a civil settlement of $15 million to the Financial Industry Regulatory Authority for allegedly sharing with its biggest and best clients its analysts' opinions on stocks. The problem was that those opinions contradicted their published views. In paying the fine, Citicorp followed standard practice and neither admitted nor denied any wrongdoing. Nevertheless, the settlement documents describe a private dinner that Citicorp hosted for some of its large clients. The analysts predicted a stock would fall despite having very recently upgraded their published position on the stock from sell to hold. This was Citicorp's fourth settlement involving alleged research violations since the start of 2012. It appears that Citicorp was continually favoring their investment banking clients and other large customers at the expense of both their smaller customers and the public. When caught, Citicorp paid what for it are small fines. This practice had been going on for over a dozen years. In the early 2000s, New York's attorney general found that Citicorp issued biased opinions in favor of the stocks of its investment banking clients. Citicorp paid over $400 million to make those claims go away. In a similar fashion, Wells Fargo Advisors paid a fine of only $1.5 million for failure to comply with anti-money laundering requirements over a nine-year period.

How effective are these fines in discouraging bad behavior? Unfortunately, not very. Wall Street firms pay the fines and then go right back to work, clearly viewing these fines as a cost of doing business and passing them along to their customers or shareholders. Most of these fines are trivial for the companies involved. A settlement of $15 million might seem large to an average person, but what is $15 million to Citigroup, with annual revenues in 2014 of $77 billion? It's the equivalent of someone who earns $100,000 a year having to pay about $20 to stay out of jail. But wait, it's really better than that for Citicorp's employees, since that $20 is being paid by someone else. The people who broke the law don't have to pay those fines; the company that employs them pays. Its earnings are slightly decreased, and the shareholders foot the bill. Do you really think an employee engaged in wrongdoing cares if the massive financial institution that employs him is found guilty of a crime or pays a fine or civil judgment that has no effect on his individual status or compensation?

In November 2012, the SEC stated that it had no intention to charge any individuals in its enforcement action against JPMorgan Chase for the fraudulent sale of mortgage bonds. It declined to pursue individuals even in the face of one of its commissioners stating that the lack of individual accountability had caused a "significant amount of public concern, and understandably so." Any number of people have observed the obvious—that lack of serious individual consequences for even the largest and most egregious abuses only encourages more. Matt Taibbi, writing in *Rolling Stone,* quoted a lawyer as saying, "There's no therapy like sending those who are used to wearing Gucci shoes to jail. . . . But when the attorney general says, 'I don't want to indict people,' it's the Wild West. There's no law."

As a condition for the bailouts and certain other federal loans and guarantees, many of the large financial institutions had restrictions placed on the dividends and share buybacks allowed. But interestingly enough, once early pronouncements about executive pay were disavowed, there were no restrictions whatsoever on compensation. The government must approve a one-cent-per-share increase in a dividend rate, but eight figure bonuses can be paid with no questions asked.

The failure of the law and enforcement as well as a lack of individual accountability was well summarized when Richard Fuld, CEO of Lehman at the time it went under, testified before Congress. Congressman Henry Waxman stated, "Your company is now bankrupt, and our country is in a state of crisis, but you get to keep $480 million." Then he asked: "I have a very basic question: is that fair?"

Let's ask ourselves a couple simple questions: what would we do if we knew we could earn more by breaking the rules, and if things went wrong, someone else would pay the consequences? What would we do if bad behavior was rewarded with bigger salaries and bonuses and prudent actions lowered our compensation? The incentives are all wrong, and drastic changes are needed.

But too many rules can cause their own problems. Government regulation requiring too much disclosure or too much detail is usually counterproductive. Unfortunately, government requires more and more paperwork, often resulting in less real protection for the public. If required disclosures are not concise and somewhat limited in scope, no one will read, let alone understand, them. About two years ago I signed documents to refinance a simple home mortgage. When I finished, I couldn't believe how many documents were required. So I counted—forty-seven. Since I am a lawyer and have worked in finance for many years, I understood what each document represented. But how many non-lawyers would know or even care? Wouldn't it be smarter to have maybe five or six signatures and make sure the borrowers understood the key points instead of zoning out as they sign a stack of documents they don't comprehend? For example, wouldn't it be helpful to truly understand if and by how much your monthly mortgage payments could increase?

Lengthy documents are now needed to comply with regulatory requirements. General Electric's 2013 annual report filed with the

SEC has approximately 110,000 words, the equivalent of a 400-page book. In 2011, Glencore, the world's largest commodities trading firm, prepared its IPO prospectus—about 1,600 pages.

A number of years ago an experienced investment professional told me a story that he claimed was not an urban legend. I'm not sure, but here's how it goes. A company was filing for its IPO with the usual prospectus of a few hundred pages. This was in the days before electronic transmission of documents, and the controlling shareholder told his lawyer he would personally deliver the final prospectus to the printer. On the way he stopped at his office and somewhere in the middle of the document inserted a sentence that said any reader could call the toll-free number he listed and receive $5. About 50,000 prospectuses were printed, and he received four requests for payments. So we could ask the question: does anyone really read the fine print?

In 2013 Wells Fargo Securities issued a monthly report containing sixteen pages of information for its customers and eight pages of fine print of "Required Disclosures." These materials included the names of hundreds of companies with which Wells Fargo Securities or its affiliates had done business. I'd sure be interested in learning how many people changed their relationship with Wells Fargo Securities because of that disclosure.

Often the government encourages or even mandates foolish actions, but then issues regulations to minimize the risks of the very behavior its policies foster. In May 2010, just two years after the collapse of the subprime lending market, Standard & Poor's issued a report entitled "Evaluating the Impact of Far-Reaching U.S. Financial Regulatory Reform Legislation on U.S. Bank Ratings." The legislation was obviously intended to make banks stronger and decrease the chances that mortgage defaults would ever be as high as they were in 2007–2008. This report observed that the legislation called for "new rules that encourage lenders to focus on the borrower's ability to repay a mortgage." What? We have to legislate to be sure that when banks make loans they will pay attention to the borrowers' likelihood of repaying? Banks, of course, did that for years. When did they stop? When the government encouraged, or even mandated, that they make loans to people who under prior standards would never have qualified and obviously had no ability to repay the loans.

I saved my favorite government figure for last. The Dodd-Frank Act was passed in 2010 to provide financial reform that would hopefully avoid a repeat of the subprime debacle, the resulting market crash, and the subsequent Great Recession. By the Act's second anniversary, 244 rules had been written by government agencies to enforce the terms of the Act. The House Financial Services Committee estimated the number of hours that private entities would have to spend each year in order to comply with those rules. And the answer was (drum roll, please) 24,180,856. That was the official government figure. I feel good knowing they can see the future that accurately. We should all sleep better.

The SEC's deficiencies when enforcement really matters are well illustrated by its failures in some of the biggest and most egregious fraud cases. It spends way too much time, effort, and expense going after the smaller guys for technical violations. They are easy prey because they cannot fight the government, which has limitless resources. Even when the small guys are right, they cannot afford to pay hundreds of thousands if not millions in legal fees when a quick settlement will result in substantially lower costs and not divert time away from business.

The Madoff case, discussed in Chapter 6, is the most prominent example of the SEC's failures. What does it say about the effectiveness of the SEC and other regulators' examinations when Madoff, who operated a $50 billion Ponzi scheme, was examined at least eight times over a sixteen-year period and no actions were ever taken?

Allen Stanford ran what was later discovered to be the second-largest Ponzi scheme ever. He had all the accoutrements of the nouveau riche: mega-mansion, private planes, huge yacht. He also had a couple of unique features: multiple families and sponsorship of a world-class cricket team. The whole empire was phony, yet he stayed in business for years. *Vanity Fair* reported that "the S.E.C., the F.B.I., and others mounted investigation after investigation of his shadowy business," but did nothing.

Based on my one personal experience with Stanford's firm, I am surprised his scheme lasted so long, especially since government regulators had investigated him. Many professional athletes had been advised by their agents and financial managers to invest with Stanford. One of my clients was approached and asked my advice. A single phone call convinced me that Stanford's operation made no sense. His representative couldn't coherently answer very basic questions, while at the same time promising high returns. So we passed, but a lot of pro athletes didn't. Somehow, when Stanford went under, the agents and financial managers who advised their clients to invest with him avoided all responsibility.

Another government enforcement failure came to light in July 2014 with a company run by two Belize-based individuals previously accused of money laundering and stock manipulation. Somehow Cynk Technology Corp., a purported social network operator, traded on the US markets with a $6 billion valuation. But the company had no reported assets, no revenue, and one employee. Within days of this information becoming available to the public, the stock fell 99.9 percent. (And even after that the stock was probably still too high.)

How can the government effectively regulate the financial system if its top officials don't even comprehend basic principles or problems when they're right in front of them? Ben Bernanke, when chairman of the Federal Reserve, became one of a long line of financial experts who predicted that prosperity would last forever, this time because the Federal Reserve had tamed the business cycle. In addition, Bernanke testified in March 2007, when the subprime debacle was clearly coming to light, that "it seems likely to be contained."

SIXTEEN

# Protecting Yourself and Fixing the Wall Street Mess

For Wall Street, 2012 was a special year at Burning Man, the annual free-spirited get-together in the Nevada desert. An artist spent $100,000 building replicas up to 90 feet tall of the headquarters of Goldman Sachs, Bank of America, JPMorgan Chase, and Merrill Lynch. At the end of the week, he torched the buildings while the crowd cheered. The participants at Burning Man were symbolically burning down Wall Street. As we have now seen, Wall Street is fleecing you and ruining America. It's important that we put an end to this behavior.

Good news! Despite all of Wall Street's shenanigans, we all have the power to protect ourselves and prosper in our great private enterprise system. If we all work hard together to prevent Wall Street from enriching itself at our expense, we can prevent it from hijacking the system. But it won't be easy. We will have to start by owning up to our mistakes and acknowledging that too many of us have been happy consumers of Wall Street pornography, willing gamblers, and accessories to Wall Street's selfish interest. We will have to come to grips with the unpleasant realization that we have voluntarily surrendered too much of our money and attention to Wall Street. We do need Wall Street to provide liquid markets for real investments. We do not need it to foster gambling that needlessly increases our risks and to serve as a toll-taker that makes us poorer. Wall Street should be reasonably compensated for providing needed services, but it shouldn't be allowed to withdraw huge sums from the economy for wealth it does not create. Market forces can still work. If enough of us say no, then things will change rapidly.

Most importantly, replace your retail broker with a discount brokerage firm. It won't be easy because many of us have had long-standing relationships with our brokers. They have spent a lot of time and money convincing you that they provide a valuable service. As we've seen, it's almost never true. You will need a lot of courage to admit you have been manipulated for all these years. How many of us are willing to admit that we been victims? How many of us are willing to admit that we put our trust in the wrong people? How many of us are willing to admit mistakes? I certainly find it hard, and I know I'm not alone. But we must if we are ever going to get out of Wall Street's grip.

Some time ago a client's husband prematurely died and left his stockbroker (and best friend) as the trustee for her and her children. The broker proceeded to manage the account to maximize his commissions at the widow's expense. Finally, on my advice she fired her husband's best friend and demanded that the brokerage firm refund her losses. Confronted with an untenable situation, the brokerage firm paid up, and the widow took her business elsewhere. Obviously this was very difficult for her, but it changed her life for the better.

When it comes to Wall Street, many of us are going to have to admit that the problem is not just some other guys' brokers or advisors. How can you be sure it's time to fire your broker or advisor and move on? Here are some questions to ask and prior practices to evaluate.

1. **Start with a simple question:** If the firm you use would have failed without government intervention in 2008–2009, why would you want them in charge of your assets now? If it couldn't even manage its own affairs, why in the world would you trust it with yours? Don't accept the excuse that no one could have predicted the market crash and prepared for it. There were many

firms that survived the crash of 2008 without any help from the government. The firms that would have gone under without government intervention were those that gambled the most. Do not take advice from a firm that only survived because of crony capitalism.

2. Would you hire a firm that had done any of the following:
   a. Sold you products that were designed to fail in order to benefit other clients?
   b. Recommended that you buy stocks that its internal memoranda referred to as "dogs" and "crap"?
   c. Paid a $2.5 billion fine for failing from 1996 to 2008 to alert the government, as required by law, of suspicious activity in the accounts of Bernard Madoff (the operator of the largest Ponzi scheme in history)?
   d. Overcharged some of its wealthy customers for many years on foreign-exchange transactions?
   e. Operated a fixed income hedge fund that lost 75 percent of its value?
   f. Paid fines to the government of over $40 billion for duping investors into buying mortgage securities, foreclosure abuses, and sales of deficient mortgages to Fannie Mae and Freddie Mac (quasi-government agencies)?

   If you would refuse to do business with a firm that did any of these things, why would you continue to work with Goldman Sachs (a), Merrill Lynch (b), JPMorgan Chase (c), Bank of New York Mellon (d), Citigroup (e), Bank of America (f), or numerous others? Just because a firm is well known, huge, and successful does not mean it serves your interest or has any special expertise to offer.

3. Has the Securities and Exchange Commission (SEC) or the Financial Industry Regulatory Authority (FINRA) taken disciplinary action against the firm? Has the firm ever been found guilty of a crime or paid fines to settle criminal matters, with or without admitting guilt? Fines, suspensions, and other forms of discipline from these government and industry regulators do not

come easy. You want to know what complaints the regulators and clients made and how they were resolved. Investors can research brokers and advisers on the SEC website (www.sec.gov/investor/brokers.htm). And the Financial Industry Regulatory Authority offers BrokerCheck (www.finra.org/Investors/ToolsCalculators/BrokerCheck/index.htm).

4. Has the firm, as a matter of its policy, cheated its clients or customers? Too many firms have gone out of their way to foster practices that result in their benefiting at the clients' expense. If the problem truly arose because of a rogue employee, that's one thing. But if it arose because of express policy and the culture of a firm, then why would you stay? Don't fall for the delusion that "My guy is okay; he's the exception, so I'm in good shape." If he works in a bad environment, why should he be different? Don't you think he is under pressure to conform to company policy and culture? Poor corporate culture breeds poor client service—it's that simple. Once again, the SEC and FINRA websites are the place to begin your research.

5. Has your investment advisor ever been terminated from a brokerage-firm's financial advisors platform (a service that allows investment advisors the ability to manage their clients' accounts through the brokerage firm)? If so, you need to know the real reason why. My firm was part of the nationwide Schwab Advisors Network. Schwab referred clients to local independent investment advisors for personalized guidance. Participating on a brokerage-firm platform is often coveted and lucrative for an advisor. And the brokerage firms do not want to sever ties with advisors who can send them lots of business, so terminations are rare. My firm was treated extremely well by Schwab, as were our clients. But we saw Schwab terminate its relationship with some firms that were many times larger than we were. Why? If I were a client, I would certainly want to know. Trouble is, the Wall Street system makes finding information of this sort extremely difficult. If a firm is forced off a platform, it will move its clients to another brokerage and suggest that it changed for better service or lower fees.

6. Has your advisor or firm told you that an investment is "guaranteed" to succeed? Run away fast if you hear phrases like "you can't lose on this" or "it's a sure winner." If it really is, get a guarantee in writing. When you don't receive one, you'll understand why.

7. What fees will you pay when you make an investment, and what will you pay over time? What markups will you pay, especially on fixed-income securities? If the markups are high, it's time to go elsewhere. You can find out how much your broker intends to mark up bonds by simply asking. In most cases, if the markup is greater than one half of 1 percent, then you are probably being overcharged.

8. Has your broker or advisor put any annuity policies into your IRA, profit-sharing or pension account, or any other tax-exempt vehicle? This is a big no-no. (See Chapter 4.)

9. Has your broker ever suggested you invest in derivative contracts? Why? Do you like to gamble with your assets? Unless your circumstances are extremely unusual, you shouldn't own derivatives. (See Chapter 14.)

10. Has your broker ever sold you class C shares in mutual funds? If yes, then she is making extra commissions at your expense. (See Chapter 4.) Why would you want to stay with someone who could have invested your money in the same fund at a lower cost to you?

11. Has your broker or advisor suggested he has an opportunity for you to make a quick profit? Why does this firm have access to information that no one else does? Was the information legally obtained?

12. Has anyone suggested that an investment has no risk? Except for very short-term US Treasury securities, every investment has some risk. Similarly, has anyone suggested you can earn a high return with low risk? Legitimate high returns can be achieved only with investments that carry high risk.

13. Does your portfolio have a high turnover? The higher the turnover, the more likely you will make less or lose more. (See Chapter 11.) I would be highly suspicious of any stock portfolio with an average turnover of more than 25 percent per year.

14. Conversely, does your stock portfolio consists of very few stocks and nothing else? If it does, then regardless of the quality of the individual stocks there is additional risk. A concentrated portfolio can certainly be a way to earn higher returns, but it can also result in unexpected losses. Concentrated portfolios are for gamblers, while diversified portfolios are for long-term investors.

15. Has your firm or advisor made any significant change in their approach to investing? For example, has a firm that preached long-term investing suddenly started short-term trading? Or has a firm that has long avoided international investing all of a sudden started emphasizing it? Clearly you want your firm to react to current conditions and opportunities, but an overall or radical shift usually signals a problem. A Wall Street merger a few years ago illustrates this all too well. A large investment advisory firm had specialized in value investing. For years it had continually stressed to its clients its view that value stocks provide superior returns to growth stocks. (Value stocks are perceived to be of high quality and typically have lower ratios of price to earnings or price to book value than market averages. Value stocks often have higher-than-average dividends. Growth stocks are perceived to have potential to grow faster than value stocks and typically have fundamentals just the opposite of the value stocks described above.) That advisory firm invested only in value stocks and scrupulously avoided growth issues. The value firm was then acquired by a growth manager. All of a sudden, representatives of the former value firm started telling their clients to split their money between growth and value. Were they admitting that the previous forty years of advice was wrong? If yes, then why would the clients stay with them? If no, then why would the clients want to buy growth? Almost right at the time of the merger, value investing came back into vogue and significantly outperformed growth. A few of the old firm's clients saw the light and left. The clients who stayed and followed the "new and improved" advice suffered a lot.

16. Has your firm taken inconsistent positions at the same time? (See chapters 3, 7, and 8.) Obviously this is an attempt to deceive

clients. The problem is finding the inconsistent positions. The firms trumpet the correct predictions while the incorrect ones never see the light of day.

17. Has the firm offered excuses for poor performance rather than acknowledging mistakes? Your advisor's job is to protect you in the real world, not in some hypothetical one. If you hear excuses such as "no one could have foreseen this" or "this is unprecedented, so there was nothing anyone could have done" or "what we did for you would have worked under normal circumstances" or any other similar excuses, it is time to go. It does you no good to hear how smart your advisor is if only the world were different. (See Chapter 6.)

18. Has the firm engaged in crossing trades between customer accounts? (See Chapter 4.) To avoid falling victim to this, ask the source of the security you are buying.

19. Has your broker or advisor previously made predictions that turned out wrong? Nobody knows the future, so all predictions are fraught with peril. How certain was the advisor about his predictions? Were they definite (bad) or nuanced (good)? It's counterintuitive again, but the more certain the prediction, then the less you should listen. If your advisors insist they know the future, you should tune out and head for the exits.

20. Does the firm purport to have proprietary formulas, knowledge that no one else does, or other secret sauce? Wouldn't it be wonderful if proprietary formulas worked? How rich would the owners be? Some formulas actually may work for a time, until one day they don't. Unfortunately, no computer-generated formula works indefinitely. Do you feel good thinking you have access to some special approach that only a chosen few have? Why are you the lucky one? Maybe the "proprietary formula" is in fact a formula for trying to get your business. The most successful investors have rightfully claimed that good judgment and analysis lead to superior results, not mathematical formulas.

If your adviser or broker is guilty of some of these infractions, what should you be looking for instead? The following list gives some pointers of where to start.

1.  First and foremost, only deal with a fiduciary. Don't hire salesmen. (See Chapter 3.) A fiduciary handles your funds like they were his own; a salesman acts for his own benefit. A salesman collects commissions and profits from markups. You pay a fiduciary a fee not contingent on results or activity. If the potential advisor will not sign a letter stating he is a fiduciary, hire someone else.

2.  Find someone who preaches the proverbial "slow and steady"— just the opposite of "get rich quick." You want to consider someone who says he can preserve your wealth and make it grow. Contrast this with someone who claims he can make you wealthy and implies there is no work involved.

3.  Hire people who admit they don't know the future. Nobody does. Not you, not me, and not them! The trouble is the future is always unknown. Sure, there are trends and history and logic, but new things happen all the time. A good advisor weighs the tugs and pulls and reaches a nuanced conclusion for what might happen. Contrast this with the person who makes predictions with precision. How can that be? If anybody really knew the future and had access to even modest wealth, he would soon be unbelievably rich. Feel comfortable with the person who sees numerous possibilities and tries to sort them out. Pay no attention to the one who claims to know precisely where we're going.

4.  Find someone who stresses quality and diversified investments. Diversification serves as a defensive mechanism to protect you against unexpected downturns that affect one class of investment but not others. Diversification also offers the opportunity to gain by owning one or more classes of profitable investment when other classes may be flat or down. A diversified portfolio will enable you to be at the right place at the right time. A

concentrated portfolio will cause you to miss opportunities. Diversification reduces volatility.

5.  Hire people who are not afraid to put what they tell you in writing. And don't be afraid to ask for this. Talk is easy, but written statements (especially those for more extreme claims) are not. Go with someone who can back up claims of past success for themselves or the failings of others. This reminds me of an attack I suffered at the hands of a big-time broker from New York. Our competitors often tried to steal our clients or compete for new ones by saying we were too conservative. Actually, that was a reputation I could live with. We had conservatively allocated a portfolio for one of our star football players. That conservative allocation nevertheless had an equity component because of our commitment to diversification. Our client was later introduced by his team's owner to the owner's broker. The suggestion was clear: fire us (the little-known firm in San Francisco) and hire the big shot at the prominent firm in New York. As this was unfolding, the stock market had just gone through a significant decline. The broker then proceeded to analyze our client's portfolio and told him that it was too aggressive. That was the first time in my twenty-five years in the business that I had ever been accused of being too aggressive. I reviewed the portfolio to determine the percentage of the assets invested in equities for the prior three years. I then did something that no good lawyer is supposed to do. I asked a question that I did not know the answer to (although I had a really good guess). I told my client to go back to the broker and ask him if he would send a letter signed under penalty of perjury. The broker would merely state that during the prior three years his average client had a lower percentage of equities than my client had. I am happy to report that a letter like that never materialized and the client stayed with me for many years, until the date I sold my firm. He continues to be advised by one of my younger partners.

With 24/7 cable and satellite television and the Internet, we are constantly bombarded with financial predictions, suggestions, and advice. What should we listen to and what should we tune out? What might be informative and helpful and what might be misleading and dangerous? Unfortunately, most of what is available through the media is entertainment and noise.

A few years ago I was delighted to get an unsolicited phone call from Dan Dorfman, the superstar columnist then at the *Wall Street Journal*. The performance of the mutual fund I managed had been quite strong. He said he wanted to interview me about my views of the current markets. I was obviously delighted at this opportunity. He asked for my two favorite stocks. I told him that I would never recommend just two stocks, but that I was happy to talk about my favorite thirty stocks. He said that wouldn't fly. He asked me if I could identify my one or two favorite sectors of the market. I indicated that we always maintain positions in all or essentially all sectors of the market, but that I could discuss the ones that we thought were worthy of slight overweighting. He indicated that approach would not particularly interest either him or his readers. He then asked what he could write about. I suggested that perhaps he could write about our unorthodox style of high-quality, diversified, and low-turnover investing—and how that worked so well. He said he would think about it and get back to me. Unfortunately, he never did.

So, what should we listen to and what should we avoid? How do we determine what's reasonable and what's nonsense? How do we distinguish good analysis from hype?

We can start with the counterintuitive. The more precise a prediction, the less likely it will occur. Let's consider the following possible predictions for the S&P 500 Index at a time when the index is 2000:

1. The market is poised to take off, and within a year the S&P 500 Index will increase by 15 percent to 2300.
2. The market is poised to take off, and our proprietary models show that within a year the S&P 500 Index will be 2413.
3. Although the market is at an all-time high, we see room for growth and fundamentals remain strong. The relatively high price-earnings ratios and possible rises in interest rates could

lead to a market decline, but on the whole we think the market will be higher over the next year.

Your money should be with the person who made the third prediction. It shows consideration for counterbalancing forces and does not have any specific target, which in all probability would be wrong. The other two predictions are designed to make you feel comfortable and happy believing that you will make a lot of money.

The prediction that the S&P 500 Index will increase to 2413 is truly amazing, but I assure you that statements like that are made all the time and by prominent people who work for important firms. How can anybody suggest that the market will be 2413? That specificity jars me, and it should jar you too. What is Miguel Cabrera's batting average going to be next year—over .300? Probably? How about .317?

We need to avoid listening to predictions that are overly optimistic. I am troubled when I see statements like "the market is poised for a melt up." Sounds good, but how would anybody really know? Statements like that remind me of the letter a prominent investment advisor sent to his clients when he thought the dot-com bust was over. He indicated a "unique buying opportunity" awaited his clients. He then significantly increased their exposure to equities. Within six months the S&P 500 Index had declined about 25 percent, one of its most substantial declines in history. I am still baffled by how anyone can keep clients with performance like that.

Predictions of extreme results should generally be dismissed. Examples include both the doomsday predictions and those of the rosy future. Although it is certainly possible that the markets will increase by massive amounts or that they will experience unprecedented losses, neither is likely. Predictions like these are generally made to get your attention and your business. They are not designed to educate you, nor are they usually based on sound analysis. There is a simple reason why people make predictions knowing that they are extremely unlikely to occur. It's called marketing.

You should listen to people who are calm and measured and thoughtful. Sorry Jim Cramer, but we don't want to take advice from people who throw chairs. That's good entertainment and leads to higher ratings, but I don't think it leads to better investment strategies.

One last counterintuitive consideration for evaluating predictions: the more prominent the predictor, the *less* likely the predictions are to be accurate. Exhaustive studies across many disciplines have reached that conclusion. (See chapters 7 and 8.)

What can you do to protect yourself and prosper in the face of Wall Street's selfish interest, Wall Street's propensity for gambling, and Wall Street pornography? Fortunately, there's much to do. Despite Wall Street's hijacking of the system, free enterprise continues to provide great opportunities. You can take advantage of those opportunities and not become a victim of Wall Street.

1. Take control of your own situation and do not let Wall Street pursue its selfish interests at your expense. Stop paying unreasonable fees and don't invest in complicated or risky products you don't need. Follow the old KISS principle (Keep it Simple, Stupid). Stop Wall Street from collecting fees when it's providing no real service. This is like a truck driver stopping every twenty miles and paying bribes to proceed. Unfortunately, it's much the same when Wall Street takes high fees and commissions and gives you little or nothing in return. To combat this, you must not be shy about asking about and understanding what fees you're paying. Do your due diligence to learn the appropriate fee structure for investments you make. Don't be afraid to shop around.

2. Once and for all, you must stop gambling and start investing. Own investments that are claims against real assets. Do not just bet against somebody else that the price of a security or commodity or interest rates will rise or fall. Stop thinking that you or anyone else can outsmart the market. This means no to short sales, no to derivatives, no to options, and no to the next great new idea Wall Street concocts. Stop buying on credit or leveraging your exposure by buying options. Stop combining gambling

with debt by buying funds that move at two or three times the value of the underlying securities.

3.  What to do with the media? Turn off, or better yet never turn on, CNBC, Fox Financial, CNN Financial, or similar outlets. You'll save a lot of money by watching the Comedy Channel, and it's much more entertaining. Okay, maybe I slightly exaggerated. In fact, the financial media can tell you what investigations are underway, what fines and penalties have been imposed, and what wrongdoing needs correcting. But don't listen to their predictions or advice. If you insist on watching, listening, or reading, do not make investments based on the advice offered. Giving good advice is not a priority for most media stars.

4.  Don't delude yourself into thinking you can invest on your own and compete against the pros. If, as we have seen, the investment professionals consistently fail to beat the markets, why in the world do you think you can? Do you seriously think that you can research investment opportunities on a part-time basis and compete with well-educated and experienced full-time professionals? Such arrogance will lead to trouble, not success.

5.  If you are really wealthy and qualify to make private investments (those not registered with the government and not publicly traded), don't be tempted. (See chapters 2, 4, and 6). With private investments you sacrifice liquidity and there is a high probability that your returns will not exceed those of publicly available alternatives. Sure, the cocktail party talk is always about the ones that did well. Who among us talks about our investments turned sour? Invest in instruments traded on established securities markets.

Some private deals are sold directly by their managers without any assistance from Wall Street. Unfortunately, many of the private deals are sold to unsophisticated (although wealthy) investors because no one with any sense would buy them. Wall Street is now making available more private deals to the public. Despite what Wall Street tells you, you don't need them.

6. Stop falling for Wall Street's false claims that everyone would be less prosperous without Wall Street's new and improved products. They want us to believe that the great wealth developed over the last fifty years is the result of Wall Street's genius rather than the natural consequence of the innovation and improvements made by the free enterprise system. Too many people believe that the best decade to have owned US stocks was the 1990s, when many of today's Wall Street innovations were developed. But it's not so. The best decade for owning stocks as measured by the S&P 500 Index (with dividends) was the 1950s. Why did the value of stocks increase so much then? Because companies were rapidly growing their sales and earnings. This translated rationally into higher stock prices. And somehow that was achieved without all of the gambling that is part of Wall Street today.

How was it possible that the great growth in the 1950s could have been accomplished without derivatives, publicly traded options, day trading, computer-driven trading, or high-frequency trading? How was it possible for stocks to have increased in value and investors to have made huge profits without hedge funds, "2 and 20" fees, 24/7 chatter on television, or companies issuing guidance on earnings (imagine having to wait for actual numbers)? This was accomplished in the 1950s with much less debt than today, lower trading volumes, fewer short sales, and less accounting fraud. It was a time when the CEOs of major corporations made perhaps thirty times what the average workers did rather than 300 times, which they do today. Somehow executives faithfully served their companies without massive grants of stock and options.

We can change our individual behavior, and the free market system will force Wall Street to behave better. We can also act collectively to strengthen the legal system—to encourage behavior we desire and to penalize those who act badly. Those who attempt to manipulate markets, illegally take advantage of their customers, or violate rules designed to protect the public and thereby put us all at risk need to

know that we will no longer tolerate this behavior and that consequences will be both likely and significant.

Likely criminal prosecutions, forfeiture of illegally gotten gains,
and civil penalties will cause changes in behavior. Anything short of
legislative change and stricter enforcement will do nothing to change
the current situation when Wall Street employees risk nothing when
they pillage.

Bondholders, too, need to know that they will be on the hook
if they make poor choices. Implicit guarantees just provide more
incentive for both debtors and creditors to act irresponsibly. If we
truly think that a major financial crisis would ensue if particular
companies were not bailed out by the government, then perhaps the
government should step in. But if it does, why shouldn't the existing
shareholders see their equity vanish? I don't get to keep my equity
if the value of my business disappears. Why don't bondholders take
a haircut? Why should investors in large institutions get favorable
treatment?

Regulation should be strengthened in meaningful ways. (See
Chapter 15.) We need regulations and laws that require all client representatives in the securities business to act in a fiduciary capacity.
Again, client first—no excuses. If, as an investment advisor, I must
act in my clients' best interest, then why should the rule be different
if I am a broker at Citigroup or Goldman Sachs or JPMorgan? Why
have the banks and brokerage firms fought and fought against legislation requiring them to exercise a fiduciary duty? Could it be they
see lower fees and profits if they must adhere to the standard?

Many firms are able to mislead investors by claiming prior success
that they did not have. We see this with both claims of good performance and correct predictions. I have no objection to people making
whatever predictions they want, but I object strenuously to those
who then fake the results. Rules and regulations need to be adopted
to protect consumers from this type of fraud.

Legislation and regulation are needed either to ban or substantially curtail most of the gambling that takes place on Wall Street.
As a practical matter, I think an outright ban will not be achievable.

So let's use the tax law to improve investing. Let's start by imposing either a significant excise tax or an additional income tax on short sales, derivatives, and options. A tax to discourage either that behavior or the use of those products would start to compensate us all for the societal harm. An excise tax on all securities transactions might work. It would certainly dampen short-term and high-frequency trading. That in turn would bring more stability and fairness to the markets.

Now, I know Wall Street will cry "wolf," suggesting that even a small transaction tax will kill the markets. I have no idea what evidence they have to support that claim. There was no significant securities transaction tax in the United States in the 1950s, 1960s, or 1970s. But there were, by today's standards, very high brokerage commissions—often 1½ percent of each transaction. Both the economy and the stock market prospered during those many years. Do you think the market can tell whether an added charge is a commission going to the brokerage firm or a tax going to the government?

The government could use its taxing authority to discourage less productive activity and to encourage more productive activity. What if the government substantially increased the capital gains tax rate on investments held less than six months and offset any resulting revenue gain by reducing the capital gains tax rate on investments held for more than five years? This would encourage long-term investment instead of short-term trading, making for a more stable system. With the appropriate reduction in the capital gains tax rate for investments held more than five years, this would be revenue neutral and not a tax increase, which is unpopular and even unacceptable in some quarters.

The government could also use its taxation authority to set standards for tax-exempt or charitable organizations since they have the special privilege of not paying income and other taxes. For example, charitable organizations could be subjected to substantial taxes on gains realized from short-term trading, short selling, derivative trading, and other activities we wish to discourage. The government could restrict the percentage of its assets that a tax-exempt entity could invest in nonmarketable securities. There could be restrictions on fees paid for managing securities, including those held through hedge funds or other vehicles. Tax-exempt entities could be prohibited from paying incentive fees on investments in marketable securities. Obviously, the boards of directors of tax-exempt entities could make government action unnecessary by adopting such rules for themselves. Unfortunately, history tells us that's too much to ask.

Forcing tax-exempt organizations to drop aggressive investment strategies may be the proverbial blessing in disguise. The actual investing experience of many tax-exempt organizations has been poor indeed. The trend has been away from traditional investing in stocks and bonds and toward relying much more on alternatives such as private equity, venture capital, derivatives, and hedge funds. Data compiled by the National Association of College and University Business Officers for the five years ending in fiscal 2013 indicated that university endowments of all sizes underperformed a simple mix of 40 percent bonds and 60 percent stocks.

Unions, pension plans, and other entities representing many members, and thus large pools of assets, could adopt policies to rein in Wall Street. Because of their size, many could get results and set trends by just setting the example. The California Public Employees' Retirement System, the largest state pension fund, recently decided to divest itself of all hedge fund investments. Finally, an influential organization has seen the light and is willing to say "enough." Hopefully this will encourage other large pension funds to follow suit.

Accomplishing meaningful changes on Wall Street will be difficult. Wall Street has incredible sums of money to invest in making sure no reforms take hold. Everyone has difficulty in breaking with tradition and the established order. Cleaning up the Wall Street mess will require an incredible amount of effort and dedication by those who want to try. We will not be able to rely on the government to do this for us. We have to force Wall Street to cease pursuing its selfish interest. We must end gambling and falling victim to the ultimate con job. We have to stop the seduction of Wall Street pornography. Enough is enough.

This will be a difficult task, but one we should pursue. Join me by doing your part. With moderate success in this quest, our free enterprise system can regain its footing, and there will be more economic security and prosperity for us all.

# Acknowledgments

I need to thank so many who have helped me so much for so long. We must start with Samuel Taylor (posthumously). He was *the* tax attorney in San Francisco who took a chance on a brand-new law school graduate. He was an exceptional mentor and eventually made me feel like a son. His guidance was extraordinary, and he offered me the independence to succeed both as a tax attorney and investment counselor.

Then there are those who encouraged me to tell this story. Steven Lanter, Myron Sugarman, and Kathy Jacobson believed in my message, with Kathy using her experience and skills as a publicist to help me reach a wider audience. For years Donald McQuade urged me to write this account. He continually told me that with my background and real-world experience, I offered a unique perspective on the issues.

As an investment counselor I owe much to Steve Cutcliffe, Bill Osher, Bill Hageboeck, David Hudson, and Michael Alpert for helping me manage accounts and for sharing with me their great knowledge of the investment world. Steve also provided invaluable assistance through his suggestions and careful review of my text. I am forever indebted to Don Hill, Charles Banks, Steven Kravitz, Todd LaRocca, Gary Scharf, Justin Bass, Adam Keefe, and Stephen Clark for their tireless efforts in building with me the biggest and best sports counseling firm in the country. Peter Rockefeller and Bruce Cameron worked so hard and so effectively in representing us in the sale of our firm. Their success gave me the time I needed to devote to this project.

Attorneys are very important in today's world. For so many years Christopher Rupright, Jeffrey O'Connell, and Geoffrey Haynes have told me how to get things accomplished, not what I couldn't do.

Neil Shapiro has long guided me through the slalom course of what I could and could not say. David Schmerler steered me through the contract for this book while his colleague and my long-time great friend Kenneth Benbassat has for many years been incredibly helpful in providing both legal and business advice.

Joseph Marshall has been exceptionally supportive and encouraged me to be a "Wall Street soldier" to get the word out to the people.

Jack Anderson has not only encouraged me to communicate on this subject, but has helped me become a better public speaker. Peter Novak has spent so many hours with me working on content, style, and delivery. He has advanced my efforts significantly.

Kate Taylor, the consummate professional, provided encouragement to write this story and thought enough of my project to introduce me to Robert Asahina. I cannot imagine working with a better writer, editor, and collaborator. He contributed greatly to improving my text, while the depth of his knowledge on Wall Street matters added so much. Perhaps most importantly to me, his assistance and suggestions were always consistent with letting my voice be heard and telling the story in my own inimitable style.

David Diamond and Tia O'Brien were so helpful in teaching me how to write for a public audience. Their valuable assistance with some of my earlier pieces helped launch my writing for the public. Lois Kozakoff of the San Francisco Chronicle has been so gracious in providing me space to communicate with the public. I appreciate her having the confidence to provide an opportunity to a new voice in the community.

Christopher Weills has published more of my articles than anyone else and still encourages me to do more. We've had a lot of laughs together while developing stories around sports and economics.

Waleska Morales and Audrianna Alvarez have for many years maintained so well my personal files, which were crucial to this project.

Thank you to super agent Jan Miller for believing in an unpublished author and then bringing this project to a successful conclusion. Shannon Marven, Lacey Lynch, and Nena Madonia Oshman helped so much in pushing this project to the finish line.

My son Aaron Faust assisted in numerous ways—many years of constant encouragement, asking questions, making suggestions, and reading manuscripts. Thanks also for coming up with the title for this book. Blye Faust provided continual support and encouraged me to contribute to the public discussion of these issues. My son Jeremy Faust, a regularly published writer himself, made valuable recommendations over the years both as to style and substance.

Lisa Yang, my tireless administrative assistant, helped so much in both the research and the editing processes. She also provided a much-needed younger point of view on both the subject matter and the way to communicate it. She's been a vital part of the whole process from start to finish.

Marie Eiland has been so important to me for over twenty-five years. She is the quintessential administrator, doing a thousand tasks and seeing me through office travails.

Susan Randol, my editor at Skyhorse, has been wonderful in both working on the manuscript with me and guiding me through the publication process. I could not have asked for more.

Don Hill pointed me in the right direction and was the first to introduce me in a systematic way to the foibles of Wall Street. I am grateful for learning so much from him and having the opportunity to work together for almost forty years. Without him my career would have been quite different, and this book would not exist.

No one writes more concisely and communicates more clearly than my wife Susan, who has published her monthly children's book reviews in the *San Francisco Chronicle* for over thirty years. She has tried hard (and I hope successfully) to teach me to use each word carefully to express its desired meaning. She always wants nothing but the best work product and is the logic police. To the extent this work conforms to her high standards, we have all benefited.

Finally, I want to thank the numerous Wall Street players for all the "wonderful" things they do.

# Index